Comments about *The Buddha in the Jungle*

"*The Buddha in the Jungle* is a wonderful read! We have been using it in our morning Dhamma readings to the Sangha here; everyone appreciates it. The themes flow very naturally along as one goes from one chapter to the next (bandits, elephants, snakes, healers), and the combination of colonialists' diaries and monastic recollections work extremely well. Kamala found just the right mix."
—Amaro Bhikkhu, co-abbot of Abhayagiri Monastery in California, and author of *Silent Rain* and *Small Boat, Great Mountain*

"This is a wonderful work of scholarship and story telling. *The Buddha in the Jungle* will please the voyager, the backpacker, the undergraduate, the embassy wives looking for another good read about their new assignment, the embassy officers unsure just where Thailand came from and how it differs from its neighbors. By introducing nearly every tale with comments by one or more western writers, Kamala helps English-reading students of Thailand and Buddhism understand the translated material she introduces. This book is a well-researched scholarly contribution that is written in an accessible fashion for the general reader. Here alternative thinkers from every kind of society can capture the sense of sophisticated and disciplined methods of healing in a society where science-based medicine is not commonplace, but where monks carried knowledge into everyday, practical matters. They, perhaps more than any other individuals, were the glue that held the community together."
—John Badgley, Asianist and retired curator of the Southeast Asian Collection, Cornell University

"This is a fascinating account told by both the Siamese themselves and their Western contemporaries of how the living dharma permeated everyday life in Siam for both monastics and laity before the advent of the 'rational' scholastic and bureaucratic approach developed in the mid-nineteenth century. Kamala relates how the monks traditionally embodied bodhisattva principles through their relationship with the laity: at that time the bhikkhus were the teachers, healers, artisans and counselors, so the sangha had a pivotal role to play in the lives of the people."
—Bhiksuni Tenzin Palmo, head of Dongyu Gatsal Ling Nunnery in India and author of *Reflections on a Mountain Lake*

"Kamala wrote so vividly that I recalled that Akira Kurosawa, the great Japanese movie director, occasionally filmed Buddhist stories with somewhat the same flavor by showing village life of a bygone day."
—Sister Dharmapali

"We had several days of doing readings to the community from *The Buddha in the Jungle* and people were very interested and appreciative. . . . This will be a very important book in showing the depth and diversity of Buddhism in Thailand. So often Theravada is presented as monochromatic, both in its practice and philosophy—which it is not at all."

—Pasanno Bhikkhu, co-abbot of Abhayagiri Monastery and co-author, with Amaro Bhikkhu, of *Broad View, Boundless Heart*

"Kamala's approach to history in *The Buddha in the Jungle* is well worth reading, especially for Westerners who are largely unaware of the real life contexts of the Buddhism they practice. The mix of Thai and nineteenth-century Western sources helps us see a different world—beliefs, values, customs—through various eyes. The early chapters also say much about the beliefs and behaviors of ordinary Buddhists. This is not the elite 'forest tradition' that is known in the West in an idealized form, nor canonical Buddhism, nor State Buddhism. We have glimpses of Buddhism as real people lived it; that is, Human Buddhism. It is the lived Buddhism of an era that has largely faded. Those of us concerned with the vitality of Buddhism today do well to ponder its past vitalities. Many thanks to Kamala for her warm, sympathetic weaving of compelling human sources into richly textured cloth."

—Santikaro Bhikkhu, Liberation Park, Chicago

"For Westerners, the process of reading these stories is an education in *how* to read the history of Thai Buddhism. Some stories remain entirely within a Thai perspective, and some are dominated by Western colonial voices. Still, the themes interweave themselves with no need for Westernized categories. *The Buddha in the Jungle* gives us a Jataka-like collection of exemplary stories that instruct us about the lives of traditional and non-centralized monks—a strategy that honors those monks by using their own story methods rather than the academic rationalism of western historiography or its counterpart in state-sponsored Buddhism."

—Joel Fredell, Professor of Literature and Medieval Studies at Southeastern Louisiana University

"The facts revealed in *The Buddha in the Jungle* will be of interest to all historians and Western Buddhists who have a connection with Thai tradition and may open a few eyes to the scope of the monastic sangha in former times."

—Laurence Khantipalo Mills, co-founder of the Bodhi Citta Buddhist Centre in Australia, and author of *Noble Friendship*.

THE BUDDHA IN THE JUNGLE

KAMALA TIYAVANICH

SILKWORM BOOKS
CHIANG MAI

UNIVERSITY OF WASHINGTON PRESS
SEATTLE

ISBN 974-9575-27-x

First published in Thailand by Silkworm Books in 2003

Silkworm Books
6 Sukkasem Road, T. Suthep
Chiang Mai 50200, Thailand
E-mail address: silkworm@silkwormbooks.info
www.silkwormbooks.info

Published in the United States of America by
the University of Washington Press
P.O. Box 50096, Seattle, Washington 98145, U.S.A.
www.washington.edu/uwpress

ISBN 0-295-98372-8

Typeset by Silk Type in Jensen 11 pt.
Cover: Mural Painting, Wat Boromniwat, Bangkok
Painter: Phra Ajan Inkhong, art master of Wat Liap, Bangkok, 1850s
Photographer: Chatchaval Srisla
Cover Design: Robert Manchester

Printed in Thailand by O. S. Printing House, Bangkok

10 9 8 7 6 5 4 3 2

CONTENTS

CONTENTS

LIST OF MAPS AND ILLUSTRATIONS

FOREWORD

THE WESTERN encounter with Buddhism has taken place primarily in the context of the psychology of meditation and comparative philosophy of religion. Buddhism has been evaluated in terms of its universal relevance, beyond cultures and their histories. The problem with such an approach is its tendency to abstraction and lack of connection to the realities of actual human lives, which of course are always lived in particular cultures and geographies. Now that a second generation of Western Buddhists is coming to consciousness, the question arises of what it means to live in a Buddhist culture.

Kamala's *The Buddha in the Jungle* is a richly evocative tapestry of stories about nineteenth- and early-twentieth-century Siam that vividly brings to life the Buddhist culture of the land now known as Thailand. The stories gathered here—of village monks encountering giant snakes, a Christian missionary gored by an elephant, bandits and boatmen, a dog-bodhisattva, midwives, and guardian spirits—collectively portray a Buddhist culture in all of its imaginative and geographical concreteness. It is a culture subject to the vicissitudes of historical change, both in terms of the presence of Westerners in the pursuit of their own economic and religious agendas, and in the changing politics of Buddhism itself as the Bangkok-based state attempts to impose a normative centralization on diverse local traditions. *The Buddha in the Jungle* thus accomplishes the feat of portraying a premodern Asian

Buddhist culture in its difference from both the West and its own later modernization, while resisting an idealism that lifts tradition out of historical time and space. The book is both a lament for a lost world and an act of recovery by which that world speaks again to the present. Old stories of this bygone world, here told anew, have striking relevance today as we become more aware of the destructive shadow side of the modern culture that displaced this particular Buddhist past.

As a teacher of religious studies, I am grateful for *The Buddha in the Jungle*: with its vivid narrative and imagistic detail (the snake stories alone will keep students riveted!) it offers an ideal text for the study of Buddhism in specific cultural contexts. And beyond the classroom, Western Buddhists seeking to imagine ways of embodying Buddhism in Western culture will learn how Buddhism has been lived by one traditionally Buddhist Asian society. Cultures cannot imitate one another; they can, however, cross-pollinate and inspire new hybrids. As we in the twenty-first century experience the cultural changes brought about by globalization, *The Buddha in the Jungle* offers Buddhist wisdom for such transformations, not as abstract philosophy or meditation teaching, but as an elder culture telling its tales to the young, transmitting the experience of the past to a present always in danger of falling into collective amnesia.

Brian Karafin
Professor of Religious Studies
Ithaca College, Ithaca, New York.

Reading *The Buddha in the Jungle* transports us beyond the smooth surface of the contemporary Thai nation-state into a premodern world of almost bewildering physical and cultural diversity. The centripetal forces of consumerism, easy communication, centralized government, state-sponsored education, and national language are not yet in ascendancy. The modern map with its tight boundaries and flat color dissolves into something like confetti.

Drawing on a wealth of ephemeral and overlooked sources such as cremation volumes, monks' life stories, diaries, gossip, folklore, and interviews, Kamala restores the physical and spiritual world of the nineteenth and early twentieth centuries. Through a remarkably fresh and ingenious use of apposition, she also gives us parallel European accounts by naturalists, engineers, missionaries, and business people who participate in the same events and landscapes but view them through very different interpretive frameworks. Together with them we find ourselves in a Thailand formed from wood and fiber, powered by water and human and animal energy, spatially knit together not by paved roads and train tracks, but by canals, rivers, boats, and the wandering feet of ascetic monks on pilgrimage. We search for sacred caves, flee rampaging elephants, explore traditional medicine, acquire a dharmic education through recitation of the Vessantara Jataka and Phra Malai stories and witness firsthand the disciplined equanimity of Buddhist monks.

This is a world receding into shadow, and Kamala has caught it as it vanishes. Her book will certainly be read by anthropologists, historians, and specialists in Theravada Buddhism, but it deserves a wider audience which should include introductory courses on Southeast Asia and, for that matter, virtually anyone curious about the intricate forms life has taken on this planet.

Stanley O' Connor
Emeritus Professor of the History of Art
Cornell University, Ithaca, New York.

ACKNOWLEDGMENTS

I WISH to express my thanks to Cornell University's Southeast Asia Program, directed by Thak Chaloemtiarana, and the Religious Studies Program, directed by Jane Marie Law, for appointing me a visiting fellow during the years of my research at Kroch Library. I am grateful to the Society for the Humanities, directed by Jonathan Culler, for awarding me a Mellon Postdoctoral Fellowship in 1993 to do research for this book.

This book is the first volume of a series on Buddhist monks and village life in old Siam. The research and writing of this book took place in two countries, Thailand and the United States. I am deeply grateful to the monks, lay ascetics, and village elders whom I interviewed over the last fourteen years. Many of them have now passed away. The finished book benefited from the discerning eyes of teachers and friends in various disciplines, and to them I owe my gratitude. Ajan Amaro, Ajan Laurence Khantipalo, Ajan Pasanno, and Ajan Santikaro gave the manuscript close readings, offered insightful comments, and made helpful corrections. Collectively they helped me clarify the Thai and Pali terminology for readers who may not be familiar with Dhamma teachings, meditation practices, and Buddhist customs. Sister Dharmapali and Bhiksuni Tenzin Palmo offered concrete insights about what they learned from local Buddhist practices in old Siam. Valuable suggestions from John Badgley, Joel Fredell, Brian Karafin, and Jack Kornfield confirmed my decision to structure the book to reflect the oral tradition.

For helping with field research I am grateful to Ajan Sommai Premchit, Ajan Srisaka and Arpapirat Vallibhotama, Sujit and Pranee Wongthes, and Aroonrat Wichienkeeo. Special thanks goes to my brother, Pitsanuwat Tiyavanich, for his exceptional collection of cremation volumes and other relevant materials. For helping me obtain library materials, I thank Chotima Chaturawong, Ngampit Jagacinski, and Chiranan Pitpreecha. I extend heartfelt thanks to Ajan David Wyatt, who provided me with maps to help the reader follow the trails of Buddhist monks and Western travelers; to Robert Manchester, whose cover design brings out the beauty of Ajan Inkhong's painting and illuminates a theme of this book; and to John LeRoy, for his copyediting and computer expertise.

My deepest thanks also go to Dolina Millar for offering help whenever needed and for excising special terminology that would have encumbered the general reader; to Patricia Connor for thoughtfully editing various incarnations of the manuscript with careful attention to detail and consistency; and to my publisher, Trasvin Jittidecharak, for patiently awaiting the completion of this book for what must have seemed an eternity.

INTRODUCTION

THIS BOOK is a collection of loosely related stories focusing on aspects of the lives and contexts of a number of Buddhist masters. These monks lived between the mid-nineteenth century, in what was then Siam, and the mid-twentieth century, in what is now Thailand. The majority of the monks, many of whom became abbots, received their early education as children and young monastics in outlying villages and towns, some of them hundreds of kilometers away from Bangkok. Their stories have been drawn from interviews when possible, and from recollections sometimes written by them, but more often recorded by their monastic or lay disciples.

To understand the context in which the monks of this one-hundred-year period lived, it is helpful to see them in relation to 1957, a watershed year that has been singled out by Thai environmentalists. They call the period prior to 1957, which reaches far, far back in time, the Jungle-Village era. During this era Siam was sparsely populated, overwhelmingly rural, and blessed with what appeared to be unlimited natural resources. Bangkok then was really a collection of villages, not a city like New York or London as it is today. Once Siam became a nation-state and joined the international community, the urban population began to increase dramatically, but even then Bangkok retained much of its rural character. All that changed after 1957.

In the nineteenth century the vast majority of the people of Siam lived in riverine villages and small frontier hamlets scattered throughout the kingdom and its satellites. These settlements consisted of clusters of houses whose inhabitants lived off farmland, orchards, rivers, and forests. Human beings and wild animals shared the same territories, and the lives of the people were deeply interconnected with nature. For most of the hundred-year period under consideration, even town dwellers lived close to nature. Most people went around barefoot; almost every child knew how to swim and row a boat; monks paddled their own boats on almsround; villagers depended on water buffaloes to plow their fields; village boys were educated in the village monasteries; the *wat* (temple-monastery) was the local community center; and the relationships between local monks and their communities were very close.

The stories in this book illustrate the Buddhist monks' involvement with the lives of common people and their respect for all forms of life. These Buddhist masters combined spiritual pursuits with social responsibilities. All of them were involved with their local communities as teachers, healers, astrologers, psychologists, artists, and advisers on practical matters. To local people, these monks were *keng* (self-reliant in every situation), *saksit* (sacred), *khemkhaeng* (possessed of inner strength), and *mi metta* (empowered with loving kindness). The monks honored the kind of teaching that best suited the character and aptitude of the individual and taught in ways that made Dhamma (the Buddha's teachings) relevant to everyday life. They trained their minds through a variety of meditation techniques including visualization. They trained their speech by intoning chants, often of great length, and by reciting suttas, mantras, and the poetic verses of Phra Malai and Jataka stories. They trained their bodies through ascetic practices undertaken during

their long pilgrimages on foot to sacred sites or prolonged retreats in caves or forest cemeteries. These practices enabled the monks and those whom they taught to
experience a power of the sacred that is incomprehensible to the untrained mind. The Sangha Centralization
Act, passed in 1902, established uniform rules and practices for all monastics throughout Siam. Once the new
law went into effect, local Buddhist masters lost their au-
tonomy. From that time on, the diverse teachings and
practices of monks and lay ascetics throughout the land
were gradually replaced by a new, "scientific" education
system. Book learning came to be more highly esteemed
than meditation practice. Many of the beliefs that local
Buddhists had long regarded as sacred came to be seen as
mere superstition under the rationalistic orientation of
both the government and the official sangha. Under the
bureaucratized sangha hierarchy, town monks became
increasingly sedentary and bookish.

In the nineteenth and early twentieth centuries, rich
people customarily used their wealth to build or restore
monasteries. The wat was the only social institution that
benefited the whole community. Town and village monasteries served not only as places of worship but also as
repositories of knowledge, training grounds for special
skills, schools for boys, playgrounds for children, sites for
festivals, refuges for animals, hospitals for the sick, and
inns for travelers. Christian missionaries who traveled to
remote regions in the hope of converting local people
spent many a night in shelters for wayfarers built on wat
land.

Each of the Buddhist masters brought forward in this
book knew two or three languages; some knew even
more. Their parents were Siamese, Lao, Mon, Khmer,
Yuan, Shan, or Chinese. Whether they lived in towns or
villages, in keeping with their local traditions they used
the Jataka—stories of the previous births of Gotama

Buddha—as a key source for teaching the *bodhisat* (bodhi-sattva) way of life. The bodhisat strives, over many lives and through the determined practice of spiritual perfection, to attain full awakening as a Buddha for the benefit of all. The Jataka stories promoted respect for other beings and other points of view, human and animal, no matter how small or insignificant a creature might seem. That the Buddhist masters introduced here were devoted to Dhamma and embodied bodhisat principles can be seen through their relationships with the laity. Meditation and *thudong* (ascetic) practices were as important to them as scholarship and the observance of monastic rules (*vinaya*).

Many town and village monks spent part of each year in forest wildernesses to train their minds in challenging environments. From seeing how monks interacted with wild animals we can observe the power of the unconditioned mind and the interconnectedness, the interdependence of all beings. Their teachings emphasized ways of living in harmony with nature, the practice of nonviolence, the cultivation of compassion, the extending of *metta* (loving kindness) to all sentient beings, and liberation from greed, aversion, and delusion. But when these monks were assimilated into monolithic state Buddhism, their practices, skills, and teachings were undermined by the forces of standardization. The monks' stories are sad reminders that many of Siam's diverse Dhamma teachings—derived from experiential wisdom and transmitted from teachers to pupils across generations for hundreds of years—have, tragically, been lost. What little remains needs to be brought forward.

The monks who appear here, and the people of their generations, lived in a time marked by the steady incursion of Western imperial power and Western ideas, technologies, and products. Siam was forced to comply with Western principles of free trade. In the face of the for-

ward advance of colonial interests into territories border-
ing on Siam, King Chulalongkorn (r. 1868–1910) initi-
ated a series of reforms to strengthen his rule over the
tributary states. Well aware of the effectiveness of the
European colonial model, the king reorganized the government along Western lines, transforming the kingdom
of Siam into a modern state with a centralized system of
administration. The hereditary rulers of the tributary
states were replaced by governors sent from Bangkok.
Once in the hands of local monks, education was gradually entrusted to secular teachers trained by Westerners.
The social service roles of village and town monks were
eventually taken over by secular institutions. Profession-
als of every degree were brought to Siam to contribute to
its modernization. Western teachers and school administrators came to help establish secular schools. Western
engineers came to Siam to build paved roads, railroads,
and telegraph systems. Military experts were hired to
train and equip a modern army. Surveyors, legal and fi-
nancial experts, businessmen, and teachers from England,
Scotland, Denmark, Germany, Belgium, and the United
States poured into the country. Missionaries came to
Siam hoping to convert the people to Christianity.

To retell stories from the lives of these monks, I have
attempted to put them in the context of their times. I
chose these particular stories for what they reveal about
life in old Siam: about relationships between monks and
novices, teachers and disciples, monastics and laypeople,
monks and bandits, parents and children, villagers and
animals, monks and animals. The recollections and life
histories offered by local monks and laypeople take much
for granted, however; they say little about the environments in which specific incidents took place, because everyone then was already familiar with local customs and
surroundings.

By contrast, the Westerners cited here, whose writings about their travels in Siam, Laos, the Shan states, and Burma were published between 1822 and 1936, tried to describe everything they saw. These Westerners—among them Catholic priests, Protestant missionaries, trade envoys, diplomats, college professors, travel book writers, engineers, a geologist, a bank manager, and a teak inspector—were contemporaries of the Buddhist masters in this book. They encountered a diverse people speaking a number of languages: Siamese, Lao, Khmer, Burmese, Yuan, Mon, Shan, Karen, Chinese, Vietnamese, Malay, Hindi, and Portuguese. Most locals were farmers who worked and lived outdoors. Travel—whether on foot, by boat, or by elephant—was slow and unpredictable, and travelers had to expect delays and discomfort. The rivers, jungles, and mountains were formidable. People were sure to encounter all kinds of wild animals, including snakes, tigers, leopards, and crocodiles, and often faced severe weather conditions. Westerners had to depend on the skills of the local people and the intelligence of elephants to get them through the forests. The attitudes and reactions of Westerners to the seemingly inhospitable environment are interesting to compare with those of monks.

Since so much of what determined the monks' actions occurred internally, and details of outward circumstances were so often omitted, narratives concerning them are often quite sparse. The comments of Westerners have therefore been included both to illustrate points and provide context. Although the Westerners' opinions and observations reflect their own biases and cultural conditioning, they tried to describe what they saw accurately. Their eyewitness accounts are like snapshots that give us glimpses of flora and fauna, mountains, rivers and canals; of the monasteries, monks, and many religious customs and practices; and of the modes of travel, local dress, foods, festivals, and funerals of local people. Westerners often wrote in their diaries or journals at night, while the scenes they witnessed or took part in during the day were still fresh in their minds. They recorded much of what they saw, because everything was so new and exotic for them. They wrote for European and North American readers who were curious about this part of the world. Some of the Westerners included here lived and worked in Siam for as many as thirty to fifty years, and some died there. Their accounts tell us what it was like to live in a remote village, to camp in the forest, or to run the rapids of a river. Just as the Westerners' reports shed light on the Buddhist monks' recollections, the monks' accounts reveal what was invisible to the outsiders' eyes.

THAI NAMES AND ROMANIZATION

SINCE THIS is not a purely academic book, technical terms have been kept to a minimum. Names of monasteries and villages have been translated into English whenever possible to help the reader get a sense of the environmental particulars (rocks, ponds, trees, and wild animals) after which the monasteries or villages were often originally named. Proper names that cannot be meaningfully translated have been left in Thai or local languages.

The naming and renaming of the monasteries reflect the difference in languages used by the Bangkok elite and local people. Local monks and people prefer short, commonsense, local names like Wat Nai, Wat Nok, Wat Klang, Wat Pho, Wat Liap, Wat Tinlen. The elites prefer long, elaborate Pali and Sanskrit names. As they fell under the influence of state Buddhism, abbots increasingly followed the elite naming practices. In this book, I use the local names.

Since the Thai language is infused with both Sanskrit and Pali words, in this book Buddhist terms such as *karma*, *arahant*, and *nibbana* follow common Thai usage.

In addition to *Ajan* (teacher), Thai Buddhists generally call their monks *Luang Pho* (revered father) or *Luang Pu* or *Luang Ta* (revered grandfather). When referring to the monks, I try to keep the Thai terms of address.

Instead of the Pali *bodhisatta* or Sanskrit *bodhisattva*, I use the local pronunciation *bodhisat*, because the word itself has a somewhat different meaning in local traditions than its Pali and Sanskrit counterparts.

In order to comply with the publisher's preference, I have followed the romanization system of the Royal Institute. One exception is the term *ajan* (teacher). Instead of *achan*, the Royal Institute's spelling, I write *ajan*, because it reflects both local pronunciation and English usage more accurately.

The following is a guide to the pronunciation of some of the monks' names. Romanization often results in names that look like English words but fail to capture the real sound of such names that a phonetic system would help to correct.

Name	English Approximation
To	toe
Man	mun
Chop	chawp
Fan	fahn
Son	sawn
Pan (monk in Ayutthaya)	pahn
Pan (monk in Phatthalung)	pun
At	aht
Iam	eeyam

The source notes provided at the end of each chapter appear in sequential order. Bibliographic particulars have deliberately been kept to a minimum. Publication details and translations of Thai titles can be found in the list of references.

Siam was renamed "Thailand" in 1941 during the Phibun regime. The term "Siam," as I use it here, refers to the kingdom that became known by that name, and "Siamese" refers to people who lived primarily in the Central Plains. The words "Thailand" and "Thai" are used in post-1941 contexts. As a result of the nationalist

policies of the Phibun government, "Thai" came to en-
compass all ethnic groups in Thailand, not just the
Siamese.

This book is dedicated to my parents
and
to all my teachers.

1 Chainat
2 Sing Buri
3 Ang Thong
4 Ayutthaya
5 Pathum Thani
6 Nonthaburi
7 Bangkok
8 Samut Prakan
9 Samut Sakhon
10 Samut Songkhram

Map 1 Thailand

THE PALELAI BUDDHA

IN 1905 Peter A. Thompson, a British land surveyor working for Siam's Survey Department, traveled from Bangkok to Suphanburi. Soon after leaving the Chao Phraya for the Thachin River, Thompson saw from his seat in the boat great numbers of ducks and herons. Then, "a little farther on a forest of long necks appears. We can approach quite closely, but at length a mass of silvery white, edged with sable, surges from the bed of reeds and with the clashing of a hundred pinions a flock of storks mounts heavenward. At a great height they begin to circle, slowly, still rising till they become mere specks. But another and another flock have followed in the wake of the first, and they too are circling in reverse directions. So they cross and recross each other, and we follow them with our eyes to seemingly infinite depths while watching the mazes of that wonderful flight." The sound of so many birds taking flight must have been extraordinary, given the great size of the stork.

As Thompson describes the area he was passing through, we see that in 1905 the countryside beyond Bangkok was still sparsely populated. "Beyond the great marshes we come once more to cultivation, invaded by patches of jungle. Still farther west we enter a region of scrub bamboo, and this at length gives place to forest. The forest belt appears to extend north and south, and covers the low hills which form a distinct watershed between the Tachin river and the Meklong river, in con-

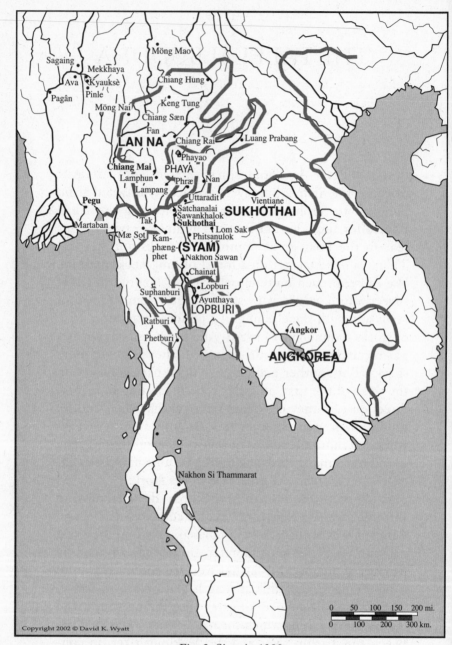

Fig. 2 Siam in 1300

trast to the cup-shaped plains which separate the Tachin river from the Menam [Chao Phraya], and the Menam from the Bangpakong river on the east."

In the course of his leisurely explorations along the banks of creeks and old canals, clues began to emerge to the area's mysterious past. Thompson learned that "farther west the natives tell of old walled cities, now buried in the jungle. Many temples were built in comparatively recent times, and their remains are scattered over the face of the country." Thompson himself came across many ruined monasteries. "Sometimes as we push through the thick undergrowth we come upon an image of the Buddha, long since forgotten, whose shrine has crumbled into ruins around him. There he sits, far from the eye of man, keeping his long watch over the jungle."

After returning to the Thachin River and proceeding northward, Thompson came to Two Brothers Canal in Suphanburi. He noticed that people living along the banks were not just Siamese and Lao. "This is a great fishing centre, and the water-way is almost choked with the weeds grown to harbour fish. Upon the banks of the *klong* [canal] there is a large Annamese population, who are Christians, and the French mission has established a little church in their midst. They do not intermarry with the Siamese, for they are all registered as French subjects, and the paternal French government imports girls from Annam to be their wives." When Thompson saw it, the town of Suphanburi was "no more than a collection of thatched cottages, but the extensive ruins of the old temples show that it must once have been a great city."

A mile inland from the Thachin River, Thompson and his party came upon a wat that he estimated to be several hundred years old. This was Wat Palelai, an ancient monastery built before the fourteenth century. Thompson and his companions were awestruck by the sight of a gigantic statue, made of plaster-covered brick, that they

Fig. 3 The Palelai Buddha in Suphanburi

discovered inside the narrow *vihara* (the principal building of a wat in which the Buddha image is kept). Thompson described the colossus in detail. "Within, at the far
end, sits a gigantic image of the Buddha, but for a moment we fail to grasp the full wonder of the sight, for we
must crane our heads backward in order to see higher
than his knee. He is seated as upon a chair, and repre-
sents 'The Buddha in the Jungle.' Upon the wall at his
side is portrayed a kneeling elephant, raising towards him
an offering in its uplifted trunk. Full seventy feet above,
the Buddha's head is dimly seen shrouded in the gloom
of the roof, amidst the wheeling bats. The image is built
upon the stump of a huge *takhian* tree."

Local people called this gigantic Buddha in a preaching
position "Palelai." The statue is 23.48 meters high and
11.20 meters wide. Archaeologists and art historians generally agree that this particular seated pose of the Buddha image was prevalent during the Dvaravati period—
that is, between the sixth and the thirteenth centuries.

By the beginning of the fourteenth century, Suphanburi
and Sukhothai in the north had become two of the most
powerful of the city-states that once made up the region
known today as Thailand. Suphanburi, which originally
meant "Land of Gold," was so named because of its
wealth. Its rulers engaged actively in trade, particularly
the ceramics trade, which extended far and wide from the
area south of present-day Laos and Vietnam, over the
trade routes to the west and south, across the Malay Peninsula, and into the Bay of Bengal. The people of
Suphanburi represented a variety of ethnic groups more
diverse than those of its neighboring city-state, Lopburi,
a hundred kilometers to the east on the Pasak River.

In the middle of the fourteenth century another city-
state, Ayutthaya, emerged and grew prominent as a center of great learning. The state's first ruler, U Thong (r.
1351–69), married a daughter of the king of Suphanburi,

who was a follower of Theravada Buddhism; from his relatives in Suphanburi, U Thong gained military know-how and manpower, very important resources for under-populated Siam. U Thong's mother was a daughter of the king of Lopburi, who followed Mahayana Buddhism; from his Lopburi relatives, U Thong gained people who were experts in law and medicine. U Thong's father was a wealthy Chinese merchant from Phetburi; from these relatives, U Thong gained experts in commerce. Gradually, the rulers of Ayutthaya brought all neighboring principalities under its influence, including Suphanburi.

In 1767 a great army assembled by a king of Burma sacked Ayutthaya and the surrounding principalities, captured local monks and laypeople, marched them to the west across the mountains, and resettled them in the kingdom of Burma. Wat Palelai, along with many other monasteries in Suphanburi, was deserted. During his reign (1851–68) King Mongkut sent a government official to Wat Palelai to begin the restoration of the ruined buildings. With the help of Ajan Klam, abbot of Wat Pratusan in Suphanburi, monks and local people worked to reconstruct the buildings, and when the restoration was completed, Achan Klam became the wat's first abbot.

At the time of Thompson's visit, Ajan Son Suwannasuk (1865–1932) was the abbot of Wat Palelai. Ajan Son was born in Suphanburi and became a temple boy at Wat Pratusan in his early teens. Under the monks at the wat he learned to read Thai and studied palm-leaf texts in Pali written in Khmer script. In 1886, when he reached the age of twenty-one, Son was ordained as a *bhikkhu* (monk). As a young monk, Phra Son studied under two other abbots, the heads of Wat Suwanabhumi and Wat Chaiyawat in Suphanburi.

In local traditions the relationship between disciple and teacher was close. Disciples served the ajan and were devoted to him. The palm-leaf texts were considered sacred, and so was the ajan. The disciple learned Dhamma not only by studying Pali texts but from living with the teacher and learning from his example and experience.

Phra Son's main teacher was Ajan Klam, the previous abbot of Wat Palelai. From him, through oral transmission, Son learned the meditation tradition and esoteric knowledge that had been passed down through the generations. The young monk also studied herbal medicine and mantras under Ajan Niam, abbot of Wat Noi in Suphanburi. He is said to have acquired the knowledge that enabled him to render himself invulnerable to weapons, cover great distances in a short time, cure snakebites, and heal victims of rabies resulting from the bite of a mad dog. With holy water Ajan Son was also able to heal people possessed by bad spirits. All this was useful and practical knowledge in a premodern society in which people lived in intimate connection with nature and had to defend themselves against all manner of dangers.

Ajan Son was also a skilled preacher. When he was a young monk he had trained to preach the Vessantara Jataka. He could perform all episodes of the Vessantara, although he is said to have been at his best in the Mahaphon, the episode in which the brahmin Jujaka traveled alone through a great forest in order to reach Prince Vessantara's hermitage. The preacher of this episode had to be good at describing the forest poetically: its trees, streams, and wild animals—tigers, deer, songbirds. Whenever he took on the character of the vile brahmin who deceived the hermit he met in the jungle, Ajan Son drew great crowds. Once the preaching hall was so overcrowded that the *sala* (pavilion) collapsed.

Thompson's visit shows that in 1905 Wat Palelai was an active monastery. "At the time of the Songkran festival (Siamese New Year) the monks mount by ladders to the roof, and copious libations of water are poured over the great image [the Palelai Buddha]."

7

The following account, also by Thompson, reveals that a few years after the imposition of state Buddhism, monks of Wat Palelai continued to follow their local practices. After the monastery was restored in the 1850s, not only did its forest tradition survive into the early decades of the twentieth century, it is also apparent that there were more than just a few branches of the Palelai lineage. "There are many wats in various parts of the country dedicated to 'The Buddha in the Jungle,'" Thompson wrote, "but of them all this is the chief. Some monks make a vow, which lasts for two or three years, never to sleep under a roof unless it be in such a wat." Local monks in the Palelai lineage followed the *thudong* (ascetic) practice of living solely in the wilderness except during the three months of the rains retreat. One of the monasteries in the tradition is Wat Palelai in Kanchanaburi, a province west of Suphanburi. Another is Wat Palelai in Rayong, about 280 kilometers southeast of Suphanburi.

Ajan Son was highly revered by local people as a meditation master and as a gifted Jataka preacher. He was the last abbot of Wat Palelai in Suphanburi who was educated according to local tradition. Ajan Son died in 1932 at the age of sixty-seven. He had spent forty-six years of his life as a monk. Local people remembered him as a physically graceful, generous, compassionate monk whose spiritual power came from deep within.

SOURCES

P. A. Thompson, *Lotus Land: Being an Account of the Country and the People of Southern Siam* (1906), pp. 277–280.

For a discussion of early Southeast Asia as a region with many centers, see Srisaka Vallibhotama, "Political and Cultural Continuities at Dvaravati Sites," in *Southeast Asia in the 9th to 14th Centuries* (1986), pp. 229–238. For the trade and other relationships among the rulers of Suphanburi, Lopburi, and Ayutthaya, see David K. Wyatt, *Siam in Mind* (2002), pp. 18–22.

For a brief history of Wat Palelai in Suphanburi, see *Prawat wat thua ratchanachak* (1982), vol. 1, pp. 604–606; for Wat Palelai in Rayong, see pp. 591–593. The main image in the ordination hall of the wat in Rayong is a Palelai Buddha that is six meters tall. In 1927 the abbot of Wat Palelai in Rayong, following Bangkok's rules requiring the renaming of the wat after the village or subdistrict in which it was located, gave his monastery the new name of Wat Pa Pradu (Monastery of Pradu Forest).

For the life story of Ajan Son Suwannasuk, see Phao Sakhuntasut, "Luang Pho Son," in *Chakrawan Phrakhruang* (January 1976), pp. 42–44.

By the end of the Jungle-Village era in the mid-twentieth century, the colossal Palelai Buddha image was no longer in the midst of the forest. The wat had lost its wilderness setting. It is only two kilometers by car from the provincial town of Suphanburi. For a discussion of events in the years after 1957, see Kamala Tiyavanich, *Forest Recollections* (1997).

Fig. 4 Somdet To, abbot of Bell Monastery (Wat Rakhang)

2

A STORK IN A SNARE

AN OLDER contemporary of Ajan Klam—the supervisor of the restoration of Wat Palelai in Suphanburi—was Somdet To (1788–72), a Bangkok monk known for his exemplary character and striking ways of teaching. His monastic name was Brahmarangsi (Sublime Radiance), but everyone called him by the name his mother gave him, To, or "Big" in English.

Before he became a Somdet, Maha To, a Pali scholar and master of the Tipitaka, was one of the teachers at Great Relic Monastery (Wat Mahathat) in Bangkok who taught Pali to the newly ordained Prince Mongkut. In the 1830s, not long after Prince Mongkut established a new school of Buddhism, later called the Dhammayut, Maha To took up a peripatetic thudong life, wandering the forests of Cambodia and the southern Lao states. It is said that he lived as a thudong monk in the Forest of Great Fires (Dong Phaya Fai) for fifteen years. This was a formidable jungle that separated the northeastern from the central regions.

In 1851 Mongkut disrobed, after spending twenty-seven years as a monk, to become king of Siam. Mongkut was then forty-seven; Maha To was sixty-three. The king ordered the Chief of the Sangha Affairs Department to track down his former teacher and invite him to return to Bangkok. In 1853 Mongkut appointed Maha To abbot of Bell Monastery, a royal wat in Thonburi. The title Somdet, roughly equivalent to that of Cardinal, was bestowed upon the abbot in 1864, when he was seventy-six years old.

Bell Monastery (Wat Rakhang) is on the west bank of the
Chao Phraya in Thonburi, which is part of Bangkok. Like
other town abbots of his time, Somdet To was perfectly able
to maneuver boats up and down the river and in and out of
the complex network of canals that existed in his day. However, abbots of royal monasteries were usually accompanied
by a few disciples, and it was these young monks, novices, or
temple boys who did the rowing, paddling, or poling for
their abbot. On a long trip, if Somdet To saw that his disciples were getting tired, he would sometimes take over the
task of rowing or poling and let his pupils rest under the
boat's bamboo hood.

Abbots from Thonburi and Bangkok were often invited to
preach in other towns and villages on the Central Plains.
Because rivers in the region meandered, often dramatically,
it was very time-consuming to go any distance by boat. In
1885 Ernest Satow, the British consul-general in Siam, traveled by boat from Bangkok to the northern region. When
he was passing through the Central Plains he noted that in
one place a bend in the course of the river looped back upon
itself to such a degree that, as Satow remarked, "One might
walk across the neck of land here in half an hour. On my
way down in the following February it took me two hours
and twenty minutes to row round, even with the help of the
current."

Somdet To had traveled all over the Central Plains. He
knew its rivers well. One day he was invited by a lay family
from Suphanburi to give a sermon at their house, which was
some distance from Thonburi. From Bell Monastery the
abbot traveled in a boat rowed by temple boys. They spent
the night in a sala, a pavilion in a wat compound. The house
they were going to was located on the bank of the Om River.
After they had rowed around several bends in the river
Somdet To told his pupils to stop. Instead of going by boat
all the way to the host's village, Somdet To decided to take a
shortcut by walking across the paddy fields. He got off the

boat and told the temple boys to continue rowing ahead on their own.

As he was walking across the fields he came upon a stork caught in a trap. The snare had sprung and caught the bird by the foot. A strong string held it fast. The bird kept attempting to fly, but it could not escape. The bird was compelled to wait for the owner of the trap to come and complete its fate. When he saw the bird's sorrowful predicament, Somdet To released the bird from the trap and let it escape. Once the bird flew away Somdet To put his own foot into the snare.

When Somdet To's pupils arrived at the village in Suphanburi they expected to see their teacher sitting at the landing waiting for them. When the host saw the temple boys but not the monk, he wondered why it was taking Somdet To so long to get there. Thinking the old abbot might have got lost, the host sent a group of men out to search for him. Before long the villagers found the abbot out in the field with his foot in the snare. When one of the men went to release the monk from the trap, Somdet To stopped him. "Don't release me yet. I have committed a crime. I must wait for permission from the owner of the trap." Somdet To knew that by letting the bird go he had violated the second precept, for he had taken something that had not been given to him.

When the trapper came to check his snare and saw that he had caught a monk instead of a bird, he immediately released the abbot. By doing what he did, Somdet To helped the trapper gain merit both for not killing the bird and for practicing dana (charity) by releasing—giving away—the captive stork. By giving up food for the body, the trapper gained food for the spirit. Having made merit, the hunter could now dedicate his merit to his dead relatives through the act of pouring water on the ground. Right there, Somdet To performed a Buddhist ceremony, chanting in Pali to give his blessings. The old abbot then followed the men of

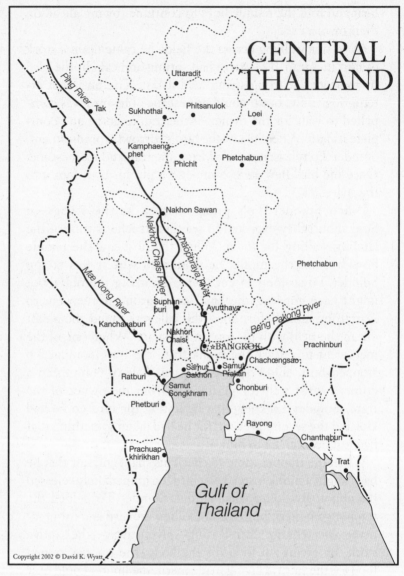

Fig. 5 Central Thailand showing places mentioned in the text

Suphanburi to their village to give a sermon according to the original plan.

Some of the Westerners who visited Siam noticed the deeply rooted Buddhist faith that enabled people to make merit for the deceased. Around 1900 Peter Thompson, the British land surveyor, observed that when villagers poured water on the ground they recited, "May this food which we have given to the use of the holy ones be of benefit to our fathers and mothers and all of our relatives who have passed away." In his journal Thompson described another local Buddhist practice that he encountered in Siam. "A man who has shown great charity, or built a splendid pagoda, sometimes desires to share the merit of his act with one who is dear to him, and there are stories of those who have desired that all the merit which they have made during their lifetime may be placed, not to their own credit, but to the advancement of the human race."

When Ajan Klam undertook the restoration of Wat Palelai in Suphanburi, he knew that without the leadership of the monks, the villagers would not have been willing to touch any of the ruined buildings for fear of being punished by the spirits who guarded the deserted wat. By helping to restore an old wat people gained merit which they could then dedicate to any beings they wished. By putting himself in the place of the stork, Somdet To enabled the trapper to make merit by giving away an animal in danger of being killed. The trapper, too, could then dedicate that merit as he wished.

Somdet To confounded aristocrats as well as commoners with his unconventional, witty ways of teaching the Dhamma. Stories of his teaching have captivated generation after generation of Buddhists. These accounts reveal that how the preacher communicates is as important as what he communicates.

SOURCES

Prawat Somdet Phra Phutthachan (To Phromrangsi) (n.d.), p. 57.

Ernest Satow, *A Diplomat in Siam*, 1885–1888 (1994), p. 28.

P. A. Thompson, *Lotus Land* (1906), p. 124.

3

A MUSLIM, HIS GOATS, AND A BODHI TREE

JOHN CRAWFURD, the Scottish trade emissary who came to Siam in 1822, estimated that the population of Siam at that time was 2,790,500, which he broke down as follows: 1,260,000 Siamese; 840,000 Lao; 440,000 Chinese; 195,000 Malays; 25,000 Peguans (Mons); 25,000 Cambodians; 3,500 natives of Western India; and 2,000 Portuguese. According to Crawfurd, of the 10,000 Malays living in Bangkok, most were war captives from the states of Kedah and Pattani in the Malay Peninsula. Crawfurd's figures may not have been accurate, but they illustrate the diversity of the population of Siam.

David Abeel, an American missionary who lived in Bangkok between June 1831 and November 1832, wrote disparagingly that "the Malays practise a species of Islamism mixed up, probably, with some of the ancient rites and customs of their pagan forefathers. They are exceedingly noisy in their devotions. At some seasons whole companies of them spend hours at a time in trilling out loud and long-drawn cries. The voices of men and women, of infancy, manhood and decrepitude, are mingled in such grating and boisterous strains as completely to disturb the surrounding region and to interrupt the repose of night."

From their residence in the crowded quarter of Sampheng, the first Protestant missionaries in Bangkok could hear the sounds of worship of at least four of the world's religions. In the Reverend Abeel's rather scorn-

Fig. 6 Bangkok in 1822

ful words, "A person may form some idea of the comparative reasonableness of these different religions without leaving his abode. One night he hears the bells and drums of Buddhism; the next, the wearisome candory cries of the Musselmans; the third, the gong, drums and squibs of the Chinese; and the fourth the bells, drums, crackers and guns of the Roman Catholics, which seem determined to confound the confusion of them all and then bear away the inglorious palm." The Muslims who settled in Thonburi also lived next door to Siamese, Lao, Mon, and Chinese residents.

In the nineteenth century the compound of Bell Monastery covered many acres of land, a much larger territory than it does today. The wat's entrance faced the Chao Phraya River. The land behind the monastery, on the side away from the river, was occupied by many Muslims who raised cows and goats. In the mornings the Muslim villagers brought their cows and goats to Bell Monastery to graze and drink water from the pond in the compound. In the evenings the Muslims would round up their animals and take them to their stables in the village.

It sometimes happened that after the Muslims let their goats and cows loose in the woods behind the ordination hall, they would go pay a visit to Somdet To (Cardinal Big). Somdet To was appointed abbot of Bell Monastery in 1853 when he was sixty-five. The Muslims called him "Reverend Father." Somdet To would tell the Buddha's story or explain Buddhist tenets to the Muslims, and they in turn told the monk about their Islamic beliefs. If the abbot was not at his *kuti* (monk's quarters), the Muslims would go to the sala to rest or take a nap. In the evening the monks usually assembled at the sala for meditation practice.

When Mongkut was king of Siam he received some bodhi tree seedlings from Bodhgaya in India, the place where the Buddha attained enlightenment. The king transplanted the bodhi seedlings with his own hands. When they had grown tall, Mongkut gave them to abbots in Bangkok and Thonburi. Somdet To carefully planted the seedling that he received in front of the ordination hall at Bell Monastery, but before he planted the little bodhi tree, he first had soil brought to the site and turned it into a mound two meters high. Then he built a brick wall around the mound, cementing the bricks to prevent the wall from collapsing. Somdet To asked the monks to see to it that the tree was watered every day and to otherwise keep an eye on it. The Muslims knew how important the bodhi tree was to the monks, and they made sure that their cows and goats did not go near it.

On a day when most of Somdet To's disciples were out and there was nobody around to keep an eye on the bodhi tree, a Muslim, Sitaram Pande, took his goats to Bell Monastery as he always did. After he saw that the goats were grazing happily in the woods behind the ordination hall, Sitaram went to rest in the meditation sala. Normally Sitaram kept a watchful eye on his goats, and if they wandered anywhere near the bodhi tree, he would chase them away. But that day he fell asleep.

When Sitaram's goats saw the bodhi tree on the mound they were drawn to it. The biggest goat leaped up to the top of the mound and started eating the leaves of the young tree. The other goats, too small to climb up, stayed on the ground making a lot of noise, as if asking the biggest goat to share the leaves with them.

From his kuti Somdet To could hear the sounds the goats were making, and he immediately knew that they were feeding in front of the ordination hall. He ordered some temple boys to chase the goats away from the bodhi tree, but by the time they got there, it was too late. The boys were so upset, they picked up dry branches left on the ground and used them to whip the goats into the woods behind the ordination hall. The temple boys then reported to Somdet To, "The goats have eaten almost all the leaves of the bodhi tree."

Somdet To asked, "Where were you? Why did you not take care of the bodhi tree?"

Kneeling on the ground, with their palms pressed together in respect, the temple boys confessed, "It's all our fault."

The abbot told the temple boys, "Go bring Sitaram Pande here. I want to find out what he has to say."

Relieved that the abbot did not yell at them, the temple boys crawled out of the kuti and ran to the meditation sala. There they saw the Muslim fast asleep, snoring loudly. They shook him and shouted, "Sitaram, Sitaram! Venerable Grandfather says you are to go see him at once!"

Sitaram sat up, rubbing his eyes. "What happened?"

"It's your goats! You let them eat up the leaves of the bodhi tree!" the temple boys shouted. "Venerable Grandfather has forbidden you to take the goats there. Why did you do it?"

Sitaram was shocked. "My goats went to eat the leaves of the bodhi tree? Why didn't you hit them?"

"We did hit them!" a temple boy shot back. "We chased them away. You must come with us. Venerable Grandfather wants to see you."

"The abbot will certainly scold me," Sitaram murmured to himself as he followed the boys. On their way to the abbot's kuti they passed the goats meandering peacefully under the trees. Sitaram shouted at his goats, "I will beat you! I will beat you!"

When Sitaram arrived, he saw the old abbot sitting on the floor of his kuti, leaning against a cushion. In keeping with the customary Siamese behavior before monks, Sitaram crawled on hands and knees to the abbot and prostrated himself. "I came to see you, Reverend Father," he said.

Somdet To asked, "Sitaram, do you know where your goats went to graze today?"

Sitaram, with his palms together, replied, "I did not know. I fell asleep."

Somdet To told him, "One of your goats climbed up on the mound and ate most of the leaves of the bodhi tree."

Sitaram begged for mercy, saying, "I really did not know."

Seeing that Sitaram did not try to defend himself, Somdet To looked at the Muslim with compassion. To make sure that this incident would never happen again, the abbot asked him, "Sitaram, do you know how important this bodhi tree is? Two thousand four hundred years ago the Buddha sat underneath a bodhi tree and attained enlightenment. People in this town revere the bodhi tree. Anybody who harms a bodhi tree will be punished."

Sitaram, his palms still pressed together in a gesture of respect, replied, "Reverend Father, the Buddha attained enlightenment under the bodhi tree over there in Bodhgaya. My goats ate this bodhi tree here at Bell Monastery. It is not the same tree as the one that the Buddha sat under."

Somdet To listened to the Muslim with equanimity. Seeing that the abbot was silent, Sitaram continued, "It is not sinful, Reverend Father. It is a different bodhi tree. It does not matter."

Somdet To couldn't help laughing. He said, "True. It is not the same bodhi tree. No harm is done. Go back to tending the goats. But from now on, do not let your goats climb up on the mound." Sitaram bowed to Somdet To and crawled out of the abbot's kuti. The Muslim sighed with relief.

Among Buddhists the belief in the sacredness of a bodhi tree still prevails. Westerners in Siam came across this belief through contact with devout Buddhists who were afraid to cut even a tiny twig from a bodhi tree. At the turn of the twentieth century Émile Jottrand and his wife were living in a house in Bangkok near Lotus Pond Monastery. The Belgian couple employed a female servant who was a Buddhist and a male gardener who was a Muslim. A bodhi tree began growing near the foundation of their house, and they were afraid it might eventually damage the masonry. On November 5, 1899, Jottrand, who was a legal adviser in King Chulalongkorn's Ministry of Justice, wrote in his diary: "In the absence of the gardener, I tell Mae Lek [the servant] to cut the rather thin stem. She answers me in complete fear saying that she could not do so because she would die as a result of this sacrilege. Since I prepare myself to cut the tree, she begs me to let go because my hand, the culpable hand, would wither and die." Jottrand's servant begged him to ask the Muslim gardener to cut the bodhi tree instead. "He is a Mohammedan and can do this without danger." In his journal Jottrand concludes his story with the words: "And I did not cut the [bodhi] to calm the fears of Mae Lek."

As a devout Buddhist, Mae Lek must have been familiar with the Phra Malai legend preached by monks at the beginning of the Vessantara Jataka Festival. The legend contains a conversation between Phra Malai, an arahant living in India, and Metteyya, the future Buddha, whose home is in Tusita Heaven. Metteyya outlined the Five Grievous Offenses that will prevent a person who has committed them from being reborn when Metteyya comes to Earth. These are "cohabiting with nuns, cutting down bodhi trees, allowing stupas to fall into ruin and letting [Buddha] images become dilapidated, causing bodhisattas to die a violent death, and killing [members of] the Sangha."

SOURCES

John Crawfurd, *Journal of an Embassy to the Courts of Siam and Cochin China* (1828; 1967), pp. 452, 449.

Early Missionaries in Bangkok: The Journals of Tomlin, Gutzlaff and Abeel 1828–1832 (2001), pp. 126–127.

Chantichai Krasaesin, *Somdet Phra Phuthachan (To)* (1964), vol. 1, pp. 264–273.

Émile Jottrand and Mrs. Jottrand, *In Siam: The Diary of a Legal Adviser of King Chulalongkorn's Government* (1905; 1996), pp. 232–233.

Bonnie Pacala Brereton, *Thai Tellings of Phra Malai: Texts and Rituals concerning a Popular Buddhist Saint* (1995), p. 212.

4

MATSI, THE BODHISAT'S WIFE

THROUGHOUT THE nineteenth century Buddhist preachers of local traditions in Siam used Jataka stories to convey the teachings of the Buddha. The Jatakas recount events in over five hundred of Gotama Buddha's previous existences as a bodhisat. In these past lives he assumed a variety of human and nonhuman forms, among them that of king, rich man, minister, brahmin, hermit, robber, monkey, elephant, deer, dog, horse, hare, lion, parrot, crow, *naga* (mythological serpent), and *garuda* (mythological bird-human). Laypeople, who had a voice in determining the subject of a sermon, generally preferred Jataka tales to Gotama Buddha's life story. These tales were full of exemplary and not-so-exemplary characters. They enabled monks to speak as animals as well as humans, and to improvise, something which they could not do in telling the story of Gotama, the historical Buddha. Back then the Jataka stories were performed at the wat, not simply read, and the monks who supplied the voices appropriate to the different characters trained for these roles.

In the Jataka stories both the young and the old found appealing heroes and heroines and exemplary spiritual models who embodied the bodhisat ideal in everyday life. This ideal of human conduct is not exclusively monastic, for it can be followed by ordinary people as well as by monks. The Jataka stories illustrate that anybody can achieve moral authority by practicing the ten spiritual perfections (Pali: *parami;* Sanskrit: *paramita*). The Ten Perfections are: *dana* (generosity), *sila* (moral virtue), *nekkhamma* (renunciation), *pañña* (wisdom), *viriya* (energy), *khanti* (forbearance), *sacca* (truthfulness), *adhitthana* (determination), *metta* (loving kindness), and *upekkha* (equanimity). Each Jataka story illustrates how the bodhisat perfected one or more paramis in each lifetime.

The object of the first parami, dana, is to inhibit selfishness and encourage generosity and selflessness. The practice of the second parami, sila, regulates the individual's behavior by requiring strict observance of the rules of conduct: the Five Precepts for laypeople living in the world; the Eight Precepts for lay ascetics; the Ten Precepts for Buddhist novices; and the 227 precepts for monks. Nekkhamma, the third parami, requires one to renounce worldly life and its pleasures by becoming an ascetic in order to inhibit the hindrances in the way of moral progress. The fourth parami, pañña, compels one to see things as they really are. With wisdom the practitioner gives freely to others whatever knowledge he or she has gained. With the fifth parami, viriya, one develops the mental vigor and strength of character that results in willingness to work unceasingly for the benefit of others.

Forbearance and patient endurance, or khanti, the sixth parami, teaches the willingness to endure unpleasant experiences, whether they result from natural circumstances, from other people's actions, or from our own doing, even if they lead to severe injury or death. We must also be willing to accept our own shortcomings and have the patience to correct our bad habits. The seventh parami is sacca. Truthfulness is always the guide of the bodhisat, who never lies and who does not break promises. The eighth parami, determination or adhitthana, requires the practitioner to be unwavering in his or her pursuit of the goals of service and perfection. Metta, the

ninth parami, usually rendered as "loving kindness," goes
beyond goodwill. The practitioner, as the embodiment
of universal love, must overcome obstacles, such as fear,
that get in the way of the bodhisat principle. The tenth
parami, equanimity or upekkha, requires nonattachment
and impartiality. The practitioner remains unmoved, unwavering in the path of principle, no matter how tempt-
ing it might be to take sides.

In every region of Siam the most important of all the
Jataka stories was the one known as the Vessantara Jataka,
which was the theme of an annual festival. It was believed
that those who sat through the recitation of all thirteen
chapters of the Vessantara Jataka in one day and one
night would be reborn as human beings when Metteyya,
the future Buddha, comes to this world. In the central
region of Siam the festival at which the Vessantara Jataka
was read took place at the end of the rains retreat, between October and November. The Siamese call the
story of Vessantara "The Great Birth." This story describes Gotama or Sakyamuni Buddha's next-to-last life,
when the bodhisat perfected *dana* to such an unprec-
edented degree that he attained Buddhahood in his next
and final rebirth.

The main characters are Prince Vessantara (Thai:
Wetsandon); his wife, Maddi (Matsi); their two children,
Kanha and Chali; Vessantara's parents, King Sanjaya
(Sanchai) and Queen Phusadi; and an old brahmin named
Jujaka (Chuchok). Vessantara is forced to renounce his
kingdom when his father banishes him for giving away a
white elephant that brought rainfall and prosperity to the
kingdom. Vessantara then gives away all his other possessions in order to live a celibate, ascetic life in the forest. The king wants Matsi and his grandchildren to remain in the palace, but Matsi chooses to take the children and go with Vessantara to live in the forest. On their
way to the forest Vessantara receives and turns down an

opportunity to become the king of another principality. Once settled in the forest, Matsi goes off every day to gather food for her family. One day while she is away, the brahmin Chuchok arrives at Vessantara's hut and asks the exiled prince to give him the children so that the brahmin's wife, Amida, might use them as servants. Soon after Vessantara gives his children away, Indra, king of the gods, disguises himself as a brahmin and comes to the hut. In order to prevent Vessantara from giving his wife to someone else, Indra asks Vessantara to give her to him. After receiving Matsi, Indra gives her back so that she can continue to take care of Vessantara. Meanwhile, Chuchok takes the two children to the court of their grandfather the king, who pays a ransom for them. Chuchok is served great portions of food and dies from overeating. The king, filled with remorse, goes to the forest with his retinue to find Vessantara and invite him to come back home. The story ends when Vessantara is reunited with his family and becomes king of a moral kingdom in which all prisoners are released from jail.

The Great Birth festival, once one of the most theatrical of all the Buddhist festivals in Siam, is dedicated to the bodhisat's fulfillment of the first parami, the perfection of generosity, accomplished in the hope of helping sentient beings free themselves from *samsara*, the cycle of birth and death. Monks and novices from various wats were invited to perform the characters in the Vessantara story. It took discipline and long training for preachers to act their roles effectively. Laypeople were particularly fond of hearing their own or visiting preachers perform those parts of the story in which Matsi and Chuchok appear. The Matsi episodes elicit great sadness as Matsi mourns the loss of her children; the Chuchok episodes elicit gales of laughter when Chuchok is shown to be a buffoon.

Somdet To, abbot of Bell Monastery in Thonburi, was a skilled preacher as well as a meditation master who followed the thudong practices. As a novice he began training to perform the role of Matsi, the most moving of all the characters in the Vessantara story. Somdet To had a soft voice that enabled him to render Vessantara's wife beautifully. The abbot's previous honorific title, Thepkawi (Heavenly Poet), conveys a hint of his gift for preaching. One afternoon, just before the Vessantara festival was to take place, a layman from Amphawa (today a district in Samut Songkhram, west of Bangkok) arrived at Bell Monastery to see Somdet To. The layman wanted to invite one of the monks to play the part of Matsi in a performance at Wat Amphawa. This layman had no idea that Somdet To had been reciting Matsi's verses skillfully ever since he was a novice, and he was convinced that senior monks like Somdet To could only deliver sermons based on the Buddha's discourses. So the layman asked that the abbot to send a monk who was a Matsi master to preach at the festival in Amphawa. Somdet To decided to go himself.

On the day of the festival Somdet To arrived at Wat Amphawa to perform in the episodes featuring Matsi, which usually lasted three hours. The laypeople, who were expecting a younger Jataka preacher, were disappointed that the old abbot was going to perform the role of Matsi himself. These same laypeople had prepared a large number of monks' requisites, made by hand, which they planned to offer to the preacher who played Matsi. When Somdet To appeared, the disappointed laypeople took away half of the requisites and put them aside to give to the next year's Matsi preacher.

Somdet To began his performance by providing the context in which Matsi finds herself. The Jataka sections concerning Matsi first describe her delayed return to the hermitage, then the awful discovery that her children have been taken away, her search for them, her great grief and suffering over their loss and, finally, her acceptance of the sacrifice. To be really accomplished in reciting an episode in the Vessantara, a monk or novice, like any good actor, had to become whichever character or characters in the story he was supposed to portray. A Vessantara preacher also had to be a master of folk poetry. His recitation of the verses could be so beautiful and so moving that it lifted the audience from their mundane lives to a different realm. Somdet To was skilled in the use of vivid words and picturesque phrases. In Somdet To, Matsi came alive. Listeners were completely absorbed in her plight, suffering, and the selflessness demanded of a bodhisat's wife. The preacher's voice and his mastery of poetic language transformed his audience. After listening to Somdet To's Matsi, the laypeople were so deeply moved that they brought out the requisites they had taken away. Somdet To ended his performance with a short sermon in which he said, "When making any offering, we should check our motivation."

Buddhist preachers often emphasized that the intention, the willingness to give, is more important than the lavishness of the gift. The quantity or value of offerings alone is not the measure of the generosity of a donor. Somdet To himself was known for his joyful giving. Whenever he returned to his wat from his preaching duties, he always distributed the requisites he had received to other monastics and to poor people.

In northeastern Siam the Vessantara Jataka festival is held after the harvest and before the beginning of the hot season, sometime between February and April. Lao Buddhists call their festival Bun Phawet. The Vessantara Jataka story was so familiar and so real to Lao villagers that they felt as if the bodhisat and his wife, Matsi, really existed in a different realm. Villagers also knew about

Vessantara and Matsi from the murals that adorned the ordination halls of local monasteries. Lao Buddhists even named a cave in Nakhon Phanom "Tham Phawet" (Vessantara Cave). As late as the 1940s this cave was still in the midst of wilderness.

Matsi has been known to appear in contexts other than the Vessantara Jataka. Ajan Chop (b.1902) was a thudong monk from a Lao village in Loei province who spent most of his life in forests. In 1930 Phra Chop (Venerable Fondness) spent the rains retreat at the forest hermitage of Woso Pond in Udonthani, in northeastern Siam, with Phra Lui, a fellow thudong monk. One day Phra Chop's mother, a white-robed ascetic (mae chi) who was living at the forest wat of Lotus Blossom Pond, also in Udonthani, came to visit her son. It had been raining hard that day and the night before. While the mae chi was resting in the sala, a beautiful woman, who looked like a princess, appeared before her. The princess told the mae chi that she was Matsi, Prince Vessantara's wife. This Matsi indeed looked as beautiful as the poetic descriptions of her that the mae chi had heard so often. In great excitement the mae chi got up and ran to her son's hut, some distance away, and called to him to hurry to the sala. Phra Chop was taking an afternoon nap, but his mother's urgent voice woke him. He jumped up, left his kuti, and began walking quickly with his mother to the sala. Just before he reached the sala, a huge tree in front of his kuti suddenly fell on the hut and smashed it to the ground. Had he stayed inside, he would probably have been killed. Once Phra Chop arrived at the sala there was no Matsi to be seen. All the monk saw were the framed paintings of her and Vessantara hanging on the wall. His mother insisted that she had in truth seen Matsi sitting right there inside the sala. Ajan Chop reflected on the incident and concluded that it must have been his good karma that a deity disguised herself as Matsi to save his life.

SOURCES

For a treatise on the Ten Perfections, see *The Discourse on the All-Embracing Net of Views: The Brahmajala Sutta and Its Commentaries* (1992), trans. Bhikkhu Bodhi, pp. 243–317. The explanation of the ten paramis is from Ashin Thittila, *Essential Themes of Buddhist Lectures* (1987). For examples of how Jataka stories illustrate the ten perfections, see I. B. Horner, *Ten Jataka Stories* (1957).

Interview with Phra Pariyatsuthi (Naep Phatthawanno), a deputy abbot of Wat Mahathat, in Bangkok, April 21–24, 1989. According to the deputy abbot, Phra Dhammakosachan (Chop Anuchari), a well-known Thai preacher and poet of the 1950s and sangha head of Chonburi province, thought that Vessantara was highly skilled in politics besides being compassionate. From Ven. Dhammakosachan's perspective, Vessantara gave his children away knowing that eventually his father, King Sanchai, would ransom them, and that this would lead to the reunification of the family. Dhammakosachan's verse rendering and explanations appear in *Parithat Vessantara Jataka* (1969).

For analyses of the Vessantara story, see Sommai Premchit, *Mahawetsandon chadok botwikhro thang watthanatham lae sangkhom* (2001). For English translation of the Vessantara Jataka, see Margaret Cone and Richard Gombrich, *Perfect Generosity of Prince Vessantara* (1977).

Chanthit Krasaesin, *Somdet Phra Phutthachan (To)*, vol. 2, pp. 227–228.

For Ajan Chop Thanasamo's account, which was written down by Suriphan Maniwat, see *Thanasamo-nuson* (1996), pp. 42–46. It was in 1928 that Ajan Chop met Ajan Man (1870–1949) and became his disciple. Years later, when Ajan Chop was wandering by himself in a forest at night, he came face to face with two tigers. For details of this event, see Kamala, *Forest Recollections* (1997), pp. 85–87.

5

MIDNIGHT VISITORS

WESTERNERS OFTEN described the agony of having to deal with clouds of mosquitoes or armies of ants. The widely traveled Jean-Baptiste Pallegoix, a French bishop whose church and residence were in Bangkok, described the misery that mid-nineteenth-century travelers endured when they had to spend a night on the water. In passing from a town on the Bang Prakong River in eastern Siam to the Chao Phraya, Pallegoix describes a memorable night spent on a canal linking the two rivers. "Unfortunately we were compelled to pass the night in the canal, where we were devoured by clouds of mosquitoes; all the night was passed in battling with them. O the misery of finding the blood sucked from every part of the body by myriads of winged insects whose venomous incision causes the flesh to swell with an intolerable itching! In the morning, the barge was covered with those plagues which we had killed during the night; and we could have filled two bushels with their remains. We were quite exhausted when we reached Bangkok, and had scarcely any blood left in our veins."

While camping overnight in a forest or on the bank of a river, travelers were likely to encounter wild animals or bandits or both. In August 1892 H. Warrington Smyth, director of Siam's Department of Mines, and his party journeyed by boat northwest of Bangkok along the river between Suphanburi and Kanchanaburi. "Boats which miss the tide remain fast in the mud until the next high tide brings water enough to release them—an event which, for the greater part of the month, occurs only once in the twenty-four hours. Armed dacoit gangs have been in the habit of waiting at these points, and making their descents at night on the boats lying helpless between the banks; and in the dry season, before the rains have raised the water-levels, the heavy-laden country boats are often at the mercy of the bad characters infesting the *klongs* [canals] for days together."

Buddhist monks, who were often invited to preach in villages far away, were used to spending the night on their boats. One day Somdet To, abbot of Bell Monastery, was invited to preach at one of the many villages along the banks of the Chao Phraya River. He traveled to the village in a boat paddled by temple boys. After a monk finished preaching, layfolk customarily offered whatever they could to the preacher. On that day the laypeople offered the abbot many monk's requisites, including pillows and hand-woven sleeping and sitting mats. These requisites were loaded into the abbot's boat. Some country folk took the opportunity to accompany the abbot back to Thonburi. Since it was a long trip, they had to spend the night in their boats, moored to the riverbank.

In the middle of the night, while the temple boys and layfolk were fast asleep, a boat approached. Somdet To had not yet fallen asleep. As he watched the men paddling quietly in the dark, the abbot could tell they were thieves. He remained silent as the thieves moored their boat right next to his and stepped on board. Unaware that the monk was lying there, utterly still, in the pitch dark, the thieves picked up the rolled mats and quietly loaded them into their boat. Somdet To thought, "These folk must really be in need of basic necessities. They must have to resort to stealing because they do not dare ask for bedding from the monks." The abbot then broke the silence. "Why don't you take the pillows, too!" The voice coming out of the dark startled the thieves. They leaped back into their boat, and as they started paddling away, Somdet To threw some of his pillows into their boat. Seeing that the monk did not object, the thieves rowed right back and accepted the rest of the requisites.

SOURCES

Jean-Baptiste Pallegoix's account is translated in Sir John Bowring, *The Kingdom and People of Siam* (1857), vol. 2, pp. 229–230.

H. Warrington Smyth, *Five Years in Siam from 1891 to 1896* (1898), vol. 1, pp. 39–40.

Chantichai, *Somdet Phra Phutthachan (To)* (1964), vol. 1, pp. 39–41.

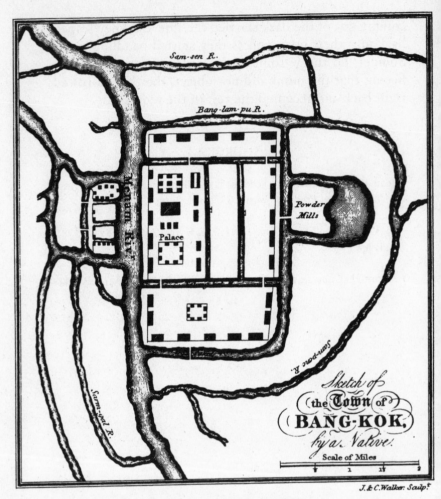

Fig. 7 Map of Bangkok in 1822

6

WHEN IN DOUBT, DO WHAT DOGS DO

SEVERAL DAYS after having argued with his abbot, Phra Thet felt ill at ease and wanted to get away, find some solitude, and regain his peace of mind. He thought of Somdet To, abbot of Bell Monastery, who was known for his ability to help people in distress. There was no telephone at the time, however, and Phra Thet had no idea whether Somdet To would be at his wat or not. But Thet got into his canoe anyway, paddled along a canal, and crossed the broad Chao Phraya River in the hope of finding the abbot.

That same afternoon while Somdet To was sitting on the porch of his kuti, he saw an unknown monk walking toward him. The visitor took off his outer robe and arranged it over one shoulder according to custom, before he approached the abbot. Then, summoning his courage, the visitor prostrated himself before the elder monk. Somdet To asked, "Who are you? Which samnak are you from?" In the nineteenth century monks referred to a monastery informally as a *samnak*—the place where one studied and lived.

The visitor, putting his palms together, replied, "My name is Phra Thet. I live at Wat Thongpu." This was a Mon wat in Bangkok.

Somdet To asked, "What is your business?"

Phra Thet explained, "I have been feeling uncomfortable for several days. I try to meditate, but my mind will not calm down. I feel so restless that even the ocher robe feels hot. I came here to bow down at your feet. Please give me advice that I can use in meditation to keep my mind at peace." That was all he said. Phra Thet did not mention that he had had a fight with his abbot.

Somdet To gave him this advice: "If you want to be at peace, just do what dogs do." Noticing that the young monk remained silent, Somdet To asked, "Do you know what I mean? Normally when two dogs get into a fight, one dog will pretend to give in and let the victor get on top, let the victor growl to show that he is in charge. Then the conflict is over."

Phra Thet bowed down to Somdet To saying, "I will follow your advice from now on."

When Phra Thet returned to Wat Thongpu he told his lay supporter, "It was amazing! Somdet To talked as if he *knew* I had had a fight with my abbot."

Somdet To's advice pointed the way to the cultivation of the second and sixth perfections: moral virtue and forbearance. By advising the junior monk to endure the unpleasant with humility, Somdet To actually taught Phra Thet about renunciation of the "self" (ego); about letting go of what we think we are and what we want. If we realize that all things are not-self, then there is nothing to defend, nothing to argue about.

SOURCES

The story told by Phra Thet is in Chantichai, *Somdet Phra Phuthachan (To)*, vol. 1, pp. 173–175. Wat Tongpu's official name is Wat Chanasongkhram (Monastery of Victory in War). It was so named to honor the Mon soldiers in Siam's army who fought Burma's armies in three battles in 1785, 1786, and 1788. Mon people continue to call the wat by its Mon name, Wat Tongpu.

7

DOGS, CATS, AND BIRDS

IN DECEMBER 1868 Henri Alabaster, interpreter for the British consulate in Siam, and his wife were rowed by boat from Bangkok to Lopburi. There were no hotels or inns at that time. Like all other travelers, the couple was welcome to stay overnight, free of charge, at guest pavilions conveniently located in wat compounds on the banks of the rivers along the way. The sala, suitable for a warm climate, was a simple roofed structure with a floor built well above the ground. It had no walls. The Alabasters slept under a mosquito net in one sala while the boat crew slept in another.

The British couple had trouble sleeping. "Our night is rather disturbed, not only by the mosquitoes, but by a number of dogs, who swarm about our quarters, and are made restless by our presence," Alabaster wrote. "Buddhists are forbidden to kill animals; so, whenever their dogs, or any other domestic animals, have the mange, or otherwise become a nuisance in the house, they take them across a river, and leave them to pass the rest of their lives in some monastery, whence it arises that almost every temple is infested with diseased and half-starved dogs; and in some cases, pigs and other animals add to the nuisance."

The compound of Bell Monastery in Thonburi was full of dogs, cats, and all kinds of birds. Back then there was no such thing as dog food, cat food, or bird food. These, mostly domesticated animals ate the same food as people.

Fig. 8 A sala (rest house), 1906

Whenever Somdet To ate at his kuti, the dogs and cats
that lived in the wat compound crowded around. While
eating with his hands, seated on the floor, the monk fed
the dogs and cats from his own bowl. Most people know
that dogs and cats can easily get into fights over food.
"Fighting like cats and dogs" is as familiar a saying in
Thai as it is in English. But when Somdet To fed them,
the dogs and cats never fought but ate together peacefully. Somdet To also gave leftover rice to the birds. Even
aggressive birds, such as crows, liked to rest outside his
hut. They were not afraid of him and did not fly away
when he approached them. Wild sparrows are hard to
tame; they are not easy to keep as pets. Yet sparrows
perched on the rim of Somdet To's almsbowl and pecked
away at the food in the bowl while he was eating out of it

himself. The abbot was full of compassion, and animals sensed this.

Temple boys, however, had a hard time sharing food peacefully with animals. Somdet Pun (1897–1973), abbot of Bodhi Monastery in Bangkok, was a temple boy at Wat Song Phinong in Suphanburi in 1909. There were a large number of cats, roosters, and hens in the wat compound. At that time there were more than a dozen cats living at the wat. Most of them belonged to layfolk who had abandoned them. Somdet Pun recalled that the cats were usually fed by the monks. In the morning after their return from almsround by boat the monks sat down on the floor of a sala and divided the almsfood evenly among themselves. The oldest monk then called a temple boy to bring a big tray for the cats' food. Every monk took a handful of rice from his bowl and put it on the tray. If the monks got any fish or fish curry they would also put some of that out for the cats. Somdet Pun recalled that as they watched the monks giving good food away, "We temple boys were not pleased that the monks gave barbecued fish to the cats, but we dared not voice our objection for fear of the rod."

In his diary Somdet Pun wrote, "Temple boys did not get along with cats. If the cats sneaked into the dining hall and stole food out of the bowls, the monks would spank us for not keeping an eye on the animals. If the cats pooped in the kutis, the monks would scold us for letting the cats into their rooms. Then the temple boys had to wash the floor. It made us so mad at the cats. When the monks were not looking we kicked the cats. Some of us threw the cats off the veranda. Others threw the cats into the water." The cats normally hid under a sala or kuti and avoided the temple boys, but in the morning, as soon as they heard the sound of a tray being banged on the wooden floor, all the cats came out of hiding. Then all hell broke loose. Somdet Pun recalled that

Fig. 9 A simple village wat

there was a fight at every meal. "Once the cats raced into the dining hall, the sala became incredibly noisy with their nonstop 'meow, meow, meow.' While some of us were preparing their food, other temple boys had to fend off the most aggressive cats. Even before we finished blending the rice with fish, some of the cats climbed right into the tray. As they fought for the food the cats bared their teeth and bit and clawed one another until all the food was gone. Roosters, too, would jump in. The cats struck the roosters with their paws. The roosters pecked back or kicked the cats with their feet. Sometimes the cats and roosters fought so hard that the food tray flew right off the veranda." Looking back, Somdet Pun sympathized with the animals. "The cats must have been really hungry. [Since monks do not eat after noontime] there was no food at the wat in the evening. In those days temple boys went home to get supper from their parents. Then they returned to the wat to sleep. Unless they found their own food, cats or dogs did not get to eat in the evenings."

Even as the urban population grew, village and town monasteries continued to serve as refuges for animals. Ajan Wanna (b. 1941) is abbot of Wat Lak Hok, located in a market gardening district laced with canals in Ratburi, southwest of Bangkok. In 1985 the abbot noticed that the population of animals in the wat seemed to be climbing. One day he asked one of his monks to tally the numbers of domestic animals in the compound. He found that there were 102 dogs, 166 chickens, and 48 cats. Rural monasteries like Wat Lak Hok, the abbot tells us, "are a place of asylum for animals. When laypeople have dogs or cats they no longer want to feed, they will leave them at a wat for monks to feed and take care of." The roosters and hens that had been abandoned at the wat were not always healthy. "Some chickens have only one leg; others have lame legs or crooked necks." These animals lived on leftover food from the monks' almsrounds. Ajan Wanna sometimes compared the difficulty of training newly ordained monks, novices, and temple boys of the 1980s with the difficulty of getting cats to follow instructions. "If you pull the cat forward, the cat will go backward. If you pull the cat back, it will go forward. If you lift the cat up, it will sit down. If you sit the cat down, it will get up."

SOURCES:

Henri Alabaster, *The Wheel of the Law* (1871), p. 275.

Phraya Thiphakosa, *Prawat Somdet Phra Phutthachan (To)* (1971), p. 65; and Chantichai, *Somdet Phra Phutthachan (To)*, vol. 1, pp. 171–172.

Somdet Pun's comments are from his diaries, published in *Banthuk Somdet Pa* (1984), pp. 11–13. Somdet Pun's disciples called him Somdet Pa (the equivalent of Cardinal Father).

Phra Wanna Wanno, *Phra Khru Wichaisilakhun* (1975), pp. 10, 77.

8

PADDLE YOUR OWN CANOE

MONASTERIES LOCATED on waterways had landings that were crowded with boats, for in Somdet To's day monks went on almsround in tiny canoes, alone. There were several types of larger boats available to abbots and other senior monks. John Bowring, the British diplomat who arrived in Bangkok in 1855, wrote in his journal on April 10 of that year that he and his party toured the city on a state barge and saw Buddhist monks begin their day by going on almsround. "We met *phra* (priests) of every grade, collecting alms, from the high dignitary in his grand boat, with umbrella and attendants, to the humblest devotees paddling a skiff only five or six feet long, upon the water." In the middle of the nineteenth century Westerners were still calling a bhikkhu a "priest," though that term eventually gave way to "monk" as the more accurate translation.

Westerners who lived in Bangkok and traveled into the countryside observed that *everyone*—men, women, and children—swam and handled boats with supreme ease. The French natural scientist Henri Mouhot, who arrived in Bangkok in 1858, described what he saw as he traveled along the Chao Phraya River. "We met a great number of canoes managed with incredible dexterity by men and women, and often even by children, who are here early familiarised with the water. I saw the Governor's children, almost infants, throw themselves into the river, and swim and dive like water-fowl."

Soon after he arrived in Bangkok in 1891, H. Warrington Smyth, director of the Department of Mines for the government of Siam, watched boat races taking place on the Chao Phraya. Smyth had nothing but praise for the female crews. "A large class of market boat, paddled by mixed crews of men and women to the number of sixteen or twenty, gave capital sport. The women crews, with their cross sashes of yellow, green, or blue, not only looked but often proved the smartest. Their rate of stroke was from thirty-six to thirty-seven for the first half-minute, after which it varied—now a long sweeping dozen to rest the tired muscles, then a spurt again, and finally they passed the line going splendidly and striking sixty-two to the minute, soaked and laughing, and ready to do it again." Smyth continues, "A race for the four-oared fishing boats was also most successful, the winning four rowing thirty-six of their powerful long strokes to the minute—a most remarkable performance."

In December 1892 Smyth was on his way to Paknam Pho (Nakhon Sawan) when his European-made "pinic" (pinnace) boat began to leak. Smyth remarked dryly, "Europeans are generally in a hurry to assume that their own methods are necessarily the best for all countries, and in the matter of boats I have seen it stated that, because the natives use dug-out trees for the principal part of their boat's hull, 'they have not yet learned the art of boat-building.'" Smyth, a well-educated geologist, rips into the inadequacies of the imported boat. "I have seldom travelled in one of these European-built pinic boats that did not leak, for after a year or two, the heat opens up all their seams beyond possibility of satisfactory caulking. For the narrow winding waterways their long straight bottom makes them quite useless, for they cannot turn. They are very crank [unstable] and desperately slow, and cannot travel on the rivers either as safely or as fast as the native craft. In a squall of wind or sharp current, with all their top hamper, they are positively dangerous."

Those Westerners likely to notice such things were quite impressed with local technical know-how, and some writers of books included beautiful engravings of mills, weirs, rice polishers, bullock carts, and, above all, boats. Smyth reveals that "in the native boats . . . the Siamese have attained a high degree of perfection, and their boats, as also those of the Lao, are admirably adapted to their purposes. With simple means every requirement has been met, so that in the Me Kawng boats the Lao have actually for centuries been in possession of the uncapsizable and unsinkable, the long-sought ideal of the Western boat-builder."

Buddhist monks were not only good at paddling boats; they were also skilled boat builders. Smyth met some of these master craftsmen in the Central Plains. In the village of Song Phinong in Suphanburi, he came across "a delightful shady wat" where, he recalled, "the monks were skilled in building the little narrow canoes in which they go their morning almsround at the river-side houses. . . . Those tiny craft have their centre of gravity so high, owing to the lofty stem and stern, that when unoccupied they will not float upright. Their beam is exactly sufficient for a man of small proportions to sit on the little stool amidships; they taper at the ends till there is hardly room for a respectable mouse, and in length they vary from seven to thirteen feet."

When he tried out one of these boats, Smyth gained new respect for the nimble skills of the village monks. "I spent the best part of an hour trying to get a boat's length from the bank in one of these ingenious craft, and in swimming ashore again to renew the attempt. I subsequently mastered a more roomy type, but I shall retain to my last day the greatest admiration for the watermanship of these Siamese mendicants, who even when bent old men go forth, and on their dexterity with their one little paddle risk their begging bowl and its contents, even on the waves of a wide windy river. For the meditation proper to a mendicant monk they seem perilous craft." The small canoe kept the young monk focused on the task at hand, and the "crankness" of the craft, Smyth adds, "makes it impossible for the paddler to turn his head to look at a pretty girl, which is doubtless just as well for some holy brothers."

As he traveled through Phitsanulok, Smyth observed, "A great deal of boat-building is to be seen all along the river, for the boat in the plains takes the place of the bullock cart and the elephant elsewhere, and forms the only means of communication and transport." The British geologist described the boats as having "flat bottoms of solid wood. . . . A wide teak log is used, or, better, a trunk of *mai-takian* [takhian tree], the most prized of boat-building woods. It is readily known in the jungle by its enormous size. Its durability, the fact that it defies all the tribes of boring worms which destroy most boats' bottoms, and the great length it grows to, cause it to be eagerly sought for all large craft, both on the rivers and on the sea-coast."

In the Central Plains, many boatbuilders were Chinese. In the southern peninsula, village monks were known for their skills as boat makers. Traditionally, boatbuilding took place in a monastic compound. In 1767, after Burma's army sacked Ayutthaya and King Taksin established a new city named Thonburi, he asked the ruler of Phatthalung to build a large number of boats for the new regime's navy and sail them to Thonburi. The dense forests of Phatthalung were full of takhian trees, and the Phatthalung ruler mobilized the villagers to fell them. Wat Palelai and Wat Khian Bangkaeo became the boatyards; all the Phatthalung boats were built at these two monasteries. (Wat Palelai in Phatthalung bears the same name as the forest monastery that Peter Thompson came across in Suphanburi around 1905, mentioned in chapter 1.)

Considerable care went into the process of procuring and preparing the wood for the boats. In all regions throughout Siam local people believed that all big trees, particularly teak and takhian, have guardian spirits. The belief that a fierce female spirit lived in every takhian tree prevented laypeople from cutting down such trees, except when they were truly needed. Tree spirits had to be propitiated and asked for permission before the takhian could be felled. Boats were carved on the sacred ground of the monastic compounds; as the monks labored at the work of hollowing the logs, the sacred power of the monastics was absorbed into the boats. When a boat was finished, a ceremony was performed to invite the tree's spirit to inhabit the boat and guard it when it went into the water.

As Smyth described it, "The hollowing process is practically the same in all dug-outs, great and small, and may be seen in all stages at the monasteries and other boat-building places on the rivers. The tree is hollowed with a narrow-bladed long-handled adze, and is then sunk for some time in water. When well soaked it is brought ashore, and turned upside down over a fire of shavings. This is regulated carefully, that the heat may be moderate and evenly distributed and the expansion gradual. When the sides have separated sufficiently, and the line of gunwale has reached an even curve all round, the ribs and knees are fastened in with hard-wood pegs. The former extend above the sides to receive the upper planks which may be added, and then the whole receives its coat of oil."

Smyth was full of praise for the local technology. "The result of this dug-out type of craft is that a vessel is obtained which never leaks, which does not hurt by running on a snag, and which lasts for twenty years without serious repair. Broad of beam, with rounded sections, no keel, and rockered ends, it is quick to turn and always manageable in any current; and, with the comfortable deck-house fittings and ample outrigged decks and gangways, the most up-to-date English boat-designer would find it hard to improve on the larger river craft."

Today far fewer young people, even among those living in rural communities, are able to swim and handle boats. During the second half of the twentieth century provincial roads increased from 2,118 kilometers in 1960 to 27,595 kilometers in 1989. Ajan Wanna (b. 1941), abbot of Wat Lak Hok, on a canal in Ratburi, observed, "In my youth boys and girls who lived along the canal knew how to swim as well as paddle canoes. Every house had a boat. Monks and novices paddled canoes on almsround. Today hardly any young monks or novices in my wat have this skill. They no longer need to row a boat on almsround." By the end of the twentieth century, the boating skills that people took for granted and the sturdy boats they used had become obsolete along with the monks' ability to build such boats. People took to the roads instead.

SOURCES

Sir John Bowring, *The Kingdom and People of Siam: With a Narrative of the Mission to That Country in 1855* (1857), vol. 2, p. 292.

Henri Mouhot, *Travels in Siam, Cambodia and Laos 1858–1860* (1989), vol. 1, pp. 41–42.

H. Warrington Smyth, *Five Years in Siam, from 1891 to 1896* (1898), vol. 1, pp. 9, 68, 43–44, 92–94.

For information on boatbuilding at Wat Palelai and Wat Khian Bangkaeo in the eighteenth century, see Thiphawan Phiyakhun, "Tamnan Ban Tale Noi," in *Saranukrom Watthanatham Paktai*, vol. 3, p. 1288.

Constance M. Wilson, *Thailand: A Handbook of Historical Statistics* (1983), pp. 172–175. During the height of the Vietnam War, these roads were built primarily for military purposes, to move troops and equipment to rural areas.

Interview with Phra Khru Siriwanwiwat (Wanna Wanno), abbot of Wat Lak Hok, Ratburi, April 16, 1989.

9

A DOG CAN BE A BODHISAT

LIKE MOST travelers of his day, Peter Thompson, the British land surveyor working for Siam's Survey Department, commented on the variety and abundance of wildlife in the country. Westerners found the snakes and crocodiles dangerous enough, but what they feared most of all were the local dogs. In 1905 Thompson wrote in his journal, "On our walks across country we really run less danger from snakes than from the fierce pariah dogs that guard every homestead. As long as we can face them, they are easily kept at bay with sticks and clods of earth, but it is unsafe to approach the homestead alone, for a solitary stranger may be surrounded and perhaps bitten before the children have time to drag the dogs off, and cuff them into unwilling submission."

Even monks were sometimes bitten by dogs when they walked into an unfamiliar village whose inhabitants did not know them. A thudong monk who had this experience was Venerable Grandfather Waen (1888–1985), a native of a Lao village in Muang Loei in northeastern Siam. In the early 1920s, when Luang Pu Waen was in his thirties, he went wandering in Tak. He noticed that villagers in Samngao district raised ferocious dogs. One day, while walking to a village on almsround, Waen was bitten by one of these dogs. He recalled in the 1970s, "When the dog chased me, the owner did not bother to call the dog back. He thought it was good that his dog was so fierce." That dog bite left a permanent scar on Ajan Waen's leg.

In the second half of the nineteenth century there were still extensive orchards in Thonburi and Bangkok. In the vicinity of Bell Monastery there were Chinese as well as Muslim communities. The Chinese and the Muslims liked to raise aggressive dogs to guard their orchards. Somdet To, the abbot of Bell Monastery, was known for his ability to pacify ferocious dogs. When Somdet To passed through Chinese and Muslim villages, he often came across these dogs. Not once did people ever see the dogs threaten or even bark at Somdet To. The dogs just looked at him. If a dog was sleeping in his path, Somdet To refused to step over the animal. Instead, he would stand right next to the dog and wait until it got up and walked away. Often he would ask the dog, "Excuse me, may I pass?" The monk's kind voice sometimes had the opposite effect. Instead of getting out of the monk's way, the dog would often get up, wag its tail, and walk up to him. Some of his pupils asked, "Why do you treat dogs with such respect?" Somdet To replied humbly, "The dog could be a bodhisat reborn as a dog in this life. I can never tell. Showing disrespect to any sentient being is an unwholesome act." People who knew him said the old abbot radiated so much metta that animals felt it.

SOURCES

P. A. Thompson, *Lotus Land* (1906), p. 195.

Luang Pu Waen Suchinno (1985), p. 45.

Chantichai, *Somdet Phra Phuthachan (To)*, (1965), vol. 1, pp. 171–172.

Fig. 10 Along the Chao Phraya River

10

VENERABLE GRANDFATHER EGG

WESTERN SOJOURNERS in nineteenth-century Siam were aware that town and village monks seldom stayed in their monasteries once the rains retreat was over. Jean-Baptiste Pallegoix, the Roman Catholic bishop who lived in Siam from 1830 to 1853, wrote, "For three months of the year, i.e., during the rainy season, the monks must stay in their respective monastery. The entire remainder of the year they are free to go from one monastery to another, to undertake long journeys and even to wander in the forest as they please and in the most distant regions of the kingdom. They know very well how to take advantage of this liberty. Everywhere one meets these wandering monks who traveled to entertain themselves, to look for medicinal plants or roots or gold and silver minerals." What Bishop Pallegoix did not mention was that monks also went wandering in search of meditation teachers and to visit sacred sites.

Westerners sometimes give us glimpses of where traveling monks went and what they carried. Between 1881 and 1882, Carl Bock, a Norwegian naturalist and writer of travel books, went on a tour through the northern states of Siam and described the Buddhist monks he saw. "During the rainy season the priests remain in the cloisters or temples, but when the dry season begins they wander about the country to different places of interest, especially the Phra Bat, where Buddha is supposed to have left his footprint. The full moon of the third month, corresponding with February, is the recognized period for the commencement of this pilgrimage, and then the priests can be seen going there by thousands."

Peter Thompson, the British surveyor who "discovered" the Palelai Buddha in the jungle, observed in 1905: "During the dry season it is the custom for monks in the village monasteries to make a pilgrimage to the Prabat mountain (on which is the footprint of the Buddha), or to some other holy spot. They carry with them nothing but the iron begging-bowl, a bag containing a few necessaries, and a large umbrella. In the heat of the day we may often see their white umbrellas dotted over the fields, and converted into little tents by strips of linen hung all round."

In the nineteenth century many town and village monks observed the peripatetic ascetic practice called *thudong*. The word *thudong* can be used as an adjective or a noun. There are thirteen thudong practices. Monks vow to wear robes made out of castoff cloth; they vow to use only one set of (three) robes; they vow to go daily on almsround for food and do not omit any house, no matter how poor the quality of the food offered; they restrict themselves to only one meal a day, which should not be eaten before dawn or after the noon hour; they eat out of the almsbowl; they do not accept food presented after the almsround; they dwell in the wilderness and there dwell under a tree or stay in the open air or in a cemetery; they vow to be content with whatever shelter is provided; and they must not lie down. It was (and still is) up to each monk how many, if any, thudong practices to follow and how long to practice each one. As one thudong master has explained, "These practices aid in the cultivation of contentedness, renunciation, and energetic effort."

Ajan Khai (1857–1932) possessed a combination of skills remarkably similar to those of Somdet To. Both monks came of age when the Jataka stories were still at

Fig. 11 Ajan Khai (1857–1932)

the heart of Buddha-dhamma teachings. They were both highly trained in the art of teaching Dhamma with drama. Besides being a Pali teacher, Ajan Khai was fond of the thudong life. Wherever he was staying during the Vessantara festival, he became a chant master for the role of Matsi or her children. Ajan Khai continued to perform Matsi when he was well into his seventies. His voice was so powerfully expressive that he could enthrall his audiences and make them weep.

Khai (Egg) was born in Egg Landing, a village east of Bangkok in what is known today as Chachoengsao province. When he was six years old, his father, following the local custom, took him to study with Ajan Pan of Wat Sothon in Chachoengsao. Khai lived at the wat as a temple boy before he was ordained as a novice. He studied local religious literature, which included the Jataka texts. Khai had a high voice, which was especially suitable for the roles of Matsi and her children. He is said to have been very disciplined and practiced hard every night when the festival drew near.

Khai was fifteen in 1872 when Ajan Pan, his first teacher, died. In Khai's day young monks usually studied under several teachers, gaining different knowledge from each. After Ajan Pan's cremation Khai traveled to Muang Phanat, a town southeast of Bangkok that had been established in 1828, just forty-four years before. The first settlers of Phanat (today a district in Chonburi province) were Lao Phuan who migrated from Nakhon Phanom, in northeastern Siam, to Samut Prakan, southeast of Bangkok, before moving again to Phanat.

In Phanat, Khai studied with a Lao monk, Ajan Chuang of Wat Noi, and attended him until Chuang died. Then Khai went to Thonburi, across the Chao Phraya River from Bangkok, to study Pali scriptures with a monk at Wat Hong (a monastery named for its donor, Hong). Khai, still a novice, spent three years at Wat Hong. He then left in order to study with Ajan Iam, abbot of Wat Latdan, a monastery on the Mae Klong River in what is Samut Songkhram province today. In 1877, when he reached the age of twenty, Khai was ordained as a monk at Wat Latdan.

In time Khai went to practice meditation with a teacher in Photharam in Ratburi, then took up the thudong life in order to find other meditation teachers. From Ratburi he wandered into a forest in Kanchanaburi, northwest of Bangkok, where he met a monk who lived at the foot of a mountain. Khai practiced meditation under this teacher for a while before wandering further on his own. In another part of the forest Khai met an ascetic monk who was living in a cave. Khai practiced meditation under the guidance of this teacher and went on himself to live in caves for another six years. He made a vow to practice for the benefit of all living beings. Here Khai encountered many wild animals that were also seeking shelter. At night the animals would lie down around his *klot* (a large umbrella with a mosquito net) to sleep but never harmed the monk. In the morning the animals left the cave and went into meadow or forest to feed; the monk went on almsround in the nearest village.

Ajan Khai continued to wander on foot all over Siam for fifteen years. He never traveled by boat. Along the way he met many people who came to him for help with one thing or another. Every year village parents who did not want their sons to be conscripted into Siam's army brought them to Ajan Khai and asked him to sprinkle holy water on them. Young men who were not conscripted attributed their good luck to Ajan Khai's holy water.

In his old age Ajan Khai returned to Bangkok and stayed at Wat Tinlen (Monastery at the Edge of the Swamp). During the first half of the nineteenth century this wat was a forest monastery located outside the city wall. The majority of resident monks were meditators, although every abbot of Wat Tinlen was also a Pali scholar. On a wall of the wat's ordination hall one can still see a row of small paintings of monks sitting in meditation, contemplating the various stages of decay of the corpses in front of them.

By the 1920s most city abbots had accepted the new curriculum developed by Prince Wachirayan. There were no longer many meditation teachers in Bangkok monasteries. This decline needs to be seen in the context of the goals of state Buddhism. Phra Paisal, abbot of Wat Pa Sukhato, a forest monastery in Chaiyaphum, notes that under the leadership of Prince Wachirayan, the final goal of striving for nibbana, "which was treated as a remote ideal by King Mongkut, was virtually ignored." Referring to *Navakovada*, the introductory text for new monks written by Wachirayan, Phra Paisal points out that the section describing the code of morality for laypeople says "nothing about the ultimate goal *(paramattha)*. In discussing *attha* (goal or benefit), only temporal and mental goals are referred to. [The Dhammayut sangharaja] considered *nibbana* unnecessary, not only for the laity, but also for the monks. This resulted in the phrase '*nibbana* realization' being removed from the statement of aspiration of the candidate in the ordination ceremony. In his teaching, the benefit of morality was emphasized only in temporal terms, without indicating any connection to the ultimate or spiritual goal. Meditation has also been ignored in the entirely bookish modern Sangha education system." The later years of Ajan Khai's life need to be seen in this context.

Although Ajan Khai had a number of followers on both banks of the Chao Phraya River, he preferred solitude and kept mainly to himself in order to practice meditation. He was known for his incredible patience and his great compassion. One day, having realized that he missed the thudong life, Ajan Khai gathered up his bowl, klot, and bag to go wandering. This was in 1927, when he was seventy years old. When the laypeople saw him getting ready to go, they begged him not to leave them. They thought he was too old to go off on a thudong. They were also afraid they might never see him again. His disciples, too, begged him to stay at the wat to teach meditation. Ajan Khai gave in to his disciples' wishes and stayed on at Wat Tinlen to teach meditation to monks and laypeople.

Bangkok in the 1920s was a melting pot. Frank Exell, an English schoolteacher who arrived in the city in 1922, observed, "Nothing could be more varied than the street scenes. If Bangkok was nothing less it was cosmopolitan. Its population represented a pretty good cross-section of Asia and Europe. If you had the energy to walk from one end of the New Road to the other, you would come across Burmese, Pathans, Malays, Cambodians, Peguans [Mon from Pagan], Laos, Japanese, Madrassees, Singalese, and of course, Chinese. Most of them dressed distinctively. There were the flowing robes of the Pathan, the sarong of the Malay, and panuang of the Siamese. And what greater contrast could you have had than the yellow robe of a Buddhist priest and the long black gown of his French Roman Catholic counterpart? It was a riot of colour, race and creed. And yet you did not sense any antagonism."

There were Chinese and Indian Sikh communities in the vicinity of Wat Tinlen. People from these quarters sometimes sought Ajan Khai's help when they fell ill or were injured. It did not matter to him whether they were Buddhists or not; Ajan Khai helped them all by giving them medicine that he had already made up or suggesting specific herbs to use as teas or as poultices. He was also known for his ability to cure people with psychological problems. Ajan Khai's training and long experience as a thudong monk made him a valuable resource for the local community because of his extensive knowledge of plants and their healing properties. A thudong monk on the trail or living alone in a cave needed to know which plants would cure him of a bad bout of diarrhea or which ones would stop an infection caused by a tick or a thorn.

To encourage people to continue the practice of Dhamma, thereby extending the life of the religion, Somdet To is said to have made as many as 84,000 *phra phim*, amulets in the form of clay votive tablets. The number 84,000, which is considered sacred, reflects the number of Dhamma teachings in the Tipitaka. Like Somdet To, Ajan Khai also made amulets by hand. Before they gave amulets to laypeople the monks reminded them that amulets protected only those who practiced moral precepts. One art historian describes votive tablets as "small Buddhist icons, usually made out of baked or unbaked clay by a press-mould technique, a process that has been used for many hundreds of years to produce religious objects. Originating in ancient India, they are called *phra phim* in Thai, but are sometimes better known in the West by their Tibetan name *tsha tsha*." The act of making *phra phim* has been considered an important religious practice from ancient times. "The stamping was repeated over and over as a method to gain merit and as a meditative devotional exercise similar to counting the rosary. Monks also left behind tablets they stamped as merit-making or as devotions as they traveled."

Like local Buddhist masters, Somdet To and Luang Pu Khai used amulets as a vehicle to teach Dhamma. Traditional masters understood that ordinary people needed the sacred for their own security. The making and use of amulets, castigated as magic or superstition by rationalists, was actually guided by Buddha-dhamma. State Buddhism, which has its roots in Prince Mongkut's reforms, is against superstition. Phra Paisal, a contemporary Buddhist thinker, has observed, however, that the reformers did not "get rid of" superstitions, they merely "expelled them from the wats." Magic and superstition fell prey to money-makers outside the influence of Buddhist masters. "This degraded form of superstition," Phra Paisal continues, "aiming to gratify any desire, does not require any morality on the part of the client. This lack of moral obligation is the main factor that differentiates malign superstition from superstition that was part of traditional Buddhism." In the second half of the twentieth century, amulets became commercial products to be consumed. Once made by hand, amulets are now cranked out in huge numbers by machines in factories. Anybody who has money can buy "sacred" amulets without any moral obligation, without any need to practice sila-dhamma (ethical conduct). Amulets that once were given away as reminders of the teachings and the protections offered by the Dhamma are now sold as commodities or collectors' items.

Ajan Khai never charged money for the amulets he made, nor did he keep any of the money that laypeople gave him. He spent it on the restoration of Wat Tinlen's buildings, which at the time were mostly made of wood, and on other improvements. Ajan Khai was able to oversee the building of new kutis and a tank to store rainwater, and he had a pond dug in the wat compound. When he was not supervising construction work, he could be found copying Tipitaka texts by hand. Although monks in Bangkok had been studying from the machine-printed textbooks written by Prince Wachirayan, Ajan Khai continued to follow the local custom of copying the sacred palm-leaf texts by hand and offering the copies to the wat, in his case Wat Tinlen. Ajan Khai even hired skilled calligraphers to help him inscribe the words on the palm leaves.

Venerable Grandfather Khai died during the reign of Rama VII. On January 7, 1932, he became seriously ill and took to his bed. Ten days later he passed away. Just before he died, he overcame his pain and asked his disciples to help him sit up and light incense sticks. He paid homage to the Buddha, then sat in meditation. About fifteen minutes later his breathing stopped completely. Luang Pu died in samadhi. His disciples then laid his body down in a sleeping position. He was seventy-four years old. For the fifty-four years of his monastic life Ajan Khai combined the study of Pali texts with the practice of meditation and various social responsibilities. In addition to Dhamma teachings and meditation instruction, he gave confidence-inspiring amulets to the worried or fearful and medicine to the sick, free of charge, and he brought comfort to the unhappy. Ajan Khai was never an abbot, a position he never sought.

SOURCES

Jean-Baptiste Pallegoix, *Description of the Thai Kingdom or Siam: Thailand under King Mongkut* (1854; 2000), p. 268.

Carl Bock, *Temples and Elephants* (1884; 1986), p. 105.

P.A. Thompson, *Lotus Land* (1906), p. 122.

The quotation of the thudong master is from *Food for the Heart: The Collected Teachings of Ajahn Chah* (2002), p. 398.

Wat Bophitphimuk (Wat Tinlen's official name) has published a large photograph of Ajan Khai Inthasaro, the reverse of which contains a life story of the monk. For a short biography of Ajan Khai, see Phatsakhon Chuthaphutthi, *Phra Phuttharup lae singsaksit* (1982), vol. 3, pp. 105–107. The abbot welcomed Ajan Khai, who became a meditation teacher at the wat, choosing to settle down at Wat Tinlen precisely because it was a meditation wat.

F. K. Exell, *In Siamese Service* [1922–36] (1967), pp. 37–38.

The citations on votive tablets are from ML Pattaratorn Chirapravati, *Votive Tablets in Thailand: Origin, Styles, and Uses* (1997), p. 1.

For a discussion of amulets in premodern Siam, see Srisaka Vallibhotama, *Phra khruang nai muang Siam* (1994).

Phra Paisal Visalo, "Buddhism for the Next Century: Toward Renewing a Moral Thai Society" (2003), pp. 5, 3; and *Buddhasasana thai nai anakhot* (2003).

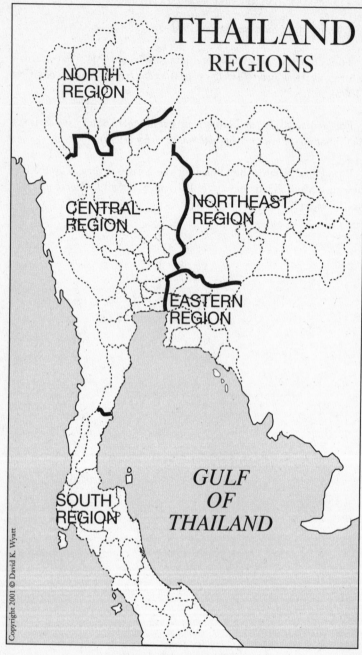

Fig. 12 Thailand regions

11

TWO LEGS MONASTERY

LIKE AJAN Khai, Ajan Butda (1894–1994), who lived to be a hundred years old, never became an abbot. The natal villages of Ajan Khai in eastern Siam and Ajan Butda in the Central Plains were inhabited, respectively, by Khmer and Lao people. They were brought to the area in response to a policy of the Siamese government that called for the forced resettlement of prisoners of war, largely captive villagers, to replace populations that had been taken away by Burma's armies. Up until the middle of the nineteenth century, whenever Siam's kings went to war with the rulers of Vientiane, their armies managed to capture large numbers of Lao people, march them to the Central Plains, and resettle them in Ratburi, Saraburi, and Lopburi, and east of Bangkok in Chachoengsao, Nakhon Nayok, and Chanthaburi. Other Lao captives were taken to parts of Nakhon Chaisi (later renamed Nakhon Pathom), Suphanburi, and Kanchanaburi, west of Bangkok.

In Lopburi large numbers of Lao Phuan people were settled in Ban Mi and Khok Samrong districts. Ajan Butda was born in 1894 in Phukha Village, Khok Samrong. His name, he said, means "son and daughter" in his parents' dialect. Like most Siamese and Lao people of their time, Butda's parents had no family name or surname. The last names that Thai people have today were acquired as a result of European influence and the trend set by the Bangkok elite during the reign of Rama VI (r. 1910–25).

Butda's parents had seven children, four boys and three girls. When he was only five Butda asked to be allowed to live at the village wat. His parents said no. Unlike most children in his village, Butda was not naughty. He willingly helped his parents do farm chores, and his parents were naturally reluctant to lose his labor. When he was ten, Butda told his mother that he wanted to be ordained as a novice to make merit for her. Again his parents said no; they needed him to work on the farm.

In 1914, when he was twenty, Butda was conscripted into the army of Siam. He served for two years at the Fort of the Big Cannon in Garlic Knoll district, Lopburi. It was while he was in the army that Butda learned to read and write Thai. When he got out of the army Butda went home to his parents, who needed his labor more than ever. According to Lao custom, when a man got married, he moved to his wife's village. Since Butda was still single, he continued to live with his parents. He worked on the farm for another six years, and then Butda's parents finally allowed him to ordain. In 1922, at the age of twenty-eight, Butda was ordained at Long Knoll Monastery in Ban Mi district. Venerable Teacher Aim was his preceptor. Twenty-five monks participated in Butda's ordination ceremony. For the rest of his life Ajan Butda considered all twenty-five monks who took part in the ceremony as his teachers. From the day he was ordained Butda began to practice meditation and vowed to remain in the robes for life.

For most of his monastic life Ajan Butda followed the traditional thudong practices. He wandered up and down both sides of the Mekong River, into the high mountains and through dense forests, visiting villages in remote areas. The ajan stayed put in a wat only for the three months of the rains retreats. The extent of his wandering can be seen from the record of the wats at which he stayed: these were in Nakhon Sawan, Chainat, Saraburi, and Lopburi in the Central Plains; in Phetchabun and Nong Khai in the northeast; in Chiang Mai and Fang in the north; in Ratburi and Phetburi in the southwest; in Chachoengsao, Chonburi, and Rayong in the east. In the south Ajan Butda occasionally stayed at Suan Mokkha-balarama (Grove of the Power of Liberation) in Surat Thani to visit Ajan Buddhadasa (1906–93), the forest master who brought nibbana back to its central place in Thai Buddhism. They enjoyed discussing Dhamma with each other. Ajan Butda's last trip to Suan Mokkh was in 1990, just before the rains retreat began.

Throughout his years of wandering Ajan Butda was often invited to villagers' houses to perform Buddhist ceremonies and give sermons. One day, as he was approaching a village, a man ran up to him and asked the monk, "Which is your wat?" Ajan Butda replied, "Wat Song Kha [Two Legs Monastery]. Wherever my two legs stand, that is my wat." In the context of the Dhamma, the two legs symbolize wisdom and compassion.

Like his village teachers, who studied local religious literature, including the Jataka stories, Ajan Butda believed that Gotama Buddha practiced paramis over many successive lives as a bodhisat before he was able to attain enlightenment. By the turn of the twentieth century the Bangkok elite of his day no longer believed that the Jataka stories had been narrated by the Buddha. Ajan Butda, however, was convinced that the Buddha had been a bodhisat in his former lives.

Ajan Butda, who followed the bodhisat practice, was able to remember his own past lives. During one rains retreat, he told his disciples, he crossed the Mekong River to stay at a Lao wat in Vientiane. While there he visited Wat Phakaeo, the Lao home of the Emerald Buddha. As he walked past three Tipitaka cabinets in the wat museum, he suddenly recollected that he had built these cabinets over three of his former lives as abbot of the wat. He recognized his own handwriting in the local language inscribed on the cabinets.

Ajan Butda also told his disciples that he had been abbot of Wat Phakaeo in Vientiane for three of his past lives. In one life he was ordained as a *samanera* (novice) and then took higher ordination as a bhikkhu. Five years later he was asked to be abbot of Wat Phakaeo. It was while serving as abbot that he inscribed the palm-leaf texts and put them in the cabinets that he had built.

In his next life he was reborn in a different village. When he was a boy his father took him to Wat Phakaeo. The little boy pointed to the Tipitaka texts in a cabinet and told his father, "These are my books!" His father scolded him, saying, "Not your books! The wat's books!" When the boy grew up, he again became abbot of Wat Phakaeo.

In his next rebirth, the little boy asked his father to take him to Wat Phakaeo and begged his parent to allow him to remain there. He was ordained as a novice. When the abbot died Butda was still in his teens and could not take bhikkhu ordination until he reached twenty. Nevertheless, the Lao locals insisted on giving the abbotship to the samanera. As abbot he again began to copy the Tipitaka onto palm leaves.

Ajan Butda tells us that he was reborn as abbot of the same monastery three lives in a row because of his attachment to the wat in Vientiane and to his handiwork there. In 1893 he was reborn in Siam. It was in this life that Ajan Butda went on thudong to visit Wat Phakaeo in Vientiane. But the Tipitaka texts he had once inscribed were no longer there. All he saw were the empty cabinets.

For Ajan Butda, as for many village monks who studied local religious literature, the Jataka stories provided a key source for the teaching of Dhamma. On one occasion a lay follower brought her friend, a thirty-year-old woman who had been unhappy for quite some time, to see the teacher. As this depressed woman prostrated herself before Ajan Butda, he said to her. "You were my mother in one of my five hundred former lives." Upon hearing this, the woman wept. With tears running down her cheeks, she asked Ajan Butda, "If I was your mother in a former life, why is my present life so full of endless suffering?"

Ajan Butda replied, "This is the way things are. You either enter another woman's womb or you allow another to enter your womb to be reborn."

On another occasion Ajan Butda was invited to give a sermon at a wedding in rural Thailand. Unlike Protestant ministers, Catholic priests, and Jewish rabbis, Buddhist monks do not normally perform wedding ceremonies. Customarily a marriage was performed by a layman versed in traditional rituals or by a respected elder. On their wedding day the bride and groom made merit by offering food to monks and inviting the most senior monk to give a sermon and offer blessings for the couple's happiness. Sometimes nine monks were invited, as nine was considered an auspicious number. These nine, together with the Buddha image, made ten, an even number considered auspicious for a wedding. On this day four couples were getting married at the same time, and Ajan Butda was invited to give a sermon.

Instead of the usual sermon about how a husband should minister to his wife and how she should reciprocate, Ajan Butda talked about supramundane happiness, the pure happiness of liberation from greed, delusion, and aversion. As Ajan Butda went on describing the joys of renunciation, the brides and the bridegrooms began to have doubts about embarking upon the married life. By the time he finished his sermon the couples-to-be had made up their minds not to enter the householder's life.

Instead of offering blessings at the wedding ceremony, the monk was asked to perform ordinations for the grooms and brides who now wished to become bhikkhus and mae chi (white-robed renunciants). Some of the grandfathers and grandmothers of the brides and grooms were so moved by Ajan Butda's teaching that they also wished to ordain along with their grandchildren. Unfortunately, since Bangkok authorities did not recognize Ajan Butda as a preceptor, he could not ordain them.

Ajan Butda had followers all over Thailand at monasteries where he spent rains retreats. Wherever he stayed, laypeople came to him to seek advice on problems they had while living in a modern society full of stress and suffering. At his Two Legs Monastery Ajan Butda was accessible to people from all walks of life. Ajan remained peripatetic until he was seventy. He lived to the ripe old age of 101, by which time he had met nearly all of the meditation masters of the twentieth century.

SOURCES

For Luang Pu Butda's life story, see *Luang Pu Lao Wai* (1994), pp. 1–5, 11, 13, 19, 44, 59.

For information on Lao settlements in central and eastern Siam, see Srisaka Vallibhotama, *Laeng Arayatham Isan* (1991), pp. 287–300.

For the teachings of Buddhadasa, see *Heartwood of the Bodhi Tree* (1994); "Nibbana for Everyone" *in Keys to Natural Truth* (1999); Santikaro Bhikkhu, "Buddhadasa Bhikkhu: Life and Society through the Natural Eyes of Voidness," (1996), pp. 147–193; and http://www.suanmokkh.org

For information on the Emerald Buddha image in Vientiane, see John Bowring, *The Kingdom and People of Siam* (1857), vol. 1, pp. 317. Vientiane was founded in 1530 A.D., and the Emerald Buddha remained in the city for 215 years. Following an attack on Vientiane,

General Chakri "invited" the image to accompany him to Thonburi. For the last three years of King Taksin's reign (1767–82) the Emerald Buddha was housed at the Temple of Dawn. Later, after Chakri became King Rama I (r. 1782–1809), he ordered the construction of the Emerald Buddha Temple in Bangkok to house this image.

Fig. 13 A Buddha image which Westerners referred to as an idol

IDOL OR GUIDE?

SOME NINETEENTH-CENTURY Westerners, especially Protestant missionaries, referred disparagingly to the Buddha images they saw, calling them idols. On April 12, 1829, on the Siamese New Year, Jacob Tomlin, a British missionary with the London Missionary Society, took a stroll around Sampheng, a Bangkok neighborhood whose inhabitants were mostly Chinese. Tomlin wrote in his journal: "Seeing the Siamese visiting the pagodas, we entered one and found several women and children sitting before the idols, worshipping and making offerings of fruit and flowers to them. One woman advanced and crouched to an idol with two beautiful lotuses in her hands. A priest [Buddhist monk] stood by and saluted us cordially on entering, but on our saying a few words to the women on the folly and wickedness of giving the beauties of Divine Providence to senseless idols he was a little sullen and evidently displeased." Two years later Tomlin and his party went to visit Bodhi Monastery (Wat Pho) in Bangkok. On January 4, 1831, Tomlin wrote in his journal, "While going round and viewing these idols a crowd of persons gathered about us, with two of whom, a boy and a young man, we had a smart contest, they contending earnestly for the honour of their idols and we for the true God. We were then in the presence of a gilded and gigantic idol, standing erect about thirty-five feet high. If he be God, we said, he is able to defend himself, for he is both big enough and old enough. We are now speaking against him in his presence, let him answer for himself; but the idol remaining dumb, the lad was obliged to admit that he could not speak; nevertheless, said he, 'he is *prah*' (a God)."

Frederick Arthur Neale, an Englishman who was made an officer in Siam's armed forces at the beginning of King Mongkut's reign (1851–68), visited many monasteries in Bangkok and Thonburi. "An ignorant demi-civilized being goes into the temple where he worships," Neale wrote, "and he sees idols [Buddha images], and hears fabulous tales [Jataka stories] rehearsed by the priestcraft of his idolatrous creed; he sees certain forms and prostrations practiced—the burning of incense, and bowing before well-lit shrines." Western Protestants, accustomed to humorless austerity, solemnity, and piety in matters of religion and places of worship, were appalled by the color, drama, and festive elements at the monasteries.

Reverend Noah A. McDonald, an American Presbyterian missionary who lived in Siam from 1860 to 1886, wrote: "The temple building proper is filled with idols which are hideous in their appearance. Some are sitting, some standing, and some are in a reclining posture. There is one temple at the old city of Ayudia, said to have twenty thousand idols in it, and the estimate cannot be far in excess of the real number. There is one reclining idol in Bangkok about one hundred and seventy-five feet long, eighteen feet across the breast, and the feet of the idol are six feet long."

Protestant missionaries were especially prone to think of Buddhists as idol worshippers, which they openly considered Roman Catholics to be as well. The average Westerner who wrote about his or her experiences in Siam was likely to uphold the banner of Western superiority in order to find the native residents wanting. Harold Hall, an Englishman who lived in Burma in the late nineteenth century, had a more enlightened view. In 1898

Hall wrote, "I have thought that the difficulty arises from the fact that there are two ways of seeing a religion—from within and from without—and that these are as different as can possibly be. It is because we forget there are the two standpoints that we fall into error." Hall continues, "The outsider judges a religion as he judges everything else in this world. He cannot begin by accepting it as the only revelation of truth; he cannot proceed from the unknown to the known, but the reverse. First of all, he tries to learn what the beliefs of the people really are, and then he judges from their lives what value this religion has to them. He looks to acts as proofs of beliefs, to lives as the ultimate effects of thoughts. And he finds out very quickly that the sacred books of a people can never be taken as showing more than approximately their real beliefs."

Ajan Butda, the thudong monk we met in the preceding chapter, prostrated himself before Buddha images innumerable times. People whom he met in the course of his wanderings liked to watch him pay respect to a Buddha image, because Ajan looked so humble, serene, and focused. When people asked him why he did the prostrations so many times a day, Ajan Butda explained, "I pay respect to the Buddha. In the morning I prostrate three times before I put on the robe to go on almsround. When I return I prostrate three more times. Before I eat my meal I prostrate again. Every morning and evening during the daily chants, I prostrate again and again. I use the prostrations to tame the mind. Once the mind knows its duty, it can stay focused. Without rigorous work to do, the mind will wander freely."

Buddhist masters generally teach that our suffering comes about as a result of our undisciplined minds, and these untamed minds are the result of ignorance, craving, and negative emotions. Using prostrations, Ajan Butda came up with a method to train his mind so that negative emotions, such as anger, could be dispelled or eliminated altogether. As he told his disciples, whenever he got angry he would get up and prostrate three times. If he got angry twice, he would prostrate six times. If he got angry a hundred times, he would prostrate three hundred times, and so on until the anger was gone. This practice served to bend his mind to the Dhamma. Ajan Butda advised his disciples, "Wherever anger arises, bow to the Buddha at that very spot. Anger is afraid of the one who bows; it won't stay with you."

SOURCES

Early Missionaries in Bangkok: The Journals of Tomlin, Gutzlaff and Abeel 1828–1832 (2001), pp. 53, 108–109.

Frederick Arthur Neale, *Narrative of a Residence in Siam* (1852; 1996), p. 37.

Rev. N. A. McDonald, *A Missionary in Siam (1860–1870)* (1871; 1999), p. 36.

Harold Fielding Hall, *The Soul of a People* (1898; 1995), p. 12.

For Luang Pu Butda's life story, see *Luang Pu Fakwai* (1994), p. 15.

VENERABLE FATHER DARK EYES

REGINALD LE MAY, an Englishman who had joined the British Legation in Bangkok in 1908, moved to Lampang as vice-consul. While stationed in Lampang, Le May traveled further north by elephant on a trip that covered seven hundred miles and took five months. In 1914 Le May arrived at Nan, an ancient principality east of Chiang Mai on the border between Siam and French-occupied Lao territory. From 1448 to 1558 Nan had been ruled by Chiang Mai, and from 1560 to 1727 by Burma. After Bangkok was established as the capital of Siam, the Nan ruler began to pay tribute to Bangkok. From 1786 on, Nan was ruled by effective kings who managed to give their people almost a century of peace. In 1893 the Nan king was forced to yield most of his Lao domains to the French. Until then the territory recognized as Muang Nan encompassed, in addition to the present province of Nan, all of what is now northwestern Laos as well as parts of neighboring China. When the last king died, in 1931, Nan was being administered, like every other province of Siam, by a governor appointed from Bangkok.

At the time of Le May's visit, Nan was still a semi-independent state ruled by its own king, Suriyaphong Phalitidet (d. 1918). Referring to the Nan ruler as prince, Le May wrote, "Nearly all the temples of Nan, and there are many, are beautifully decorated in colour and kept in good repair, more so than in any other northern town, and I was told that the aged Prince of Nan took especial

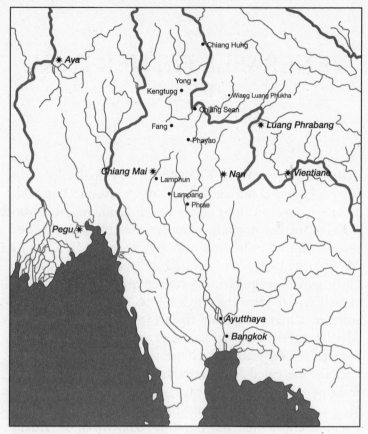

Fig. 14 Nan and its neighbors

care that they should be so." One morning Le May saw the eighty-four-year-old king "while he was being carried in state to worship at his favourite temple of Wat Cha Heng." The king of Nan "was sitting on his palanquin with his legs crossed beneath him, and looked for all the world like the Buddha himself." Le May, moved by his appearance, reported that "the old [king] was both blind and deaf, but he had a wonderfully striking face, as though chiseled in marble." Suriyaphong also had a good memory. "When I called to pay my respects, he spoke with animation of names and faces of thirty years ago, and remembered well the time when his father's seat was still at Wiang Sa, before Nan became definitely incorporated into the Kingdom of Siam. Nan was at that time a very wild place, and the [king] told me that, not so many years ago, the compound in which I was then staying had been pure jungle in which tigers roamed at will, and that the peasants could not pass through it except in bands."

In premodern societies, being blind was not necessarily considered a disability, but at the turn of the twentieth century the administrative monks sent from Bangkok to inspect monasteries in rural districts were disconcerted to find that some local abbots, although old and blind, still governed their monasteries. These monks were highly revered by local people for their spiritual power. They could be found in all regions of Siam.

Before 1902 when the sangha was centralized by the state in a decree that put all monks of local traditions under Bangkok law, village abbots were normally appointed by a consensus of local people. If a thudong monk came by and villagers liked him, and if there was no abbot at their wat, they might ask the thudong monk to stay and govern it. One such monk was Ajan At, the most revered abbot in the history of Wat Klang Khlong in Night Heron Village. Ajan At was blind. Local people called him Venerable Father Dark Eyes. Physically the abbot was strong and healthy. He was learned and strict in the monastic discipline.

Originally, Ajan At had been a resident monk at Wat Tha Mon in Nakhon Chaisi, in the Central Plains west of Bangkok. Around 1880 he went to Samut Songkhram, southwest of Bangkok, to spend a rains retreat at Wat Bang Khonthi, which was not far from Night Heron Village. When the Night Heron villagers heard about Ajan

At, they went to Wat Bang Khonthi to listen to his sermons. After the rains retreat was over, the Night Heron villagers asked Ajan At to stay longer. They were in the process of restoring a formerly deserted monastery they called Wat Klang Khlong, which was not far from their village. In 1883, after they had completed the reconstruction, the villagers invited Ajan At to be the abbot. On land adjacent to the Buddhist monastery there is a Roman Catholic church called the Church of the Night Heron. The monastery and the church still exist today.

Ajan At remained abbot of this monastery for twenty-eight years. He died in 1911. According to the traditional rules of the monastery, on the holy days *(wan phra)* that occurred during the four months of the rainy season, monks were expected to give sermons as often as three times a day: morning, afternoon, and night. Every member of each village household was thus given the opportunity to listen to Dhamma teachings at some point in the day. There were lay meditation teachers in addition to meditation monks at the wat, for it was the custom of this monastery to provide laypeople and monks with meditation training all year round. People who sought solitude liked to stay at Wat Klang Khlong.

Ajan Song (b. 1883), born the year that Venerable Father Dark Eyes became abbot of Wat Klang Klong, is another ascetic who lost his eyesight. Ajan Song was one of the teachers of Ajan Butda. This is how the two ajans met. In 1922 Butda took up the ascetic thudong practice and wandered to northeastern Siam. From the forest of Phetchabun Butda walked to Chaiyaphum and then to Nongkhai on Siam's side of the Mekong River. He spent the 1923 rains retreat at the Monastery of Rice Field Village in Tha Bo district, Nongkhai. From Tha Bo district Butda crossed the Mekong to Vientiane, in French-occupied Lao territory. The following year Ajan Butda returned to Siam and wandered to the Phu Phan Mountains, an extensive range in the northeastern region.

In 1925, while he was still wandering in the Phu Phan range, Ajan Butda met an older monk with a *mala*, or rosary, around his neck from which hung a Buddha image as wide as his hand. The monk was carrying a palm-leaf text with him. This was Ajan Song. As soon as Butda saw Ajan Song, he realized that the older monk had been his father in a previous life. From then on Ajan Butda called the monk Father Song. At the time of their meeting Song was forty-one; Butda was thirty-one. Shortly thereafter Song gave Butda the Buddha image and the palm-leaf text that he had been carrying when they first met.

Like Ajan Butda's, Ajan Song's parents were Lao. Song was born in Sisaket in the Northeast but was ordained as a monk in Prachinburi, in eastern Siam. Soon after his ordination Ajan Song went wandering on his own. After the two monks became spiritual friends *(kalyanamitta)*, they wandered together from the Phu Phan Mountains to the forests north of the Central Plains. In Nakhon Sawan they lived in Phu Kha Cave, practicing meditation and learning from each other. Ajan Song lost his eyesight when he grew old, but this was not necessarily a handicap. As Ajan Butda tells us, "Although Father Song's body-eyes are blind, his heart-eyes see clearly; he was able to 'see' truths that others could not." Ajan Song lived to the age of ninety-three.

One of Ajan Song's contemporaries, Ajan Phom, was abbot of Wat Bolo in Chianyai district on the southern peninsula. Wat Bolo is one of the oldest monasteries in Nakhon Si Thammarat. Its local history has been passed on, orally, by the elders to the young for many generations over hundreds of years and is still told by the local people today. Before he was ordained as a monk, Phom was engaged to a village woman. Like many young men of his day, Phom intended to ordain temporarily before marrying his fiancée. A year or two of living a monastic life had long been important in Siam as a maturational experience for a young man before he took on family responsibilities. Prior to the introduction of secular education, temporary ordination served that function most specifically. Not long after his ordination Ajan Phom became ill and lost his eyesight. He made a vow to remain in the robes for life and devote the rest of his days to the Dhamma.

As a young man, Phom, handsome and bold, was regarded as a *nakleng*, a word that has no equivalent in English. The word *nakleng* can be used as an adjective or a noun. Traditionally, a nakleng could be good or bad. He was a strong, fearless male, able to protect other people's property or to steal a buffalo and get away with it. A nakleng abbot was highly respected by villagers and feared by bandits. In every village there were good and bad nakleng. Villagers looked up to a good nakleng to protect them and to pursue bandits. Ajan Phom, the nakleng abbot, was skilled in settling local disputes. Before World War II, when most villages were still surrounded by wilderness, people seldom took their disputes to a provincial court. They either went to see their abbot or took matters into their own hands. Ajan Phom was respected for his fairness. The responsibilities of each abbot included educating the young and ensuring that community crises were handled in the proper way. As a meditation master, Ajan Phom was known for his clairvoyance. Whenever their buffaloes were stolen, the villagers would come to him for help. The abbot would sit in meditation and then tell the villagers who had stolen the buffaloes and in which direction the bandits had gone.

Ajan Phom had over a hundred disciples. Although he became blind, his memory remained sharp, and he recognized every voice in the village. As long as the oral tradition still prevailed, being blind did not get in the way of teaching. He continued to teach village children; just by listening to their recitations, the ajan could tell if the pupils had made mistakes. Venerable Father Phom remained a teacher until he died.

According to the history of Wat Bolo, Ajan Phom was the most revered abbot of the twentieth century. A statue of the great teacher can be seen at the monastery today. Local people still come to pay their respects and ask for the ajan's help, especially when they have lost valuable possessions.

SOURCES

Reginald Le May, *An Asian Arcady: The Land and Peoples of Northern Siam* (1926), pp. 171–172.

For a history of Nan, see David K. Wyatt, *The Nan Chronicle* (1994).

Wat Klang Khlong is located in Nok Khwaek subdistrict, Bang Khonthi district, Samut Songkhram province. Nakhon Chaisi is now a district in Nakhon Pathom province. For a short history of Wat Klang Khlong, see *Prawat Wat Changwat Samut Songkhram* (1962), pp. 403–408.

Ajan Song Brahmasaro and Ajan Butda's life stories are from *Luang Pu Lao Wai* (1994), p. 45. The Phu Phan range, which separates the Sakon Nakhon Basin to the north from the Khorat Basin to the south, begins at Na Klang in Udonthani, 80 kilometers south of Nong Khai, passes through Sakon Nakhon, Kalasin, and Mukdahan, and terminates near the Mekong River at Khong Chiam in Ubon Ratchathani.

Interview with Phra Maha Banyat Dhammadaro, current abbot of Wat Bolo, Nakhon Si Thammarat, September 18, 1998.

Fig. 15 Abbot's kuti

14

BIG BUDDHA, TOUGH HUNTER

IN THE 1860s it took several days to travel by boat from Thonburi to Ratburi, a principality southwest of Bangkok. In his later years Somdet To, abbot of Bell Monastery, spent a lot of time at Wat Klang on the bank of Khoi Tree Canal in Ratburi. He was busy building a huge image of a standing Buddha carrying an almsbowl.

Wat Klang was then surrounded by forests full of wildlife. Some of the villagers who lived nearby made their living as hunters. One day a hunter named Phran stopped by the monastery to rest in a sala. He had heard that a big Buddha image, twelve meters tall, was being constructed by a monk named To (whose name means "big"). After his rest, the hunter strolled to the construction site where Somdet To and several novices were mixing limestone plaster. The monk was of compact build and not all that much taller than the novices among whom he stood. The hunter, Phran, had never met Somdet To. He asked a novice, "Where is Monk To?" The Somdet replied, "I am Monk To. What is your business?" The hunter was surprised. "I expected to see a big monk!" he exclaimed. "You are so small! How can a little monk like you build a big Buddha image?" The villagers who were helping Somdet To with the construction work were horrified that the hunter dared to speak to the abbot so disrespectfully. But Phran had a reputation for being tough, and nobody dared criticize him openly.

The next day some villagers brought their oxcarts to

Somdet To so that he could use them to transport bricks to the construction site. Phran was hanging around the monastery when the oxen arrived. The hunter asked Somdet To, "Oh, did the villagers bring these oxen for you to eat? No problem. I'll kill one of them for you if you let me have the meat from a haunch." Somdet To said nothing; he merely walked into his kuti. Later that day Somdet To gave several lengths of thread that he had blessed to the temple boys to tie around the necks of the oxen before they were taken to a meadow to graze. At that time there were plenty of wild meadows behind the monastery where cattle could be let loose to roam free during the day. In the evening village boys would go to these pastures to round up the beasts and take them home. The uneasy villagers, who were afraid that the hunter might be tempted to kill one of their oxen when nobody was around, asked the boys to keep an eye on the animals.

One day a few oxen strayed far out into the meadow and vanished from sight. Hunter Phran followed these oxen and shot an arrow at one of the animals. He knew from the sound that the arrow had struck the ox but did not go into the hide. The ox was scared and ran away. Phran shot another ox that was still standing. The same thing happened. The arrow hit the ox but it did not penetrate the hide. The second ox turned around and ran back to the monastery. The hunter was confounded that he had failed twice. Normally he was a sharpshooter; his arrows rarely missed the target.

The next morning when Phran walked into Wat Klang, Somdet To asked him, "How was the ox meat yesterday?" The hunter, alarmed, wondered silently, "How did the monk know that I shot at his oxen?" Somdet To then warned him: "You are getting older every day. Do not kill any more animals. Watch out, the karma of violence will bear fruit."

Phran did not heed the monk's warning. A few days later he tried again. He noticed that around noon some of the oxen liked to rest under a big fig tree that sheltered them from the hot sun. Phran climbed the fig tree and hid among its branches. When the oxen came to rest under the tree, the hunter shot from the tree. This time his arrow struck an ox on the rump. Although it was not injured, the ox fell to the ground. Phran took out another arrow, but as he stretched his arms to take aim, he fell out of the tree. As soon as he got up, the first ox, on its feet again, charged him. Quickly Phran climbed back up into the tree. The two oxen lingered, waiting for the hunter to come down. As he sat in the tree Phran wondered why both arrows had failed to pierce the hide of the oxen. He speculated that perhaps he should have heeded Somdet To's warning.

That evening, when it became evident that two of the oxen were missing, five village men went out to look for them. They found the animals under the fig tree. They also spotted the hunter up in the tree. The villagers asked Phran, "Why are you sitting up there?" The hunter replied, "I am watching the oxen." Skeptical, the villagers examined their oxen and found that the skin of one of them was bruised and swollen from having been struck by an arrow. The villagers threatened to throw rocks at the hunter if he did not climb down out of the tree. Finally, the hunter gave in and walked back to the wat with the other men. On the way Phran thought to himself that since none of the villagers had actually seen him try to shoot the ox, no one would be likely to accuse him of any wrongdoing.

Somdet To had just finished taking a bath when he saw the villagers walk in with the hunter. He asked them what happened. The hunter told him his story. Knowing that Phran was aggressive and pugnacious, Somdet To said to him, "You don't think twice about killing, no matter how big an animal is. Someday when you are careless you will be attacked by these animals. Your karma will catch up with you." The hunter listened quietly to Somdet To. Just as the sun was setting he walked home.

The next day Phran came back to the wat, and Somdet To gave him a long lecture on the demerit generated by his actions. Gradually Somdet To was able to convince Phran to give up hunting. The contrite hunter even promised Somdet To that he would ordain as a monk for the coming rains retreat. From that day on Phran came to the wat every day to help the monks and novices with the work of constructing the great standing Buddha. Before the rains retreat began, Phran was ordained as a monk at the Monastery of Khoi Tree Canal (Wat Khlong Khoi).

After ordination the former hunter became known as Phran Phrotako. Phrotako was his monastic name. As a monk Phran lived up to his duty. He was diligent, highly responsible, and willing to do all kinds of work for the wat. Three years after his ordination he helped finish the big standing Buddha statue, thus completing the project that Somdet To had begun and left unfinished as a result of his death in 1872. Somdet To epitomized traditional Buddhist masters in old Siam who combined scholarship with meditation practice and social responsibility.

Three decades after Somdet To's death, monks of all traditions in Siam were made subject to the Sangha Act of 1902. Once the sangha was centralized, only monks who had passed the Nak-dhamma ("skilled in Dhamma") examinations could be appointed village abbots. The Nak-dhamma was a new curriculum of monastic education created by Prince Wachirayan (1860–1921), the head of the Dhammayut order who was named Sangharaja of Siam in 1910. It became the standard course of study in monastic education and remained largely unchanged throughout the twentieth century. All ordained monks were required to study the Nak-dhamma books instead of relying upon their teachers and the traditional Tipitaka texts from which monks of Somdet To's generation had been taught. The former hunter plunged into the Nak-dhamma and passed the highest level of the new monastic studies curriculum. Having passed the Nak-dhamma examinations, Phran was appointed abbot of Wat Khlong Khoi. As abbot, Phran was highly respected as a leader of the community. Bandits were afraid of him and laypeople on both sides of Khoi Tree Canal looked up to him for guidance.

Phran was fortunate to have had Somdet To as his first teacher. The elderly abbot recognized that aggression, a strong component of this hunter's character, caused havoc among animals and distress in people. The monk was able to channel this raw energy toward the good. A hunter like Phran spent much of his time in the forest, confronting its dangers and enduring its hardships. To be a hunter, Phran had to be fearless (willing to enter the forest alone), patient (able to sit still for long hours), adventurous (willing to take risks), single-minded (focused while stalking animals), and tough (heedless of insect bites, rain, and discomfort). The qualities that made Phran an effective hunter were the very same ones that made him an effective leader of his community, once his misplaced skills were transformed.

SOURCES

The story of hunter Phran was told by Venerable Grandfather Khamkoet (1781–1892), a contemporary of Somdet To and abbot of Wat Amarin, not far from Bell Monastery, in Thonburi for eighteen years from 1874 to 1892. See *Wat Intharawihan, Bang Khunphrom* (1994), p. 106.

15

THE BOATMAN AND THE BANDIT MONK

ONE OF the most important Buddhist traditions in nine-teenth-century Siam was the temporary bhikkhu ordina-tion when young men became monks before getting mar-ried and becoming householders. Having young men live as monks for a year or so was a way of preparing them to be mentally and morally fit to take on the responsibilities of village and family life. Thus, becoming a monk was not necessarily a lifetime commitment; for some it was only a training. Ordination served not only to give merit to the monk's mother; it was also a way for young men to obtain useful mental discipline and to receive nurture from older men.

H. Warrington Smyth, who was director of the Depart-ment of Mines in Siam from 1891 to 1896, saw the changes in attitude of his men when one of them became a monk. "Nothing surprised me more than to witness the respect with which one of my boatmen was regarded by his former comrades when he donned the yellow robe. Several times he came to visit me, and it was evident he had become a great man in their eyes, and they felt that no attention was too good for him. He was no longer called by his name; but they *Korab*'d him [yes sir'd] and *wai*'d him [bowed and saluted] as they would a noble of the land. They served him on their knees, and no trace of familiarity could be observed. The past was forgotten; he was to them a holy man, retired from the world, living the noble life of contemplation."

Like so many young monks of his day, Smyth's former boatman learned to meditate, chant, and perform rituals in addition to studying Buddhist scripture written in Pali. "He told me of his own struggles with his thoughts in time of meditation," Smyth tells us, "and of his life of real austerity; of the early repetitions before the Buddha in the first chill dawn; of the long hours puzzling over those horrid Pali texts, and of the slow orderly procession round the village, when they might not look up, nor address their friends; of how their meditations were broken by the cheerful voices of the neighbours passing by; of how one or two played football [*takro*] to work off their pent-up feelings beneath the wide-spreading banyans about the Wat grounds; and of the disapprobation of the stern old prior, who ruled with a rod of iron, and often made him wish he were back in the world again. The evident earnestness of the whole thing left a most vivid impression on my mind." Smyth also found that his workers were devout. "Often, too, it happened that one of my people asked for a day's holiday, and subsequently I found he had spent the whole of his time, and his last month's wage, in a grand merit-making festival, with all his relations, at the family Wat. One often saw these merit-making feasts in progress, and, if quaint to our notions, they are real enough to them."

Men who faced imminent death sometimes vowed to ordain temporarily if they managed to survive, and some survivors remained in the robes for life. One such monk was Ajan Bun, a well-known preacher at Wat Sawetchat in Thonburi. Before he became a monk Bun was a bad nakleng. Ajan Bun seldom revealed anything of his former life unless it served the Dhamma.

In his day local preachers still got around mostly by boat. They had little control over the time of their arrival, especially if the village to which they were going was far away from their monastery. For special ceremonies, however, preachers did need responsible boatmen to get them to their destinations on time to deliver sermons. Some preachers like Ajan Bun had to resort to threats to get the boatmen to do their duty.

One day Ajan Bun was invited to preach at a village wat some distance beyond Wat Dan Samrong in Samut Prakan, east of Bangkok. From their monastery Ajan Bun and his preaching partner first went to Wat Dan, and there they hired a boatman named Dam (Black) to take them to the (unnamed) village wat. The trip from Wat Dan to this village wat normally took between four and five hours. Once they left Wat Dan, it looked to the two preachers like Dam was doing a good job, so they took a nap to conserve their energy. After paddling for a few hours Dam stopped along the bank of the canal, took out a small cutting board, chopped *ganja* leaves into small pieces, stuffed them in a pipe, and smoked away as if he had no cares in the world. Once he finished smoking, Dam got back on the boat and started paddling with extra energy, occasionally saying to the monks, "Venerable Sirs, we're almost there." The boat swayed dangerously in the swift current. Within an hour the boatman had got the preachers back to Wat Dan, right to the place from which they had started. When the two preachers woke up they found that they had gone nowhere.

Ajan Bun, furious, yelled at the boatman, "Dam, where did you live before you moved here?"

"In a village near Hua Ro in Ayutthaya, sir," the boatman replied.

"Look at my face carefully!" ordered the monk.

"Yes sir; I notice a scar on your forehead about four inches wide," answered the boatman.

"Did you know Bandit Bun in Ayutthaya?" the monk asked.

"Yes sir, I knew him," replied the boatman.

In a voice, loud and clear, the preacher told him, "I was Bandit Bun! You must get us to the village wat before dawn or you're dead!" The boatman was so terrified of the former bandit that he rowed hard all the way to the village wat and got the monks there just before the sun came up.

Bun had been a notorious bandit in Ayutthaya. One night after a raid, just as he was about to sneak out of a house, the house owner, who was waiting by the door, hit Bun with an axe. The axe cut a deep gash in his forehead. Nevertheless, Bun escaped by jumping into the river. As he floated in the water, hiding under heavy masses of water hyacinth, he could feel himself slowly bleeding to death. All night long Bun recited a Pali mantra he had learned to stop the bleeding. By dawn the current had swept the vegetation and Bun to a monastery on the riverbank. The bandit struggled into the monastery and asked the abbot to help him. Bun vowed that if he did not die from such a serious wound he would ordain for a rains retreat. The abbot, who was skilled in herbal medicine, treated Bun and finally healed him.

Soon after he recovered, Bun went to stay with a relative and was ordained as a monk at Wat Sawetchat in Thonburi. Phra Bun's determination was exceptionally strong; he mastered all the chants and Pali texts no matter how difficult they were. Bun's teachers must have recognized the young monk's aggressive nature and harnessed it to the service of the Dhamma. The bandit, who never disrobed, became a strong, confident preacher. Bun eventually attained the fifth level of Pali studies. In 1913 Ajan Bun was appointed abbot of Wat Sawetchat. When he was sixty years old he stopped accepting invitations to preach and no longer traveled. Ajan Bun died in 1957 after having governed the monastery for forty-four years.

SOURCES

H. Warrington Smyth, *Five Years in Siam, from 1891 to 1896* (1898), vol. 1, pp. 82–83.

For Ajan Bun's story, see *Phra Khru Nonthasankhun (Somsak Nanthasaro)* (1997), p. 7.

16

TENDING WATER
BUFFALOES

WATER BUFFALOES were most important domestic animals for local farmers, who used them to plow their paddy fields. Peter Thompson, the surveyor, got a close look at water buffaloes. In 1905 he wrote, "They are formidable-looking beasts, with their immense spreading horns, which get very much in the way when they are yoked together. A pair of horns has been known to measure as much as eight feet six inches from tip to tip, measured round the curve. The buffaloes are unused to Europeans, and if we approach them they will face us, standing side by side, with heads thrown back so that their horns touch their backs. It is extremely rare for them to charge, though in the neighboring French provinces [in Laos] they are said to be very dangerous. In Siam they appear soon to lose their fear of white men, and I have been on quite friendly terms with many buffaloes. At midday they wallow in pools of semi-liquid mud, nothing showing above the surface but their heads, and whilst they are grazing small white herons perch on their broad backs and glean a rich harvest."

Tending water buffaloes was a task usually assigned to small boys. After watching a group of village boys round up water buffaloes, Thompson noted, "At night they are brought back to the homestead and shut in a pen. It is amusing to see the children run up to one of the huge beasts, and climbing on his back with the help of his tail—using the hock as a step—drive him home with shrill

97

Fig. 16a Plowing with Buffaloes, 1906

Fig. 16b Village transportation, 1906

cries and many blows from their small fists, while the remainder of the herd follows meekly after."

Most abbots of town and village monasteries learned how to tend water buffaloes when they were young boys. In traditional villages children played an important part in the economic life of the family; they contributed significantly to the welfare of the household. Children knew that they were useful, that the family could not function as well without their labor. Along with the parents, young children usually began the day with chores. Parents asked the young to work in the fields; they got their hands dirty. The thought of asking for money in return for their work never entered the children's minds.

Ajan Panya (b. 1911) has been abbot of Wat Cholaprathan in Nonthaburi since 1960. His monastic name in Pali, Paññananda, means "One Who Delights in Wisdom." His parents called him Pan, but people either call him Luang Pho Panya or Ajan Panya. When he was six years old and living in his natal village in Phatthalung, in the southern peninsula, the young Pan was given the task of taking two water buffaloes out to graze before the sun came up. Such a chore could be daunting for children who believed in ghosts, but they could not say no. Ajan Panya recalled how he faced his fear of ghosts. "The most unsettling thing was to have to get up very early during the plowing season. The buffaloes had to be in the paddy field before sunrise. I was afraid of ghosts but dared not tell my father for fear of being scolded. I didn't like it when my parents told me to do a task at night when it was pitch dark out. Before dawn I had to take the buffaloes out to eat grass to get them ready for the work of plowing. I was afraid of walking in the dark, so I hung on to one of the buffaloes. Wherever he went to eat grass, I went with him and watched him graze. I talked to him as I would to a human companion. I thought if anything happened, I could always climb on his back and make him run. But nothing ever happened. Sometimes I saw a stump. In the darkness it looked like somebody was standing there. I hung on tightly to my buffalo while eyeing 'the thing' carefully. The mystery finally unfolded when the sun came up. It was just a stump. Not a ghost as I had feared."

Young boys given the responsibility of caring for buffaloes became sensitive to the animals' well-being. These great beasts were the children's friends. Ajan Panya recalled, "The buffaloes' happiness was my happiness. I could tell at a glance if they had had enough to eat. Watching the buffaloes submerge in a waterhole gave me joy. On days when the buffaloes did not get enough to eat, I felt terrible. My heart sank."

If the rice fields were far from the village, the boys had to walk long distances to get their buffaloes fed and to the fields on time. Ajan Phut (b. 1922), the late abbot of Wat Pa Salawan in Khorat, recalled that throughout his boyhood, in a Lao village in Sakon Nakhon, "in the morning I took the buffaloes out of the pen and walked to the paddy fields, about three kilometers from the village."

What Western travelers like Thompson perceived as an amusing sight was in fact often a struggle for the village boys who cared for the animals. In the course of tending and safeguarding their domestic animals, boys had to face fear, by themselves, at an early age, since their adult relatives were usually busy with their own work. Ajan Phut remembered, when he was a boy in the early 1930s, how frightened he was to lead his buffaloes through the wilderness. "At dusk I had to round up the water buffaloes in the field and walk them back to their pen in the village. I was only twelve then, and I was really scared. The area around the village was a dense forest full of wild animals such as tigers and elephants. I did not want to walk by myself, but I could not get anyone to accompany me."

Taking care of buffaloes could be pleasant if the boys were working together in a group. The task gave the youngsters the opportunity both to be away from the watchful eyes of adults and to expend their youthful energy outdoors in the fields and forests.

Luang Ta Chi (b. 1925), now abbot of Wat Thai in Washington, D.C., remembers the chore as one of his happiest childhood experiences. Luang Ta Chi's given name is Surasak; people call him Venerable Grandfather Chi. Chi (Ji) is the first syllable of his Pali name, Jivanandho. He was born in Beautiful Mound Village, a Lao community in Mukdahan in northeastern Siam. The village is not very far from Sweet Vegetable Hill. Luang Ta Chi, recalling how he and other village boys learned about their immediate environment, tells us, "We got up early in the morning and rode the water buffaloes to the hill. There were trails going up the hill along which we could zigzag the buffaloes to the top of the hill. This hill was covered with all kinds of big trees, but the hilltop itself was a flat meadow. Once we got the buffaloes to the top to graze in the meadow, we were free to do whatever we liked. We hung out all day playing with each other, running around, climbing trees, picking mushrooms, looking at birds and other animals, and so on. In the late afternoon we rounded up the buffaloes and rode them back to our village."

Children learned from the natural world and from friends as well as family. Ajan Chang (1848–1938), who in 1906 became abbot of Wat Khiankhet in Thanyaburi, a district in Prathum Thani, learned to read and write from his fellow buffalo boys. Chang was born in a Mon village in Bang Kradi, about a day away from Bangkok by canoe. The inhabitants had migrated to this area from Mon villages in Martaban.

Chang, which means elephant, is the name his mother gave him when he was a little boy because he was so much

bigger than most other children his age. (It was not unusual for parents to wait until their infants were older
before naming them, and their names usually reflected
something about the child's appearance or personality.)
In the 1850s his mother sent the young Chang out into
the fields every day to tend their water buffaloes. Chang
carried with him, like a knapsack, a waterproof bamboo
tube in which he kept a palm-leaf book. Ajan Ong, a Mon
monk at Wat Bang Kradi, wrote down words on the palm
leaves for Chang to read. Every day Chang asked an older
buffalo boy to teach him to read. In return Chang would
round up buffaloes for the older boy who taught him—
one buffalo for each word. Buffalo boys knew well how
hard it was to round up all the buffaloes and get them to
walk home together. It took a lot of running around to
locate all of them. Chang made the older boy an offer he
could not refuse. Thus Chang learned to read out in the
field while tending water buffaloes.

During the reign of Rama II (1809–24) the largest wave
of Mon people, about forty thousand of them, fled to
Siam to escape the Burmese ruler. Since Siam was under-
populated, the king was delighted to gain such a large in-
flux of human labor. Many Mon immigrants settled along
the Chao Phraya River some fifteen to twenty miles
northwest of Bangkok. (Today these Mon villages are in
Prathum Thani province.) There is another Mon settlement, Seven-Striped Fish Village (Ban Chet Riu), in
Samut Sakhon, whose inhabitants' ancestors migrated to
Siam from Moulmein during the reign of Rama II. Up
until the second half of the twentieth century, Ban Chet
Riu remained protected, because of its isolation, from the
forces of modernization. Adults as well as children were
proud of their work in the paddy fields and the knowledge that had been passed down to them from their ancestors. Until the early 1960s the Mon in this village had

always been paddy farmers. The village elders were reluctant to send their children to the public school established by the government for fear that they would be attracted to Thai urban culture. An old saying cited by Mon
village elders conveys their pride in the traditional way
of life: "Ten merchants cannot match a farmer's life.
Twenty educations cannot compare with one farmer."

This saying refers to the movement of secularly educated young people away from farm life into the bureau-
cracies and factories in the cities. Living in the land of
natural biodiversity, old farmers, women as well as men,
were knowledgeable about their local environment. They
knew how to plow and harrow all the fields in which the
seedlings were transplanted. They knew how to create
dikes that enabled them to control the water levels in the
fields and knew which plant crops were resistant to flood-
ing. Farmers also knew how to build simple houses and
construct oxcarts, yokes, and plows; they could build
boats, make brooms and rakes, produce glue from animal
parts, and fashion musical instruments. After the harvest
season farmers also thatched roofs, wove baskets, mats,
and nets, and made fishing traps. Women raised silk-
worms, made dye from plants, and wove cloth for members of the family. They knew how to take care of domestic animals and livestock, what to do when the animals got sick, and where to locate medicinal plants in the
nearby forest. Unlike urban people, who know little or
nothing about the food they eat, farmers were skilled in
production and knew how to preserve food for long trips
or for future use. Throughout the nineteenth century
young men as well as women learned their skills by working alongside their elders in the community. The so-
called illiterate farmers in fact possessed all sorts of skills
that were especially relevant to living in a forest-village
community. In isolated villages throughout Siam, up un-

til the mid-twentieth century, knowledge of local agriculture and the environment continued to be passed down from the elders to the young.

SOURCES

P. A. Thompson, *Lotus Land* (1906), p. 181.

For Ajan Panya's life story, see *Chiwit lae ngan khong Than Paññananda* (1991), pp. 5–7.

For Ajan Phut Thaniyo's life story, see *Thaniyata Therawathu* (2000), pp. 36, 38.

Interview with Phra Maha Surasak (Luang Ta Chi), abbot of Wat Thai Washington, D.C., May 22, 1997.

For a brief biography of Ajan Chang Dhammachoto, see *Aphinihan 59 kechi achan chudang* (n.d.), pp. 28–30.

For a history of Ban Chet Riu, see *Phra Khru Khosonsakhonkit (Thongsoem Sumedho)* (2000).

17

SCARECROWS AND BABY-SITTERS

KING RAMA III (r. 1824–51) was about the same age as Somdet To, whom we have already met. During his reign the king ordered the extensive renovation of Bodhi Monastery—the largest wat in Bangkok—in order to make the monastery an encyclopedic repository of all traditional knowledge. On a wall of one of the wat buildings is a series of twelve mural paintings illustrating a Thai folk tale called "Grandmother and Grandfather."

Grandfather and Grandmother grew beans, sesame, and rice. On a day when they were called away from home, they ordered their grandchildren to scare away the crows and urged them to be vigilant. Due to the children's disobedience, however, a flock of crows descended and ate the rice crop. When Grandmother returned she shouted at the children and called them names. When Grandfather arrived, he proceeded to beat the children. In despair the children went to see a hunter and begged him to shoot those crows. To their dismay the hunter replied, "None of my business!" This made the children angry, prompting them to spot a rat, which they asked to bite the hunter's bowstring. The rat replied, "None of my business!" Then the children went to see a cat and asked it to bite the rat. The cat answered, "None of my business!" They went to ask a dog to bite the cat, but the dog said, "None of my business!" When the children asked a hammer to beat the dog, they got the same reply. And so it went. When they asked a fire to burn the ham-

Fig. 17a A village boy tending younger children, 1906

mer, water to quench the fire, a river to overwhelm the water, and an elephant to destroy the riverbank, the reply was always "None of my business!"

Finally the children came across some fruit flies. Out of sheer desperation they asked the fruit flies for help. The insects volunteered to swarm around the elephant's eyes. The elephant was thus compelled to destroy the riverbank, the river to overwhelm the water, the water to quench the fire, and so on until finally the hunter had to shoot the crows.

From this folk tale, told to them by village elders, children learned how important the task of driving off the birds really was.

As they traveled about in old Siam, Westerners often came across men, women, and children standing on platforms out in the paddy fields, waving their arms and shrieking in order to chase away the flocks of birds about to descend and feed upon the rice crop. In December 1885 Ernest Satow, the British consul-general in Siam, traveled by boat from Bangkok to the Central Plains. Satow and his party were in the habit of going for long walks in the morning before continuing their journey on the river. In his December 3 journal entry Satow wrote, "We started for a walk on the plain behind the trees that hid the bank, and found nearly all the population out in the rice field engaged in scaring birds, and making a tremendous noise about the business. Here, as elsewhere, they said the crop had been short, as the water had not risen high enough to cover the upper fields." Satow noted, "The village seemed well-to-do, and their houses well-built. We observed plenty of buffaloes and well-shaped little bullocks, from which we inferred that the district must be a fine ground for cattle-thieving, which however report says is pursued rather as an occasional pastime than as a profession."

Because there was so much work to do, as there always is on any farm, children were often assigned tasks that they had to do all alone. Girls and boys were often given the job of scaring off the birds. As Satow traveled by elephant on the way to Phichit, north of the Central Plains, he entered this record in his journal: "At 7:20 [A.M.] we passed a small village called Ban Phakaphi, and had to flounder a considerable distance along the edge of a paddy-field swamp to frighten the birds away from the ripening grain, and a young girl was seated on a small raised platform, roughly thatched with grass, whose duty was to agitate the cords now and then as if to warn the winged robbers that their enemy man was on the look-out."

Keeping the birds away was hard work that required patience and mindfulness. Children were taught to be self-reliant and responsible from an early age. They were proud of their work if they managed to safeguard the crop, but they could count on being punished if they neglected their duty and let the birds invade the fields.

Khruba Chaiyawong (1913–2000), abbot of the Monastery of the Buddha's Footprint at Huai Tom in Li district, Lamphun, began his training in patience and mindfulness before the age of six. By then his parents, who were Tai Yuan, already had five children. Chaiyawong was the third. The *khruba* (teacher-monk) recalled that one day when his parents wanted to go into the forest to dig certain roots for food, they left Chaiyawong in their paddy field, some distance from home, to keep the birds away. After sitting there by himself all day long, the six-year-old boy got hungry. He left his post and walked off to find some fruit to eat. By the time he returned to the field, a flock of doves had already devoured most of the rice. Chaiyawong went home in the evening and said nothing to his parents.

Fig. 17b A Farmer and his children

The following day Chaiyawong's father went to inspect the field. The sight of the damage made his father so angry that he picked up a stick with which to hit the boy. Chaiyawong was so afraid of his father's anger that he ran away. As the abbot recalled, "I fled into the forest and spent the night there. I got bitten a lot by mosquitoes. No blanket to cover my body. My shirt was full of holes. The next day I went to sleep at a friend's house. My mother was worried. She searched for me everywhere: in the fields, in the village, and in the forest. She finally spotted me in a tree, eating leaves. My mother was so overcome with sadness that she could not speak. She sat down under the tree and cried. Once she regained her mindfulness, she begged me to come down. I climbed down and prostrated myself at her feet. Still crying, my mother begged me to come home." Chaiyawong told his mother that he was afraid of his father. His mother promised him that she would not let his father beat him, and Chaiyawong then returned with her.

Besides scaring off birds, another task that parents assigned to both boys and girls was to baby-sit their younger siblings. H. Warrington Smyth, who lived in Siam from 1891 to 1896, observed, "In this country, where the respective spheres of action of the two sexes are so little differentiated, where women smoke cheroots and guide the plough, and where both are dressed alike, boy nurses have charge of the small children as frequently as girls. It is as often as not an elder brother, or the son of a slave, who accompanies the small charge everywhere; who gives it cigarettes and sweets, who carries it when tired, who washes it, who fans the mosquitoes off, and sleeps beside it. And except when rendered momentarily forgetful by an exciting *denouement* at a *Yike* [a farcical theatrical performance], or by the gambols of [a dog], they seem singularly apt and gentle at the business, and handle their charge with a *sang-froid* which I must admit evoked my greatest admiration. One had been accustomed to regard babies as a kind of dangerous explosive, or a variety of rare china, which must either burst or break at the first touch. But it is reassuring to know that even men folk may handle them in safety."

The yike that Smyth saw took place in a wat compound in Ratburi during the Kathin festival marking the end of the rains retreat, a time when people offered new robes to the monks. The difference between the yike, which villagers so enjoyed, and the *lakhon* performed for the nobility, Smyth tells us, is that the yike is "acted entirely by men and boys, in contradiction to the *Lakon* [lakhon], in which women only act. There are but few accessories. The dramatic instinct of the Siamese, which is largely developed, supplies them with an imagination superior to scenic effect. In the *Lakon* there is more display. Costly dresses and supple posturing are *de rigueur*. The performance is entirely pantomimic, and is accompanied by the tinkle of the orchestra, and the clash of choruses all night long. In the *Yike*, on the other hand, the point of performance lies in the dialogue."

While in the audience watching a yike in Ratburi, Smyth noted that the performance, in which a woman hides her lover in a basket, was so suspenseful and funny that it went on "with jokes and topical allusions for hours together. To the children it is the height of happiness, and many a small boy holds a fat brown baby astride his hip, watching intently every change of feature of the funny man all through the performance, scarcely noticing his burden. Occasionally he changes it from one hip to the other, throwing the whole weight of his body to the opposite side to counterbalance it."

Ajan Dun (1888–1985), abbot of Wat Burapha in Surin, had the experiences of being both a baby-sitter and an actor. The oldest of five children, Ajan Dun was born in Surin, a muang in the Northeast with a large Khmer population. As a child he took care of his two younger brothers and three sisters in addition to doing household chores such as fetching water, cooking, pounding rice, and tending water buffaloes. Dun was a healthy boy with good manners and fine features. When he was eighteen, Dun was selected to play a female character in a public theatrical performance, called *lakhon nok*, sponsored by the governor of Surin. Unlike *lakhon nai*, which were usually performed at the royal palaces in Bangkok and in which all the roles were played by women, all the roles in the *lakhon nok* were played by men. A good-looking young man like Dun would be offered a leading female role. The *lakhon nok* was very popular among townspeople before the advent of motion pictures. The theatricals in which Dun played female characters included *Chaiyachet*, *Laksanawong*, and *Chanthrakuman*. These plays were as familiar to village folk as they were to townspeople. While he was with the theater group the young Dun also had a chance to learn Bangkok Thai.

SOURCES

Historical Illustrations: Wat Phra Chetuphon (1982), p. 65. The official name of Wat Pho (Bodhi Monastery) is Wat Chetupon.

Ernest Satow, *A Diplomat in Siam*, 1885–1888 (1994), pp. 21, 57.

For Khruba Chaiyawong's story, see *Phra Chaiyawongsanussati* (2000), pp. 42–43.

H. Warrington Smyth, *Five Years in Siam from 1891–1896* (1898), vol. 1, pp. 289–291.

For Ajan Dun Atulo's life story, see Nanthapanyaphon, *Chiwaprawat Luang Pu Dun* (1985), pp. 2–3.

18

ABBOTS AND BANDITS

AROUND 1900 Peter Thompson, the surveyor, traveled by boat from Bangkok to Paknam Pho, north of the Central Plains. Along the way Thompson and his Siamese assistants often spent the night in a sala in a wat compound. Thompson wrote, "Along the river banks the wats are dotted at frequent intervals, and we could travel from one end of the country to the other and always find at night a roof over our heads, and a dry floor raised off the ground. The posts and the floor are of teak, and the red tiled roof comes low down, giving protection from the sun and rain, but the sides are quite open. Within the sala is a pulpit from which the monks read during a cremation. One or two banners painted with scenes from the sacred books depend from the rafters, and flocks of pigeons roost inside the roof. Along one side of the sala is a raised platform, and at one end is a little image of the Buddha." At one place in Ayutthaya, Thompson tells us, "The village wat is very simple. There are the houses for the monks and the *sala*, or rest-house, and perhaps there is a little *bawt* [*ubosot* or ordination hall], but often the *sala* serves also as the *bawt*."

In spite of this seemingly peaceful setting, the central region was at this time notorious for the roving bandits who plundered the territory. Thompson noted, "In some of the wilder districts bands of outlaws retreat to the jungle and levy a regular toll upon the surrounding villages. The villagers appear on the whole to regard them

Fig. 18 Forest scene in Siam

with good-natured tolerance, as long as they do not exact too much." Thompson went on to say, "More serious, and far more exasperating to the villagers, are the irregular raids or *plons*. On a fine moonlight night a band of twenty or more collect at some prearranged spot. There are some regular robbers amongst them, but many young fellows, no doubt, join purely for the fun of the thing. Their object is generally to make a raid upon their neighbours' buffaloes or bullocks, so they march off and surround the village which they have selected. Sometimes they are able to get away with their booty before the barking of the pariahs has fairly aroused the sleeping inhabitants, but should these be more on the alert a pitched battle takes place. They are armed only with rusty old muzzle-loaders, and often after an hour's firing no one on either side is hurt. This is not altogether to be attributed to the badness of their weapons or of their marksmanship, for the villagers are firing from behind their houses, and the dacoits are skillful at taking advantage of such cover as the ground offers. They execute concerted movements without audible words of command, and, indeed, these midnight marauders probably possess greater military instinct than any other section of the community."

Thompson learned that if "the dacoits succeed in driving off the cattle, the villagers speedily summon their neighbours and organise a pursuit. In the rainy season it is easy to follow the tracks across the muddy fields, but let them beware lest they tread upon sharp bamboo splinters, which the dacoits leave behind them. These splinters can make a nasty festering wound in a bare foot. The dacoits generally make for a patch of high ground on which no marks will be left, and from this they drive the herd out and back again on every side, thus making a great number of tracks going and returning, and confusing their pursuers as to the true direction which they take. Once in their own district the dacoits break up, and each man leads back a buffalo to mingle inconspicuously with his own herd. The dacoits are careful never to attack those who would cause a big government inquiry to be made, and there is little doubt that they are often hand-in-glove with the local Nai Amphurs [district officers]."

One night, around the same time that Thompson was traveling through the Central Plains, bandits succeeded in raiding Sweet Mango Village in Ayutthaya and drove off all the livestock. The very first thing the villagers did was to turn to their abbot for help. Ajan Son (1867–1957), abbot of Sweet Mango Monastery, was a meditation monk who was skilled in astrology. Villagers who had lost possessions often came to seek the abbot's help in retrieving their lost objects. The monk who succeeded Ajan Son in 1958 recalled that when the villagers came to see the abbot after the raid, "Ajan Son closed his eyes in concentration for a moment before he told the village folk the whereabouts of their cattle. People followed his advice and were able to locate the cattle. Another thing the ajan did, when villagers asked for help, was to go straight to the buffalo pen to look for traces of the marauders. Once he found the bandits' footprints he used an axe to drive a wedge into every one of them, chanting a mantra while doing so. Then the ajan told the villagers to round up strong men and track the rustlers down. However, Ajan Son urged the men not to harm the bandits once they caught them."

As it turned out, Ajan Son's prediction of the bandits' escape route was accurate. From living close to the wilderness the village men knew the terrain well, and, following the abbot's surmise, they went in pursuit of the dacoits. Ajan Son's successor tells us, "Due to Ajan Son's spiritual power, the bandits could not find their way out of the thick forest. They kept wandering in a circle until

ABBOTS AND BANDITS

they were exhausted. Consequently, the villagers were able to catch up with the robbers. After hearing that the ajan had cast a spell on them, the bandits lost their will to fight."

Ajan Son, like many village abbots of his day, played a significant role in maintaining the well-being of the community, not only as a monk capable of casting believable spells, but also as one who, in modern terms, was skilled in psychology. The ajan gave the villagers confidence that they otherwise lacked. Few would have dared go after the thieves even if a posse of sorts could have been organized. But with the abbot's encouragement, more men were persuaded to join the victims and help track down the dacoits. Furthermore, the abbot used skillful means by telling the laypeople that the mantra he used to stop the thieves in their tracks would be effective only if the villagers promised to refrain from killing any of them; otherwise, he warned them, they would be breaking the first precept. By telling the people not to harm the bandits, Ajan Son circumvented the possibility of the bandits' returning to take revenge.

Suphanburi, a central Siam town more ancient even than Ayutthaya, was known for its many meditation masters. At the time of Thompson's tour Suphanburi was also notorious for buffalo rustlers. Ajan Nong (1865–1934), abbot of Wat Amphawan on Madan Tree Canal, was venerated for his strict practice of Dhamma-vinaya and his ability to keep bandits away. Buffaloes belonging to his monastery were not subject to theft, because fear of Ajan Nong's curse discouraged thieves from daring to steal or kill the animals. Local people believed that he had supernatural powers. These spiritual powers also served as protection for the buffaloes in Madan Tree Village. A fire once broke out in the village. The smoke could be seen from the wat, two kilometers away from the fire. Monks and laypeople hurried to help extinguish it. Ajan Nong, accompanied by a young monk, Fung, got there first. Practicing kasina meditation, Ajan Nong gazed at the fire and stood in silence. Then he grasped his bathing robe with one hand at each edge of the cloth and slowly waved his robe up and down three times. The fire, miraculously, stopped burning.

When Ajan Nong died in 1934 his followers made a statue of him that shows him reclining on his right side wearing monastic robes. This was the resting position he was in when he died. On the wall of the pavilion that houses Ajan Nong's statue, his followers inscribed the following words: "You have qualities worth revering. It is not easy to find anyone today who could match you. Although you departed from this world, only your physical body disappeared. Your name and your legacy will always remain in our hearts."

SOURCES

P. A. Thompson, *Lotus Land* (1906), pp. 168, 263–265.

For the story of Ajan Son, see P. Bunsanong, "Luang Pho Son," in *Sun Phrakhruang*, March 1991, p. 34.

The story of Ajan Nong putting out the fire was told by Fung Chaibun, an 82-year-old former monk and village elder, in *Prawat Luang Pho Nong Inthasuwanno* (n.d.), pp. 15–16. For short biographies of Ajan Nong Inthasuwanno, see Phatsakhon Chuthaphutthi, *Phra Phuttharup lae singsaksit* (1982), vol. 3, pp. 97–102; and Sujit Wongthes, "*Pai Song Phinong*," in *Sinlapa Watthanatham* 13, no. 10 (August 1992): 92–98. In 1917 a twenty-two-year-old novice named Maha Pun took higher ordination as a monk at Wat Song Phinong in Suphanburi. Ajan Niang Inthachoto was his preceptor and Ajan Nong was his examination master. Three decades later he became abbot of Wat Pho in Bangkok. A gifted writer and preacher, Maha Pun was highly respected for his ability to make the Dhamma teachings accessible to all. Maha Pun went on to become Sangharaja of Thailand in 1972.

19

BANDITS AND THE PRACTICE OF GRATITUDE

IN OLD Siam each male villager was required to pay a head tax of four baht per year. This was a lot of money for subsistence farmers to pay, especially if they had several sons. Siam was still underpopulated, and those men who could not afford to pay the head tax were made to work for the government instead, usually at hard labor. Frank Exell, an Englishman who was working for Siam Bank in Nakhon Si Thammarat, visited Phatthalung in 1931 and called on the governor, who showed him around the government buildings. Exell wrote, "I had seen men working on the roads near the prison, without any chains or fetters, and I asked if any attempts were made at escape. The Governor hurriedly explained that the people working on the roads had nothing whatever to do with the jail. They were poor unfortunate people who had been unable to pay their annual head tax and were putting in a suitable amount of labour in lieu of payment. This was apparently quite common in the provinces and carried no stigma. During this period of work they were housed by the local authorities and provided with food. Houseroom usually consisted of sleeping on the ground under the local government offices but there was not much hardship about this in a tropical climate."

Exell tells us that "the Governor was surprised" when he told him that "no such system existed in England and that a man could be sent to prison for non-payment of taxes and, unkindest cut of all, still be liable for the taxes.

He considered, not unfairly, that the Siamese were, therefore, much more advanced and there was not much I could do but agree. I imagined myself walking down the main street of Torquay and passing the time of day with well-known residents who had come on hard times and were labouring cheerfully on a drainage scheme. The possibility of a vicar or a local squire being employed publicly on such jobs appealed to me immensely."

The Phatthalung governor took Exell on a tour of the jail. "Prisoners convicted of crimes of violence were housed in a large airy building and shackled to the floor at suitable intervals." As he walked around with the governor, Exell noted, "The prisoners were allowed to talk and some relieved their feelings by hurling abuse at the Governor as he passed. He did not appear to mind this in the least but understandably begged to be excused from translating. He seemed to regard a bombardment of abuse as a safety valve which did him no harm and the prisoner much good."

Paying their annual tax was not much of a problem in the household where Ajan Panya (Pan) grew up. Ajan Panya, abbot of Wat Cholaprathan since 1960, was the third of four children. His parents were farmers who owned twenty water buffaloes and over a hundred oxen and cows. They also owned fifty acres of paddy fields. Some years they leased other people's land to farm, paying twenty baht per year. With this amount of money one could buy an ox or two. His parents considered themselves financially comfortable, since they had more than enough to eat.

"My parents spoke little," Ajan Panya recalled. "They never fought or argued, never used bad words. I never heard them quarrel with neighbors. They were friendly and helpful to anybody who had problems. They helped others according to their ability. Although they owned twenty water buffaloes, they were willing to lend eigh-

Fig. 19 Siamese women

teen of them to neighbors who needed to plow their fields. My parents used only two buffaloes to work their own fields. Nevertheless, if anybody was in need of buffaloes, they would lend out their last one." His parents showed the young Pan that other people's needs came before their own. "Those who turn to us," they told him, "must be really in need. For our needs we can always look to some other source." At the end of the plowing season neighbors usually returned the buffaloes without offering any payment. His parents never complained.

Pan's parents extended their hospitality even to strangers. Sometimes as many as fifteen people from far away might show up unexpectedly in their village. His parents willingly offered them shelter and food. Ajan Panya recalled that on the day the visitors were to leave, "My mother would get up earlier than usual to prepare breakfast for these travelers and also give them lunch to eat on the way. Mother was a good and resourceful hostess, she did it so often. Offering shelter and food to strangers made mother happy. She gained friendship. These travelers often gave her unusual foods or gifts from other places. Their gifts were not given as payment but out of affection."

In Pan's village there were ten households. All the villagers knew each other; they were like one extended family. There were two monasteries near the village. Pan's house was located between Wat Nanglat and Wat Khoknian. Wat Nanglat was the monastery of his ancestors. When Pan's relatives wanted to be ordained or make merit they would go to Wat Nanglat. Pan's parents practiced *sanghaha-vatthu* dhamma. The principles of *sanghaha-vatthu* (the Four Bases of Assistance) were taught to children by adults who lived the teachings. Children learned to practice generosity *(dana)*, to speak kind words *(piyavaca)*, to render service for the benefit of others *(atthacariya)*, to treat everyone equally, and to behave properly in all circumstances *(samanattata)*. Pan grew up in an agrarian society in which family, friends, and neighbors truly depended upon one another. In a traditional subsistence economy such as Pan's, money played a minor role and was used primarily for paying taxes and buying cattle or tools. "During the plowing and harvesting seasons farmers took turns helping each other with the physical work in their fields. The labor one needed was given free of charge. It was considered rude to pay money for such help."

Villagers of all generations worked and played together. During festivals they would cook special dishes or desserts together. They would then take the food to the wat and distribute it. Even when there was no special occasion, if a man killed a deer or caught a particularly large fish—food the villagers seldom had—he or his wife would cook a large curry, then send their children to distribute bowls of it. This environment of sharing and generosity formed Pan's character, although when he was still very young he did not always appreciate village customs. "As a child I got tired of walking to every house to distribute curry or desserts. Whenever my parents got some special food, such as a piece of meat, they would cook a big pot of curry. If they got a few durian fruit, they would make a big bowl of dessert with coconut milk. If they caught a lot of fish, they would divide the fish into portions. Then we children would have to walk from one end of the village to the other to distribute meat curry, durian desert, or raw fish to every house. This happened often. As kids we could not really avoid this duty. Whenever I saw my folks putting fish in piles, I thought, 'Oh dear! More work for me today! Have to run around again!'"

The village where Pan grew up was surrounded by high hills, wide pastures, and dense forests. Ajan Panya tells us, "The air was clean. Villagers worked on farms. The soil was fertile. No need for fertilizers. It rained according to season. Rainwater was used for drinking and farming. Once we finished planting rice, we grew vegetables and fruit trees. Then it was time to harvest the rice. Once the harvesting season was over we gathered vegetables and tended fruits to eat and distribute to neighbors. Surplus produce was used in exchange for necessary goods. The way of life in the agricultural societies was free of competition. All produce was shared. People lived off their farms. Life was simple and straightforward."

But even in this small peaceful village, full of friend-

Fig. 20 A Shan woman

ship, danger sometimes lurked. Villagers could never feel entirely secure. They lived in fear of cattle rustlers. Phatthalung had a reputation for being home to many naklengs and bandits. In the 1920s, as Ajan Panya recalled, "Bandit gangs known as Black Shiny Head, Dawn Sand Hill, Silver Skin Red Mustache, and Dark Skin Black Mustache got their names from whatever villagers managed to notice about the marauders at the time of a raid. There were a great many of them. Almost every night some village was raided, and buffaloes were taken from the fields. The bandits came, fired guns in the air, and rounded up all the buffaloes. As many as twenty might be taken away."

After the bandits stole the buffaloes they simply disappeared into the forests, and it was hard to track them down. In spite of frequent raids Pan's parents' cattle and buffaloes were never stolen, whether the animals were kept at home or left in the field. Neighbors who lost cattle or buffaloes to the thieves sometimes got some of them back, thanks to Ajan Panya's parents. "For example, if ten buffaloes were stolen, my parents were able to get back eight out of ten. The bandits killed two buffaloes for food." As Ajan Panya explains, "This was not because my parents had power over the bandits or that the bandits felt deferential toward my folks. This was due to my parents' kindness to everybody. They lent their buffaloes to anybody in need. It did not matter how many buffaloes or for how long. It was my parents' generosity that protected their buffaloes. Some of these bandits had been guests at our house and might have been lenient out of gratitude for the free food and shelter they once received." Ajan Panya concluded, "Back then the bandits were not horrible men; they had their own code of ethics."

Buffalo banditry was either a profession or a sport men engaged in order to prove their manliness. Monks who grew up in the southern peninsula recall an old local saying: A real man knows how to steal a buffalo. Ajan Panya explained, "In the old days parents would not allow their daughter to marry a man who did not know how to steal a buffalo. Local people believed that if you knew how to steal a buffalo, you would know how to keep your own buffaloes from being stolen." As the English proverb says, "An old thief makes a good gaoler."

Before Siam became a cash economy the custom of sharing food and other resources with one's neighbors was widespread in every region. Phra Bodhirangsi (b. 1918), abbot of Wat Phantong in Chiang Mai, reminds us of this fact. Bodhirangsi, the oldest of ten children, was born of Tai-Yuan parents in Ban Chang Khatab, a village southeast of Chiang Mai city. He learned the Yuan language from his father. At the age of nine, according to the local custom, Bodhirangsi was ordained as a novice at Wat Muang Chang near his village. While still a novice he attended the central government's primary school, which required that all children speak Bangkok Thai. In 1938 Bodhirangsi took the bhikkhu ordination at Wat Phantong. He then went to live with Khruba Inthachak, abbot of the forest monastery at Great Pond in Sanpatong district.

While Bodhirangsi was studying and practicing meditation under Khruba Inthachak, two of his brothers and his father were also ordained as monks. At the end of a rains retreat the four monks—Bodhirangsi, his brothers, and their father—went on thudong through the forests of Chiang Mai. They walked to Mae Sot (in Tak) and went as far as Chiang Rai at the border of northern Siam and the Shan states. In their wandering the thudong monks depended on alms from villagers whom they met along the way. As late as the 1940s, Bodhirangsi recalled, the sharing of food was still common. "People did not need to cook so many dishes. Each household would cook only one pot of curry and distribute part of it to other houses; other dishes came from neighbors. There were hardly any murders in the villages in which people shared food."

Buddhists in northern Siam were a diverse mix of Tai-Yuan, Shan, Lao, Khoen, and Lu. In their sermons Buddhist preachers often used local stories to teach people how to practice generosity. Stories and legends useful in teaching the Dhamma were kept in local wat libraries. W. W. Cochrane, who was writing an anthropological study of the Shan for the British Association for the Advancement of Science, began collecting and translating Shan legends. Cochrane was in the Shan states between 1910 and 1912, just around the time Ajan Panya was born.

This is Cochrane's translation of a Shan story:

"Ages ago, in the land of Kokkulu, there lived in a certain village a rich man named Sawtika. He had many buffaloes and cattle in his pasture, and in his treasure-house much silver and gold. The king, hearing that the Buddha had come to a neighbouring place, and wishing to see him, called all his able-bodied people to go with him, leaving in this village only the aged and the children, with servants to look after them.

"In another part of the country there lived a very wicked robber chief who, on hearing that the king and the able-bodied had gone, called his band together to rob the village. Sawtika, too old to go with the king, heard that the robbers were coming and commanded his servants to arm themselves with bows and spears and go forth to drive the marauding band away. His little daughter, Sammoktasa, hearing the command given, thought of a better way. Coming to her father she said, 'Father, you have great riches in buffaloes, cattle, horses, mules, silver, gold, and precious gems. Besides this, there are with you many old men and women and children. You have much to lose. The robbers have nothing to lose and much to gain—and are as fierce as wasps. Your servants cannot drive them away. Let me therefore go and conquer them with kindness. If they are pleased, they may go away, for men and angels like to hear sweet words. No one drives a buffalo by scolding, but gently leads him with a string and coaxes him on; so may I do with the robbers.'

"The aged Sawtika saw the wisdom of her words and said, 'It is well. Go, my child, with your maidens, and meet the robbers. Offer them water to drink. They will be thirsty. And speak kind words to them.' The maidens filled their water jars with water, fresh and cool from the well, and carrying them on their heads went forth from the village. They found the robbers resting in a shady grove of mango trees. Approaching the robber-chief, Sammoktasa said, in words of polite greeting: 'Whence have you come? and what do you, with all these good men, seek? Take a little water, please, for you must be thirsty.' Thus gently did she speak to him.

"The chief, thinking in his heart that the little lady mistook them all for good men, did not want to tell her that they had come to rob her father and the whole village. So he, dissembling, said, 'My little lady, the king and his people have gone to see the great Buddha; we too were going with them; but coming too late we camped here. To-morrow we will go on to hear the golden words of the great teacher.'

"Sammoktasa, undeceived, put her water jar on her head again and said, 'It is very good to go and thus acquire merit; but let me help you, for you are all weary and hungry, that I too may share by hospitality the blessing that will come upon you.' Receiving graciously the thanks of the robber-chief, she returned to her father who had already prepared for her coming. In a few moments, Sammoktasa, with her companions, was on her way back to the robbers, taking with her four carts loaded with rice, fish, onions, pumpkins, salt, tea, and tobacco. With their own hands they divided the food among the robbers, saying as they did so, 'By using our gift you will increase our merit in all worlds to come.' As the robbers were eating, they heard the sound of drums—bur-r-r, bur-r-r—from behind the village, where old Sawtika had stationed a few servants. The chief asked, 'What is that?' and the little lady answered, as she had been instructed to do: 'O, that is only the sepoys whom the king left to protect the village during the absence of the able-bodied.' Then with many kind words she returned with her maidens and the empty carts to the village. As soon as she was gone, the chief said to his followers, 'It would be cruel to attack the village after all this kindness; neither are we able to fight against the king's police' [for he thought that they were already there]. 'Let us go,' said he, 'and seek booty elsewhere.'"

Like monks of Siamese and Lao traditions, Shan preachers, too, used simple stories such as this one to teach Dhamma. As the story unfolded it was often accompanied by sound effects. In this story a group of Shan novices probably put in a few drum rolls while their teacher was telling the story.

Cochrane, who also found the tale edifying, concluded his translation with the words, "Thus it was that one little girl by her kindness overcame a band of robbers and saved a whole village from pillage and its people from slaughter. This teaches that soft words are better than swords and kind acts than armies. There is nothing so great as gentleness and hospitality." Sammoktasa provided a good role model for Shan girls and boys in the audience, for the story tells us that regardless of gender or age one can contribute to the welfare of the community.

SOURCES

F. K. Exell, *Siamese Tapestry* (1936; 1963), p. 134.

Chiwit lae ngan khong Than Paññananda (1991), pp. 1–6.

Interview with Ajan Paññananda, abbot of Wat Cholaprathan, Nonthaburi, January 17, 2001.

For an explanation of *sanghaha-vatthu* in English, see Ajahn Pasanno, "Illuminating the Dust: Brahmaviharas in Action with Guided Meditation," in Ajahn Pasanno and Ajahn Amaro, *Broad View, Boundless Heart* (2001), pp. 25–26. See also Phra Maha Prayudh Prayutto, *Dictionary of Buddhism* (1985), pp. 167–168.

The southern saying "A real man knows how to steal a buffalo" emerged in interviews with three monks who grew up in southern Thailand: Ajan Paññananda (January 17, 2001), Ajan Banyat of Wat Bolo, Nakhon Si Thammarat (September 18, 1998), and Phra Maha Sombun Saekho, Wat Khuhasawan in Phatthalung (April 7, 1989).

Interview with Phra Bodhirangsi, abbot of Wat Phantong, Chiang Mai, July 13, 1989.

W. W. Cochrane, *The Shans* (1915), vol. 1, pp. 181–183.

20

AN ELEPHANT ON A RAMPAGE

IN THE nineteenth century not many Westerners traveled to Nakhon Lampang, which is six hundred kilometers north of Bangkok. Those who did were likely to have been managers and other employees of corporations extracting teak from the region or missionaries stationed there to convert the natives. In 1914 Reginald Le May, the British vice-consul, made the trip by elephant from Muang Ngao to Lampang, a distance of some eighty-four kilometers that normally took four days. "Muang Ngao," Le May wrote, "derives its importance solely from the fact that the Anglo-Siam Corporation for many years had their northern headquarters there. In fact, the small town was almost entirely settled by their contractors and dependents, most of whom were Shan and Khamu. There was also, however, a small Lao population, cultivating rice and selling local produce from their booths in the market."

Reginald Campbell, after a seven-year career as an officer in the British navy, was hired at the end of World War I by a British-owned teak company then logging in Muang Ngao. When Campbell first arrived at the forest in 1920 his new boss, a man named Orwell, showed him around. The forest in which he was to begin working, Campbell tells us, "consisted of the whole of the basin (or watershed) of the river Mae Ngow [Ngao] and its numerous tributaries. From the sources of the Mae Ngow to where it ran out into its parent river, the Mae Yome,

Fig. 21 Working elephants, 1880

was a distance of a little over thirty miles, while in places its tributaries extended for twenty miles to right and left. Thus the total area under Orwell was not far short of one thousand square miles, a no mean responsibility."

Campbell learned how long it took for a log from Muang Ngao forest to reach Bangkok. "The lower half of the Mae Ngow basin was closed for afforestation purposes . . . , but the top half, which was open, had contained originally about a hundred thousand marketable teak trees, all of which were being gradually felled, logged, measured, hammered and then dragged down to the Mae Ngow river for 'ounging' into the big main river Mae Yome by elephant. Once, I learnt, the logs had reached the Mae Yome, they would float more or less unattended down to the rafting stations some two hundred miles to the south, where they would be made up into rafts before completing the final three-hundred-mile journey to the saw mills of Bangkok. The average time, I gathered from Orwell, it took for a log to reach Bangkok after being placed in the Mae Ngow was five years."

Orwell first showed Campbell how to inspect felled trees. Next, Campbell wrote, "We moved to another part of the forest to watch and inspect elephants working at the stump," a relay system in which the elephants "engaged in pushing and prodding the logs down the steep and sodden hills to where more elephants were dragging more logs along specially constructed paths."

As soon as the logs reached the river they were measured and "hammered," or stamped, with the name of the company that had felled them. "When the logs had all been hammered," Campbell tells us, "more elephants . . . came on the scene and rolled them down the bank into the river-bed, where they would await the next 'floating rise.'" Orwell had one hundred and eighty elephants working for him. From his boss Campbell learned that the elephants "lived almost natural lives in their natural surroundings, working only a few hours a day and then being hobbled to rest and graze at will in the jungle."

Male elephants were preferred, Campbell wrote. "Males are more valuable for timberwork than females, partly because of their strength, partly because they are not so timid, and partly because their tusks are useful for levering and pushing the logs."

There was one major drawback to keeping male elephants, however, which Campbell soon discovered. "The male has periods of disturbance known as 'musth,' during which he is highly dangerous and has to remain securely shackled to a tree. One can tell when an attack is coming on by an oily discharge that starts exuding from a hole on the temple; when the oil, which comes out very gradually, has trickled down to a level with the eye—then look out! If he's not properly secured the chances are he'll try to kill anyone in sight."

Campbell was assigned the task of neaping (counting) logs along a twenty-kilometer stretch of the Mae Wang River between Great Village and Lampang. While he was away from the base camp, one of Orwell's hired elephants ran amok. This was a male elephant called Pukamsen, whose name means "one hundred thousand pieces of gold." When Campbell reached Lampang, Orwell, who had also gone there, told him about the incident. Lao workers later filled in the details. Before retelling Orwell's story, Campbell, who knew his boss well, said of him, "There was no more modest man than Orwell, consequently the story as he told it to me did not do justice to the matchless courage he must have displayed; but I had seen [Pukamsen], and I knew every inch of the locality where the scenes were enacted."

One morning Pukamsen, who had come into musth, broke the chain that bound him to a tree and got free. Two of Orwell's working elephants and their mahouts were walking at the time along the nearby road to Lampang.

When Pukamsen advanced upon them, Campbell tells us, "Even they, the elephants, feared him, and, turning, they fled sideways into the jungle, shedding howdahs and mahouts in the process."

The elephant continued up the road, coming up behind "a Lao husbandman, walking alone. . . . He hears a faint sound, the slur of the broken chain, behind him, and casually looks round. A scream of horror rises to his throat, strangles as a mountain surges upon him. He is knocked down, crushed, and left a shapeless mass of flesh and blood on the road."

Except for the noise of the dragging chain, Campbell says, the elephant in musth "makes not a sound; that is the terrible thing about him and his kind: he may be a foot or two behind you, and you won't know he's there, so noiselessly does he move."

Pukamsen destroyed everything and anything that got in his way. Campbell continues, "Nearer and nearer he draws to the village of Muang Ngao. Two bullock-carts appear ahead. The drivers just have time to flee, and he is on them, smashing the carts to matchwood and killing the patient bullocks."

The news spread like wildfire, and soon the whole village knew that Pukamsen had turned killer. Campbell explained that Pukamsen was not Orwell's elephant, but the chief who owned the animal was probably ten days' journey away, and Orwell had to be responsible for the safety of the village and the inhabitants. Orwell told the village headman to order his people to stay home. Since the tuskers owned by the British company were also in danger (for Pukamsen would likely attack them), Orwell ordered his elephant overseer to move every tusker near the village at least ten miles away.

On his way back to his bungalow, Orwell, on horseback, encountered the elephant. "Suddenly a bomb seems to burst on his left. [Pukamsen], hiding unseen in the fringing jungle, must be charging him." The sudden sight and smell of the horse, an animal elephants prefer to avoid, stopped Pukamsen, and the pause was just long enough for Orwell to see the telltale oil at the elephant's temples. Orwell galloped his mare back to his compound as fast as he could to work out a way to trap the raging elephant.

According to Campbell, Pukamsen was clearly a rogue. Although Siamese law protected elephants from hunters, rogue elephants could be shot on sight. But Orwell "is a man who loves elephants and would not willingly take the life of one. He dwells on [Pukamsen]'s matchless strength and mighty grandeur. Shall he be the man to lay low such magnificence, when in the course of two or three weeks' time the 'musth' will in all probability have passed, leaving [Pukamsen] as harmless as the very bullocks he has slain?"

Orwell went to his office at dawn and summoned the village headman, the teak company's chief headman, and a number of other workers and mahouts. He told them to get all available men to dig a pit nine feet deep and six feet wide in the center of the "harvested paddyland opposite the company compound on the other side of the river." Orwell told his workers, "When the pit is finished, conceal it with a covering of leaves and bamboo, then place a plank across the middle so that a man may get over in safety and an elephant may not."

Orwell next instructed that when everything was ready the mahouts were to drive two cow elephants into the field to lure Pukamsen after them. Then Orwell, who spoke Lao, explained that one man was needed to complete the plan. "A man will go into the middle of the field, and the elephant, seeing him, will charge. The man will then make for the pit and run across the plank." The plank would not support the weight of the elephant, who would fall into the pit. None of the Lao or Khamu workers wanted to take the risk. The job fell to Orwell.

Pukamsen reacted as Orwell had anticipated. The bull elephant thundered after him as Orwell ran toward the concealed pit. "Crash! With a thud that literally shook the earth the vast body smashed into the pit." Immediately, "The coolies and mahouts leap forward, their object being to secure [Pukamsen]'s legs and thus render him helpless against the company elephants that will shortly arrive to drag him to a tree; but the awesome spectacle of the huge leviathan, bellowing and trumpeting and rumbling and bubbling, smashing and heaving and goring at the sides of his prison causes their hands to tremble and the ropes to get confused."

The Lao workers were horrified, Campbell wrote, to see that the elephant "has actually managed to tear down

Fig. 22 An elephant in musth under restaint

part of one side of the pit and is beginning to heave himself up over the falling earth. Up he comes, up, up . . . then the coolies and mahouts wait for no more. Dropping their ropes, they flee in terror across the Mae Ngow river. Orwell, finding himself alone and helpless, has no course left him but to follow them."

Campbell continues, "The party gain the further bank of the river and run up into the company compound. There they see [Pukamsen] sullenly rolling off into the jungle beyond the paddy-fields. But the fall has evidently shaken him, for he walks with a limp."

That evening Orwell learned that Pukamsen has killed another man. Campbell wrote, "Owing to the menace of the killer the work of the whole Muang Ngow teak forest came to a standstill; those of the Laos who were employed in distant, safe corners of the forest came in to the village to see the fun, while those who were employed near the village rushed off to the forest to get away from it; as for Orwell himself, he was far too busy trying to trap the cause of the trouble to be able to straighten things out."

Finally, somebody must have located the elephant doctor, a local man who appears to have been employed by the teak firm. "At last there came to Orwell the company's elephant-medicine maker, bearing a bundle of arrows, the tips of which were stained with a greenish fluid, and a buffalo horn filled with powder." The medicine man told Orwell, "These are poisoned arrows, and if they are put in guns and fired at [Pukamsen]'s legs, then he will become so lame that he will scarcely be able to move at all; at which your servants the coolies and mahouts will surely have the chance to rope him."

Orwell followed the native's advice and succeeded in shooting several arrows into the elephant. "The great brute," Campbell tell us, "was rolling and staggering like a drunken man, what with the pain of the poison and the musth going out of him. Wasn't even necessary to get elephants to drag him to a tree; his mahout eventually came along and he obeyed him like a lamb. Will he get over it, did you say? He was almost himself again by the time I left to come in here."

In conclusion Campbell wrote, "Thus ended the running amok of [Pukamsen]. And if ever a man showed courage and resource in a trying time, with no one to help him and a great responsibility upon his shoulders, it was Orwell."

SOURCES

Reginald Le May, *An Asian Arcady: The Land and Peoples of Northern Siam* (1926), p. 253.

Reginald Campbell, *Teak-Wallah: The Adventure of a Young Englishman in Thailand in the 1920s* (1935; 1986), pp. 32–34, 126–138.

Fig. 23 Venerable Grandfather Doem, abbot of Wat Nong Pho,
Nakhon Sawan

21

HOW TO TAME ELEPHANTS

IN THE 1920s, when Orwell and Campbell were working in Muang Ngao forest, there were still a few village abbots skilled in handling elephants in musth. These meditation masters had mastered the Khotchasatra, a collection of palm-leaf texts on elephants containing information about the personalities, habits, and behaviors of elephants; instructions on how to train them, care for them, heal them, and handle them in musth; and advice on how to train domestic elephants to capture wild elephants.

One such elephant master was Ajan Doem Buddhasaro (b. 1861), abbot of Bodhi Pond Monastery (Wat Nong Pho) in Paknam Pho, Nakhon Sawan province. Ajan Doem, sixty years old when Orwell's elephant, Pukamsen, went on a rampage in the jungle, would have been able to subdue the elephant without having to use poison arrows.

Ajan Doem taught a large number of monks, but he did not teach the Khotchasatra to just anybody. In 1948 a young monk named Charan Thithadhammo, who was from Singburi, south of Paknam Pho, found his way to Ajan Doem's wat. During that year Phra Charan (b. 1928) had been ordained as a monk to make merit for his parents. It was his intention to remain in the robes for only one rains retreat. After he passed the middle level of the Nak-dhamma, Phra Charan decided to wander in the forest for a while before disrobing. He wanted to see the north and felt sure he would find an abbot there who

would perform the disrobing ceremony for him. Just before he was ordained, Charan's grandmother urged him
to do the right thing. "The timing of your disrobing is
very important. If the time is bad, after you disrobe you
might get killed or end up in jail. Some people's lives
have been ruined. Remember, choose the time to disrobe
carefully." Perhaps his grandmother, who had raised him
since he was a young boy, tried to warn him because she
knew that Charan was very stubborn and determined to
do things his own way.

Ajan Charan, who is now abbot of Wat Amphawan in
Singburi, recalled that it was his good karma that brought
him to Venerable Father Doem. After getting permission
from his preceptor to leave his home wat, Phra Charan
traveled to Lopburi and bought a train ticket to Phitsanulok,
intending to get off there and wander in the nearby forest. On the train he met several laypeople who were going to visit Ajan Doem of Bodhi Pond Monastery (Wat
Nong Pho). The pilgrims said they were getting off at
Bodhi Pond, a very small station, and they asked Phra
Charan if he would like to accompany them. He accepted.

The pilgrims called Venerable Father Doem "the bodhisat
of Four-Stream Muang." The four streams refer to the
Ping, the Wang, the Yom, and the Nan rivers that join
together at Paknam Pho to form one single river. From
Chainat southward these streams combine with tributaries of the Tha Chin on the west and the Chao Phraya on
the east.

Phra Charan followed the pilgrims on foot along the
road to Bodhi Pond Monastery. At the gate of the wat
the pilgrims invited the young monk to walk before them
so that he would be the first to pay respect to Ajan Doem.
When Phra Charan entered Ajan Doem's kuti, he was
immediately struck by the abbot's appearance. "Venerable Grandfather Doem sat on the floor with his back
straight. Graceful. Big and tall. Reddish dark complex-

ion. His body was all wrinkled. He was very old, yet his eyes sparkled, unlike ordinary old people's eyes. I could feel the power, the energy, and the mystery. When my eyes met his I felt as if I was drawn into this mysterious energy. It made me afraid."

Phra Charan, feeling renewed faith, prostrated himself before the abbot. The young monk thought, "So this is the Venerable Father Doem, whom people respect so much! He is very old, yet I can feel his inner strength and power. Why is that? Is it because he is an ascetic monk strongly grounded in sila, samadhi, and pañña?" When Ajan Doem asked Charan which monastery he was from, Phra Charan noticed that the abbot's voice was loud and clear, unlike the voices of most people over ninety. Before Phra Charan could answer the first question, Ajan Doem fired off another one. "Have you traveled all the way here merely to disrobe?" he asked. Deeply disturbed, since he had not told any of the pilgrims about his decision, Charan wondered, "How did Venerable Father Doem *know*? Better be honest with him!" After Charan told Ajan Doem that he was from Wat Phromburi in Singburi and asked him to perform the disrobing ceremony for him, Ajan Doem replied, "All right. Stay here with me for a while. Today is not a good day to discuss disrobing." Ajan Doem then called a lay leader to take Phra Charan to a kuti reserved for guests.

One of Phra Charan's good qualities was that wherever he stayed he offered a massage as a way to reciprocate the kindness of his host. While living in Ajan Doem's wat, Phra Charan attended the abbot by giving him a massage at night. While giving the massage, young Charan had the opportunity to ask the abbot about local Buddhist customs and practices that puzzled him. Ajan Doem had a way of explaining things, Phra Charan tells us, that made him want to know more.

At the monastery Charan noticed that there was a

steady stream of people, all day long, coming to see the abbot. Young and old asked the ajan to blow on their heads, an ancient form of blessing usually performed by a meditation monk or abbot. As Phra Charan describes it, "Venerable Father Doem blew the sounds '*om* [the mantra syllable Om] *phiang* [the noise made by the expulsion of the breath], *om phiang, phiang di* [good], *phiang di*' over each supplicant while holding their heads with both his hands. I was afraid he might lose his strength." Performing such a blessing a few times is one thing: doing it all day would be exhausting.

People brought amulets and knives for Ajan Doem to bless, which he did by chanting mantras into the objects. Luang Pho never turned anyone away. The laypeople then returned home with these sacred objects, fortified with the belief that the items that Venerable Father had blessed had the power to protect them from bad spirits. "Luang Pho was already too frail to walk around much," Phra Charan reports, "yet he still accepted invitations to travel by oxcart to laypeople's houses to perform ceremonies for them. When his disciples tried to stop him, he told them that he wanted to serve people until the day he died."

One night, while massaging the abbot, Phra Charan asked, "Venerable Father, your *phiang di, phiang di*, can it really bring good things?"

Ajan Doem smiled before replying, "I can't tell you now what good it will bring. You must stay with me longer to find out."

Outside the monk's bedroom Phra Charan saw a collection of several kinds of swords and wooden sticks used in warfare as well as in dramatic presentations, and a musical instrument called a *ranat*, made of wood with bamboo keys and played much like a xylophone. One evening Charan gave Ajan Doem a massage as usual. Out of curiosity, Charan asked, "Venerable Father, these swords and wooden sticks, why do you keep them here? Do monks know how to use them?"

Upon hearing Charan's questions, Ajan Doem laughed, saying, "Be patient! Be patient, young man. You have only been ordained for one rains retreat, and already you are in a hurry to disrobe. Listen carefully and think about the things I'm telling you." In Phra Charan's words, Ajan Doem explained that "in the old days the monasteries were schools for all kinds of knowledge. These monasteries were like the famous Samnak Thisapamok and Samnak Taksila in India during the Buddha's time. Laypeople came to the monasteries not only to make merit but also to seek knowledge from the monks."

Phra Charan asked, "What's the difference between ordaining for one year and several years?"

Ajan Doem again laughed as he replied to Charan's innocent question. In central Siam, he explained, "It is said that ordaining for three years is the equivalent of studying for a bachelor's degree. Spending seven years in the robes is like training for a master's degree. After ten years in the robes you earn the equivalent of a doctorate. Monks who disrobe after only one or two years in the robes are not called *thit*." The Thai word *thit*, derived from the second syllable of the Pali word *pandit* (scholar), is an informal term of respect applied to disrobed monks who had been in the robes for many years.

Phra Charan then got to the point. "What about these *krabi-krabong* [steel swords and wooden sticks]? What are they for, Venerable Father?"

Ajan Doem replied, "The *krabi-krabong* were at the heart of fighting." Luang Pho then went on to explain the traditional role of monks in old Siam: "The monasteries in the kingdom of Ayutthaya taught statesmanship, law, economics, arts and crafts, medicine, music, astrology, and swordsmanship. Monks in those days had all kinds of skills; they could teach anything. Sons of the nobility who studied the art of government at the monastery learned to discipline themselves as well as to lead people." Ajan Doem reminded his young pupil that "living in the wat teaches you to master yourself and to live in harmony with others in the community. You learn self-discipline that can guide you when you disrobe to live a householder's life."

Ajan Doem then explained the importance of swordsmanship and the prestige that once attached to those who studied it. The sword was the weapon of choice in the days before guns. Warriors fought in order to protect the people in their kingdoms. In ancient times every man who was not a slave had to serve as a soldier when called upon, and every man had to learn how to use the sword. Bodhi Pond Monastery had once been famous for teaching the art of swordsmanship. Monasteries were known for the specialized training they offered. One wat might be famous for teaching Pali scripture. Another wat might be known for carving, casting, and sacralizing potent amulets or for the teaching of music. Young people went to a particular wat to train in those skills that interested them. The monasteries were truly schools for all subjects. There were no secular schools until the very end of the nineteenth century, and even after the Bangkok government's education reforms changed the way things were taught and what was taught, local monasteries continued to offer both primary education and special skills. Parents knew which monasteries were good at what subjects, and they took their sons to be ordained and trained according to the local monks' specialty. If a young monk mastered one skill at a certain monastery and wanted to have training in another field, he could go elsewhere for further study.

Ajan Doem went on to tell his pupil that Ajan Thao, the first abbot of Bodhi Pond Monastery, had been one of the generals in Taksin's army. In 1766 Taksin was

serving as the Governor of Tak, a principality northwest
of Ayutthaya, when he was summoned to the city of
Ayutthaya, which Burma's troops had surrounded. Thao
was among the officers in Taksin's army when the governor-general marched his forces south. Thao fought
alongside Taksin when the army reached the battle-
ground. Seeing the hopelessness of the situation, Taksin
escaped with his troops just before Ayutthaya fell in April
1767. The men made their way southeast toward Chanthaburi, near the Cambodian border today.

When Taksin settled in Thonburi, where he established
a new center for Siam and became its king (r. 1767–82),
Thao resigned from the army. As a soldier he had killed
many people; in old age he wanted to devote his life to
the Dhamma. The retired warrior then traveled north
from Thonburi to ordain at a monastery in Paknam Pho,
a journey of some ten days by boat.

Ajan Thao had been living as a monk in Paknam Pho
for some time before he discovered the ruins of Bodhi
Pond Monastery. He restored the old wat and became its
abbot. There Ajan Thao established a school of swordsmanship called the Sword School of Bodhi Pond (Samnak
Dap Nong Pho). Ajan Doem told Phra Charan that "Ajan
Thao wanted to impart the art of swordsmanship to the
next generation so that knowledge of the martial arts
would not disappear. Future men would thus know the
art of swordfighting, be able to protect themselves from
their enemies, and avoid becoming war captives." The
ajan reminded Phra Charan, "Before King Taksin could
liberate the kingdom of Siam he had to struggle. He lost
a large number of soldiers. Remember that Ajan Thao
was one of the officers closest to the king."

Ajan Doem next described how Ajan Thao trained his
disciples. "Before he taught the techniques of swordsmanship, Ajan Thao first laid the foundation by teaching
each young man to practice meditation. To be trained as

a soldier, a young man first had to learn to master his mind. Only then could he master the art of swordsmanship." In the monasteries the sons of the nobility, as well as the sons of commoners, lived a spartan life: they rose early, practiced their skills daily, and lived frugally. Monastic discipline helped prepare future soldiers for life on the march and on the field of battle. The aged ajan spoke from experience. He was one of the last living teachers in Siam of the ancient art of swordsmanship.

After some weeks had passed, Charan reminded Ajan Doem that he wanted to disrobe. The abbot replied, "You should wait. It is not the right time yet."

For a while Charan did not dare bring up the subject again, thinking, "While I'm still in the robes I might as well learn a metta mantra from the ajan. After I disrobe I can use the mantra to court women. I want to get a pretty woman to marry me."

Charan next asked Ajan Doem to teach him metta mantras of the kind that would make women fall for him. Ajan Doem laughed and told Charan to bring him a pencil and several pieces of paper. "Luang Pho then wrote down all kinds of mantras, good for a lot of different situations that I might encounter in everyday life. I'd never run out of mantras to recite. In order to learn each mantra by heart, I had to recite it every day." Looking back, Ajan Charan realized that "this was Luang Pho's way of dealing with a person like me. I wanted the mantras, and he gave me so many mantras that my mind became completely preoccupied with mastering them, so much so that I forgot that I came here to disrobe."

Phra Charan noticed that when people came to Ajan Doem's kuti to ask the abbot to blow on their heads, "Luang Pho did not recite any mantra for *them*, yet he gave *me* all those mantras to learn. I wondered if I was wasting my time reciting these mantras."

When Charan expressed his doubt about the value of

learning all the mantras, Ajan Doem explained, "By themselves the mantras are meaningless. They are used as a means to focus the mind to be at one point. A mind that is constantly wandering is a weak mind; it has no power. Reciting the mantras keeps the mind focused. It is difficult to walk across a swift-running stream. The focused mind is like a bridge that helps you cross the stream to the other shore. Once you cross, you no longer need the bridge. A mantra serves as a bridge to get the mind to samadhi. Once your mind knows how to get to samadhi you no longer need to recite the mantra, because the mind has already gained incredible strength due to your power of concentration. Once you have reached this attainment you can blow on people's heads, breathing 'om phiang, om phiang' while wishing that good things will happen to them. Do you understand? Now go back to reciting the mantras until your mind can cross to the other shore."

After six months had passed by, Charan realized, "The more I talked with Venerable Father, the more I enjoyed learning from him. It seemed like he knew that I was like a wild horse that needed to be tamed." While learning to keep his mind focused by reciting the mantras, Phra Charan had been meditating all along, although he did not call it that.

One day Ajan Doem told Charan, "You have been with me long enough. Are you ready to learn meditation practice? I will teach you. Do not disrobe. A man like you is better off in the ocher robes. You will make greater progress by living the monastic life rather than a lay life."

Seeing that Phra Charan was still dead set on disrobing, Ajan Doem sighed, "Please don't go away. I will die within the next three months. You are the first person to know this. Stay with me. This is the most important time in your life." Phra Charan saw that many monks and laypeople came to visit Ajan Doem, and yet Luang Pho had never told any of them that he was going to die soon.

One day, while getting his massage, Ajan Doem told Phra Charan, "I want to pass on an important body of knowledge to you. I have been observing you, and you are well suited to be the recipient of this knowledge." Phra Charan was elated to hear such praise, but his heart sank when he heard what Ajan Doem had in mind for him. "The knowledge that I want to give you is from the Khotchasatra, on how to subdue elephants in heat, rut, or musth. Not everybody can master this knowledge. Only people with parami, and you are one of them. I learned the Khotchasatra from my grandparents, who learned it from my great-grandparents. My ancestors were skilled elephant trainers. My great-grandfathers told us that they once captured two white elephants in a forest in Kamphaengphet that they presented to the king of Ayutthaya."

Feeling disappointed, Phra Charan told his teacher bluntly, "I do not want to learn elephant lore. I would rather learn a mantra that will make women fall in love with me or one that will enable me to envision the Buddha entering me."

In an instant Ajan Doem, who had been lying down, sat bolt upright. Pointing a finger at Charan and speaking in a firm voice, the abbot said, "Listen to me. You are too young to know what you want or do not want. When an elder offers you something, just take it. Why refuse the knowledge? You are too stubborn." Ajan Doem then cited a Thai proverb: "Knowledge is not something lugged around on the shoulders."

"Still," the stubborn Charan argued, "what is the use of learning how to train a domestic elephant to capture a wild elephant in the forest? We live now [in 1949] in a modern society; we no longer need wild elephants. Besides, learning how to subdue elephants in heat or in rut is not my business. I am never around such animals."

To get to the young monk, Ajan Doem, who had never owned a shirt in his entire life, used a modern analogy. He asked Charan, "Which would you prefer? Having one shirt or ten shirts?"

Phra Charan replied, "It's better to have ten shirts."

"That's right. If you are not wearing the spare shirts, you can iron them and hang them in a cupboard ready to be used any time you need them. Our ancestors gave us many kinds of knowledge. Why not keep this learning? Some day it might come in handy."

Finally, with a heavy sigh, Ajan Doem revealed his true feelings. "Listen to me carefully. The elders have vision that the young do not have. They think carefully before they do anything. I want to teach you the Khotchasatra because you have taken good care of me. I have never given this knowledge to anybody, not here in Nong Pho or anywhere else. I want this knowledge to live on after I die. Do you understand?"

Before learning how to subdue an elephant in musth, Charan first had to be skilled in meditation. It was at this time that the ajan taught Charan a method of meditation called kasina. This meditation method consists in focusing one's full and undivided attention on one object related to earth, water, wind, or fire or on a disk of a blue, red, yellow, or white color.

The kasina meditation could only be learned under the guidance of an experienced teacher, and Ajan Doem began by supervising the young monk. After weeks of sustained effort Phra Charan was able to see the meditation object as clearly with his eyes closed as he could when they were open. While still persevering in his concentration upon the object, Charan reached a state of mind where all sense activity was suspended, where there was no more seeing and hearing, no more awareness of the body, no more feeling. In this state the truly focused mind is calm and completely serene, and the practitioner has achieved the one-pointedness known as "purity of mind." It is not easy to attain this first mental absorption. It can take weeks, months, or even years.

It was only from such a state of mind that Phra Charan would be able to see the deity that guarded the elephant. At this stage Phra Charan and the deity would become one. No longer would there be any distinction between the observer, the meditator, and the observed, the meditation object—that is, the image of the elephant's deity. It was at this point that the meditator would be able to radiate metta to the deity.

As he watched Phra Charan make progress in meditation, Ajan Doem reminded him, "See? If you had refused to learn the Khotchasatra, you would never have mastered the kasina meditation practice. You entered the monastic life empty-handed. [By quitting too soon] you'd be leaving it empty-handed. Don't be stubborn like a scorpion. The elders know what they are talking about."

Phra Charan became so absorbed in the practice of the meditation that the thought of disrobing no longer entered his mind. Once Charan demonstrated his skill in kasina meditation, Ajan Doem imparted knowledge of the Khotchasatra to Charan by oral transmission. "Most elephants have divine ears. Using kasina meditation you will find out if the elephant has a *devata* [deity] who guards him. Then you will know that the elephant has divine ears. To subdue an elephant that is on a rampage, you must first visualize the deity who is guarding the wild elephant. Then you radiate metta to the deity. Once the deity receives the metta radiated by you, the deity will convey this to the elephant and then guide the animal away from you so that it will not harm you."

Ajan Doem emphasized the importance of maintaining a still, empty mind: "While radiating metta, your mind has to remain absolutely still for a long time; otherwise the metta will not reach the deity, who must be relied upon to convey the metta to the elephant. Make sure that your concentration is at least 80 percent powerful; a weaker concentration could be fatal. The most important thing is to focus on the deity, not the elephant. An elephant in musth is unable to receive metta. If you focus on the elephant it might step on you."

The aged ajan warned Phra Charan to take extreme caution. "From *jhana* [a state of deep meditation] you will be radiating metta far and wide, in every direction, not only to the deity who guards the wild elephant but also to all sentient beings. If your concentration is weak, you'd better not go near an elephant in musth. Such an animal is ferocious. If you make a mistake, you will be dead. When a male elephant is in musth, even the mahout who has cared for him for a long time could be killed, never mind a stranger. This is not a method recommended for beginners. Many thudong monks have been killed by being stepped on by elephants while trying to spread thoughts of metta to them." It was not all that long ago, Ajan Doem continued, that a thudong monk went wandering in the Great Mountains (Khao Yai), claiming that he was unafraid of elephants. "One day he encountered one in musth. Having been a wandering monk for a while, he thought he could handle the situation. Not knowing anything about the behavior of elephants, the monk walked toward the animal for a closer look. The elephant trampled the monk and gored his body with its tusks."

By the time Phra Charan mastered the knowledge he received from the Khotchasatra and the ten kasina meditations, his character had also been transformed. He no longer wanted to leave the monastic life. Teaching the young monk an ancient skill meant imparting more than knowledge, he was also passing on an aspect of the history of his lineage. After he had completed the transmission, Ajan Doem became visibly ill, and his condition quickly deteriorated. He died in 1951 at the age of ninety-one. He had been a monk for seventy years. Ajan Doem was one of the last elephant masters in Siam, and the last master swordsman of his lineage. His death marked the end of the sword school at Bodhi Pond, and the few other remaining schools of swordsmanship vanished as well. Swords—and the art of swordsmanship with its discipline and spiritual training—gave way to guns, cannons, bombs, and tanks requiring nothing of the modern warrior other than obedience and technical know-how.

Phra Charan was twenty-three when Ajan Doem died. It was then that the young monk vowed to remain a monastic for the rest of his life. Ajan Charan laments, "It's a pity I did not meet Luang Pho long before this. But due to my karma, Luang Pho died just six months after I became close to him."

After the seven-day wake for his teacher was over, Phra Charan went wandering in search of another meditation teacher. Although young monks usually had company when they went on such trips, Phra Charan chose to risk going alone. "I went on wandering on my own to train myself. When I was walking in the forest one day, a huge elephant spotted me and came charging head on, ears cocked, trunk up, screaming with rage, intending to trample over me. I immediately focused my mind firmly in kasina meditation as Luang Pho Doem had taught me. From the mind unified in a single point, I radiated metta to the deity who guarded the elephant. Just before he reached me, the big bull halted and turned away." To Phra Charan's relief, "The deity was able to restrain the elephant. It told the elephant not to harm the monk who had no intention of harming the elephant."

In this terrifying situation Phra Charan could have been killed. When he experienced the truth of Ajan Doem's teachings and realized that his teacher had saved his life, Phra Charan felt immense gratitude. He could still hear

Ajan Doem's words ringing in his ears: "Do not turn down knowledge that the elders offer you. Some day it will come in handy." Until he met Ajan Doem, Phra Charan's life had no direction. As Phra Charan came to discover the power of the unconditioned mind, all his doubts began to dissolve.

Fortified with the power of metta parami, Phra Charan continued his wandering in search of meditation masters. Within a decade after Ajan Doem's death, Phra Charan had met some of the most revered Buddhist masters of the twentieth century. Among the village abbots under whose guidance Phra Charan practiced in the 1950s were Ajan Chong (1872–1964) of Wat Natang Nok in Ayutthaya and Ajan Chat of Wat Ban Sang in Prachinburi. The latter passed away a year after Charan met him. Phra Charan also learned from other thudong monks such as Venerable Father Dam, whom he met by chance in a forest, and Ajan Li Dhammadharo (1907–61) of Wat Asokaram in Samut Prakan. Phra Charan spent three months practicing meditation in the wilderness with Ajan Li. Phra Charan also studied with Ajan Techin, a Burmese master in residence at Bell Monastery in Thonburi.

In the late twentieth century Ajan Charan became a meditation master in his own right. At Wat Amphawan in Singburi the abbot has trained a large number of children as well as adults in vipassana meditation practice and in living virtuous lives. In a tribute to his teacher Ajan Charan wrote, "Venerable Father Doem was a great master. It is rare nowadays to find a master like him. He gave me my monastic life. Every day during the daily chant, after I pay respect to the Buddha, I prostrate myself to Ajan Doem with deep gratitude for making me what I am today."

SOURCES

Ajan Charan, *Buddhology: Luang Pho Charan laoruang Luang Pho Doem* (2001).

Interview with Ajan Charan Thithadhammo, abbot of Wat Amphawan, Singburi, February 6, 2002.

Holt Hallett, who traveled through northern Siam in the 1880s, learned that in time of war virtually every male was still expected to become a soldier. Hallett wrote, "Every man from eighteen to seventy years of age who is not a slave, is reckoned as a fighting man." See *A Thousand Miles on an Elephant in the Shan States* (1890), p. 202.

For a detailed explanation of kasina meditation, see Buddhaghosa, *The Path of Purification (Visuddhimagga)* (1979), pp. 122–176.

22

A BODHISAT ELEPHANT

BEFORE PAVED roads were built, people got around on foot and by boat. Those who wished to travel overland depended on elephants. Archibald Ross Colquhoun, a Scotsman who explored the Shan states in the 1880s, tells why. "The elephant is an absolute necessity during the rainy season throughout the mountainous districts of Siam and the neighbouring Shan country to the north, the rivers and streams being without bridges." Carl Bock, the Norwegian travel book writer who journeyed northward from Rahaeng (Tak province) in 1881, adds another reason why elephants were indispensable. "On the second day we came across immense granite blocks scattered over the ground in great abundance, while here and there the forest gave place to open patches of country in which the grass grew to a height of from ten to fifteen feet, often overtopping not only the backs of the elephants, but even the roofs of the howdahs. Nothing but an elephant could have got through such country without immense difficulty."

Western travelers had nothing but praise for the strength, patience, and intelligence of elephants. On the way from Lampang to Lamphun, Bock and his party "entered a fine forest, and the travelling became very rough. We crossed the Metan, I should think, twenty times in the course of the day, and in the alternate ascents and descents I had ample opportunity of noting the sureness of foot of the elephants, which seemed quite to enjoy the excitement of climbing and descending the steep acclivities, mounting rugged slopes where a goat would seem hardly to find a foot-hold, and sliding down-hill on their bellies, with their forelegs spread straight out in front, and their hindlegs behind, with an ease and self-command which a mule, using all his legs, might have envied."

Colquhoun noted, however, that elephants could be very difficult. "In the jungle neighbouring Kiang Tong [Kengtung or Chiang Tung], about two hundred elephants were roaming in a wild state, having been freed from labour, let loose, and devoted to the pagoda in that town. At the time of our visit they had become a terror to the people and a cause of devastation to their fields. Owing to their religious servitude, or rather emancipation, they were not allowed to be recaptured, and had become as fierce as those roaming wild in their native haunts in the wilder parts of the valleys of the Salween and the Mekong."

Samuel House, an American missionary and physician, had a close call with his elephant. One day near the end of the nineteenth century, on his way from Rahaeng to Lamphun, south of Chiang Mai, the missionary noticed that his elephant was in a bad mood. Lillian Curtis, wife of the American Presbyterian minister in Lampang, retold House's story, which she had heard from other missionaries. Upon reaching Lamphun, the elephant "gave vent to his distemper, shook his driver and Dr. House from his back, and enraged, gored the latter severely, wounding him in the abdomen. The natives managed to get the elephant away, and then, because of their superstitious fears, fled, leaving Dr. House alone, wounded, and in the fierce sun blaze. Fortunately," Curtis continues, "one of the spectators ran to Chieng Mai and informed Dr. McGilvary of the accident. In the meantime Dr. House, realizing his critical condition, tried to drag himself to the shade, but could not, as he was too weak. He could just reach his satchel, which he opened, and by means of his hand mirror sewed up the wound—a dangerous condition under the most favorable circumstances—and there he lay in the heat and the dust, with parched lips and weakened from loss of blood and pain. In due time, Dr. McGilvary arrived, and he was borne to Chieng Mai, where he was tenderly cared for and nursed back to life." In retelling this story Curtis comments that the incident "reveals a phase of mission life and shows the necessity of a missionary's being an all-round-about man."

Most Westerners who traveled by elephant were accompanied not only by the elephants' mahouts but by supply packers and bearers as well, since local people were reluctant to make elephants carry too much. Western travelers rarely dared to venture out on their own. Thudong monks traveling on foot had to contend with elephants, too, and had little hope of being rescued if they ran into trouble. And they were sometimes quite alone. A few monks left records of their encounters.

There is a vivid elephant story told about Ajan Pan Sonantho (1875–1938), abbot of the Monastery of Cow's Udder Village (Wat Bang Nomkho) in Ayutthaya. Like many village abbots of his time, Ajan Pan studied at his village wat, went away for a number of years to seek knowledge from other teachers, returned to his natal village to teach, and eventually became abbot of the village monastery.

Pan was born in Cow's Udder Village. In 1896, at the age of twenty-one, he was ordained a monk at the Monastery of Cow's Udder Village and was given the monastic name Sonantho. Ajan Sun, abbot of the Monastery of Mo Fish Village, was his preceptor. Pan studied Buddhist texts under the monks at his village wat and learned meditation practice from Ajan Sun. Pan's preceptor was a meditation master who was skilled in herbal medicine. In 1899 Pan traveled by boat to Bangkok to further his studies. At that time there were quite a number of monasteries in and around Bangkok that were still known for their meditation traditions. Among these were Wat Saket, Wat Sangwet, Wat Chakrawat, and Wat In. At Wat Saket the young Pan lived with Ajan Choen, under whose guidance he studied Pali texts and practiced meditation. He also

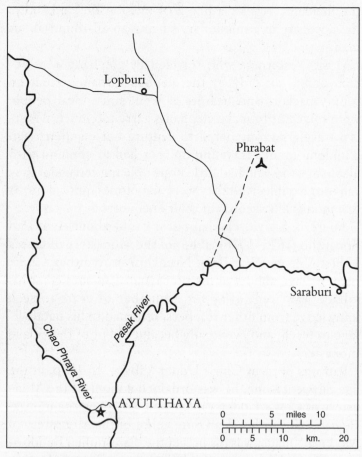

Fig. 24 The route to the Buddha's Footprint from Ayutthaya

went to Wat Sangwet to practice meditation and learn herbal medicine. After five years in Bangkok, Phra Pan returned to his village wat. He was fond of the thudong practice and did not become abbot of Wat Bang Nomkho until he was sixty.

Before he became an abbot, in between rains retreats Ajan Pan often led his disciples on a thudong to pilgrimage sites. On one occasion he led a group of four monks to the Buddha's Footprint north of Saraburi in the Central Plains. From Ayutthaya the monks walked more than sixty kilometers in order to reach the sacred shrine on the hill. One evening, after they had been following an elephant trail through a forest, they came to a savannah-like area known as a *thung* in Thai. Lucien Hanks, an American anthropologist who saw a thung in the Central Plains in the middle of the twentieth century, described it as "a vast space covered with tall grasses, sedges, and in this region, on the higher points, with thick bushes." Hanks noticed that villagers generally avoided this area. Those who traveled through a thung reported that "when they were mounted on the backs of water buffaloes, only grass was visible to right and left. Besides, snakes 'as big around as an arm' slithered in the thickets, occasional crocodiles lurked near permanent ponds. However, these creatures were not as fearsome as the elephant herds that might charge and kill the man who surprised them. In the proper season, deer [searched] for tender shoots near water holes, and following them the tiger."

Ajan Pan and his disciples reached the forest after passing through a hamlet of five households and walking about two kilometers across a thung. There was a pond nearby, but there was no water in it at the time. Surveying the terrain, Ajan Pan told his monks they would stop there for the night. He issued a stern reminder. "Once

Fig. 25 The Temple of the Buddha's Footprint in Saraburi

you pitch your klot, do not move. No matter what happens you must be willing to die for the Dhamma."

For solitude, the monks left some distance between each klot, which they put up close to the edge of the forest. Not long after they had finished putting up their shelters, a group of villagers turned up. They made an offering of sugar water. After the monks drank the water the villagers urged them to spend the night nearer their settlement rather than out in the open. They told Ajan Pan, "Venerable Father, this is elephant territory. A herd of elephants lives in this forest. A while back some monks who pitched their klots in this pasture were gored and trampled by wild elephants. It would be safer if you moved to the village. Then if anything happens we can help you." Ajan Pan did not accept their invitation. He told the villagers, "It is our rule that once a monk has put up his klot he is not supposed to move it. Come what may, we have to face it." The ajan insisted that his monks stay right where they had already made camp. Knowing the habits of the wild elephants, the villagers warned, "If the elephants turn up, please bang the lids of your almsbowls loudly. We'll rush here to help you as soon as we hear the signal." Then, before nightfall, they walked back to their village.

After the villagers had left, Ajan Pan told his monks to do the *brahmavihara-bhavana* or meditation on the four sublime states: loving kindness *(metta)*, compassion *(karuna)*, sympathetic joy *(mudita)*, and equanimity *(upekkha)*. Since Maha Wira, who narrated Ajan Pan's story, did not describe this practice, let us turn to Nyanaponika Thera (1901–94) for clarification. These four meditations, he says, are intended to help the practitioner achieve jhana. The mind that has attained the boundlessness of the Brahmavihara will not harbor any hatred. As Nyanaponika explains, "The practical aim is to achieve, with the help of these sublime states, those high stages of mental concentration called *jhana*, 'meditative absorption.' The meditation on love, compassion and sympathetic joy may each produce the attainment of the first three absorptions, while the meditation on equanimity will lead to the fourth *jhana* only, in which equanimity is the most significant factor." Nyanaponika continues, "The ultimate aim of attaining these *Brahmavihara-jhanas* is to produce a state of mind that can serve as a firm basis for the liberating insight into the true nature of all phenomena, as being impermanent, liable to suffering and unsubstantial. A mind that has achieved meditative absorption induced by the sublime states will be pure, tranquil, firm, collected and free of coarse selfishness. It will thus be well prepared for the final work of deliverance which can be completed only by insight."

To return to our story, once the meditators gained the absorbed concentrations, their minds full of loving kindness, wide, unbounded, free from hatred and ill will, they extended loving kindness out toward all sentient beings. With each monk sitting in samadhi according to his level, the atmosphere surrounding them was quiet and still. Around 10 P.M., just as the villagers had warned them, the monks saw a herd of elephants, led by a huge bull with short tusks, come out of the forest. The moon was almost full, so the sky was bright. The monks could see each elephant clearly. Ajan Pan's klot was the first one on the trail. When the bull elephant came to Ajan Pan's klot, he stepped right over it and stood motionless. Ajan Pan was practically under the elephant's big belly, which widened out on either side. To come out of the forest each elephant in the herd had to go around the klots blocking its path. Sidestepping each shelter, one by one the elephants squeezed their way past the monks and began crossing the thung leading to the forest at the far end of the field.

The last elephant, however, was mischievous. The villagers called him Twist, since one of his tusks was crooked. Instead of following the rest of the herd across the thung, Twist turned around and began to run back to the monks. He charged Ajan Pan's klot. In this terrifying moment the ajan was not disturbed. He later told his disciples, "With aspiration toward awakened understanding (bodhinyana), my mind was equanimous; if I were to die in this mind state I would go straight to Tusita Heaven and be watching the elephant from there." Having attained the third state of jhana, Ajan Pan directed his mind to penetrate the minds of his disciples. "I then looked into the minds of my four companions and saw that they all aspired toward awakened understanding. I felt relieved that my fellow monks all had the same intention."

Maha Wira, one of the thudong monks who witnessed Twist's attack, later retold this story. "As Twist ran up to Venerable Father Pan's klot, the lead bull [which must have followed Twist] attacked him. Using his trunk, the bull slapped Twist on the backside. Venerable Father heard the slapping noise three times. With each slap Twist's head was pushed toward the ground. But that did not stop him from coming closer. Finally, the great bull grasped Twist's tusk with his trunk and pulled hard. Twist fell to the ground. That stopped him. Twist got up and ran across the thung. The bull walked slowly around the thung for a while. After seeing that there would be no more trouble, the bull turned to the ajan's klot, kneeled down and lifted his trunk up as if he were paying respect. Then he followed after his herd and disappeared from our sight." Ajan Pan told his disciples, "I think the bull must have been a bodhisat."

The elephants left. The sky was beautiful. The moon, shining brightly, was surrounded by stars. But more trouble was to come. When living in the wild monks not only had to contend with dangerous animals, such as tigers, elephants, and big snakes, they also had to cope with the forces of nature. Maha Wira recalled, "Less than half an hour after the elephants had gone the sky suddenly turned dark. No more moonlight or stars. Water began to drip from the sky. And then it poured and poured. Gone were the elephants; now came the heavy rain. The monks observed the rule that they must not move their klots. Ajan Pan wondered why the bull didn't come to rescue us. The elephant was probably looking for shelter himself to get out from under the heavy downpour." Once the monks could no longer sit inside their klots, they stood up. It rained for about two hours.

Fig. 26 Venerable Father Pan, abbot of Wat Bang Nomkho,
Ayutthaya

Since the five monks carried only one set of robes each, which they were wearing, their robes were soaking wet. When the villagers arrived early the next morning to offer almsfood and saw how soaked the monks were, they took off their plain-colored sarongs and gave them to the monks to wear so that the monks could hang their wet garments out to dry. Normally monks are not allowed to wear lay clothing, but as Ajan Pan explained, "Under the circumstances, necessity must rule. The Buddha would have given his permission."

After the villagers had offered food to the monks and heard what had happened, they said they thought it was miraculous that the monks had survived the elephant's charge. The local people were in awe and eager to learn the secret mantra they believed the monks used. Before leaving the thung they invited the monks to spend three days in the vicinity of their village and asked Ajan Pan to give them amulets to protect them from the aggressive elephant. Ajan Pan understood their fear because the monks had just been challenged to face such fear themselves. The abbot used this opportunity to bring the Buddha's teaching closer to the laypeople's experience. Instead of amulets, Ajan Pan gave them the mantra "Buddho" and taught them two protective meditations, *buddhanussati* and *metta bhavana*. For the practice of buddhanussati Ajan Pan selected one of the many qualities of the Buddha. He told the villagers to reflect on the Blessed One as the exemplar of metta, reminding them that with the perfection of loving kindness the Buddha could tame wild elephants. Then he taught the villagers how to cultivate metta. By reciting the mantra "Buddho," Ajan Pan told them, they would also be able to send metta to Twist to let the elephant know that from now on they were friends and that they should not bring harm to one another.

Before the monks left, the villagers asked Ajan Pan to

return to their village every year on his way to the Buddha's Footprint. Their faith in the thudong master's spiritual achievement moved the villagers to act. The recollection of the qualities of Buddha helped them overcome their fear. The practice of metta bhavana created a friendly atmosphere around the village. With devotion they practiced the two protective meditations and experienced for themselves the fruits of the Dhamma.

The following year Ajan Pan returned to the same thung and put up his klot. The villagers came out to see him and told him they were no longer harassed by the elephant. "In the past," they told him, "Twist was always coming into the village, destroying rice plants and property. Whenever he saw us he would charge. Ever since you gave us 'Buddho' the elephant has ignored us. Twist merely walks past our village now without wrecking anything."

SOURCES

Archibald Ross Colquhoun, *Amongst the Shans* (1885; 1970), p. 89.

Carl Bock, *Temples and Elephants* (1884; 1986), pp. 144, 188.

Lillian Johnson Curtis, *The Laos of North Siam* (1903), pp. 278–279.

Phra Maha Wira Thavaro, *Prawat Luang Pho Pan, Wat Bang Nomkho* (1997), pp. 50–53.

Lucien M. Hanks, *Rice and Man* (1972), p. 73.

For an explanation of the interrelateness of the four sublime states, see *The Vision of Dhamma: Buddhist Writings of Nyanaponika Thera*, edited with an introduction by Bhikkhu Bodhi (1986), pp. 185–200.

For a discussion of the stages of jhanas, see Henepola Gunaratana,

The Path of Serenity and Insight: An Explanation of the Buddhist Jhanas (1985).

For a glossary of Pali terms on *dhutanga* (thudong) practices, see *Food for the Heart: The Collected Teachings of Ajahn Chah* (2002).

23

TEACHING PRECEPTS TO AN ELEPHANT

IN 1861 the French naturalist Henri Mouhot and his men traveled by elephant to Luang Prabang. At Pak Lai, north of the principality of Nan, Mouhot wrote, "The district is very mountainous with rice-grounds on some of the slopes. We several times had to cross the Laie, which is 35 meters wide, and rushes along like a torrent, with a great noise. There are, about here, many precipices. It was wonderful to see the elephants climb, descend, and hang on by their trunks to the rocks without ever making a false step." He continued, "I have quite an admiration and regard for these noble animals. How remarkable are their strength and intelligence! What should we have done without them amidst these vast forests and rugged mountains?"

Frank Exell, a former schoolmaster, had been living in Siam for ten years before he had the experience of staying out in the jungle. In 1932 Exell went to visit a fellow Englishman, a Mr. Hartley. Hartley was in charge of the forest belonging to the Anglo-Siam Corporation near Muang Phong, a Lao village north of Muang Ngao and Lampang. After three weeks at the camp, living among the working elephants, Exell noted, "I found the elephants of unending interest and I could spend all day watching them at work." There was one large tusker called Punoi Phiba (Crazy-Spirit Bull) which Hartley would not allow Exell to approach because, as Exell continued, "It had already killed several mahouts and was of very uncertain temper. Its very name told you that it was mad or occupied at times by a malevolent spirit. But it was a magnificent worker and too valuable to be destroyed. It never lacked for a mahout since to ride it was a distinction. The mahout would be known as the fearless rider of [Punoi Phiba] and that put him in a class by himself. I was quite content to study the animal at a safe distance."

During this same period Ajan Khao (1888–1993) and a fellow thudong monk spent a rains retreat in a forest in the northeastern region. At night Ajan Khao usually stayed in a hut meditating inside his klot under its mosquito net. One night an elephant wandered to the back of his tiny hut. Only a stone bench behind the hut separated the elephant from the monk. The elephant stopped at the bench and started exploring the hut with the tip of its trunk. It extended its trunk through the window, sniffing at the mosquito net above Ajan Khao's head. The klot and the net began to sway back and forth. Sitting in meditation, Ajan Khao was mindful; he could feel the elephant's breath over his head. Ajan Khao remained seated in meditation, mentally reciting "Buddho, Buddho, Buddho." Knowing that he could not really get away, he kept his mind focused on the mantra. More than a few hours passed. The elephant stood stock still, as if it were waiting to grab the monk when he stepped out. Once in a while Ajan Khao heard the elephant snuffle around, and then, once again, there was silence.

Eventually the elephant ambled to the west side of the hut and took a sour tamarind from a basket hanging on a tree. A day or so earlier a villager had given these tamarinds to the monks. They used them to polish the covers of their almsbowls. Hearing the elephant chewing the tamarinds, Ajan Khao thought, "Big Fat Belly is eating the tamarinds with gusto! Wonder if there will be anything left for us monks to polish the lids of our almsbowls with. If I sit here until the elephant finishes eating, he might come back to the hut and trample me to death. Better step out to talk. Elephants are intelligent; they can understand human words. They have been living with human beings for a long time. I might be able to reason with him. But if he charges in here, I'll be killed. One way or the other, he will get me. Might as well step out to face him. There's no choice anyway. So dark, it's hard to see to get around."

Ajan Khao stepped out, stood at the base of a tree in front of his hut and started talking to the elephant. "Older Brother, I would like to talk to you. Please listen to me." The elephant stood in silence as Khao continued, "You are a domestic animal. You have been with people for a long time and learned human words. I'm sure you understand me perfectly well. You know our customs: what to do, what not to do. When you are given instructions and you don't follow their commands, people might hit you on the head or even kill you." Ajan Khao explained to the elephant that the practice of moral discipline (*sila*) insured that we will be reborn as a human or a deity. "Listen to me carefully, I am teaching you with compassion. Your brother-monk will give you the Five Precepts. Please undertake the precepts so that when you die you will go to a higher realm. At worst you will be reborn as a human being. At best you will be reborn in a heavenly realm. In any case, it's better than being reborn as an animal only to be a vehicle like a horse or a beast of burden like an elephant. If you don't work hard, people will beat you."

In a tender voice full of humility, Ajan Khao then proceeded to teach the elephant how to abandon non-virtuous actions. "Older Brother, please undertake the Five Precepts from your brother-monk. The first precept is to abstain from killing either humans or your fellow animals. The second precept is to abstain from taking things that are not given to you, such as the tamarinds that you just gobbled up. Villagers gave these tamarinds to me so I could polish my bowl lid. Since you did not know the precept you won't get bad karma this time. I just want to let you know that it is not right to take tamarinds without asking permission from the owner. The third precept is to abstain from taking another elephant's mate. The fourth precept is to be honest and abstain from dissembling. The fifth precept is to abstain from drinking any intoxicants. . . . Now that you have undertaken the Five Precepts, please go away and forage to your heart's content. Leave me alone here to meditate. I will generate metta to you every day."

Ajan Khao was amazed that the elephant stood still the whole time. Once the monk finished preaching, the elephant turned around and walked away. Its footsteps made the earth shake from the force of its weight. The elephant did not return to the forest hermitage for the rest of the rains retreat.

SOURCES

Henri Mouhot, *Travels in Siam, Cambodia and Laos, 1858–1860* (1989), vol. 2, p. 157.

F. K. Exell, *In Siamese Service* [1922–36] (1967), p. 205.

The story of Ajan Khao Analayo was written down by Ajan Maha Bua Nanasampanno in *Patipatha phra thudong kammathan* (1973), pp. 184–187.

For a discussion of how elephants, in the early nineteenth century, were fed "tonic herbs" (something like amphetamines) to prepare them for battle, see David K. Wyatt, *Siam in Mind* (2002), pp. 27–33.

24

LORD BUDDHA AND KING COBRA

IN 1881 King Chulalongkorn (r.1868–1910) celebrated the 100th anniversary of the Chakri dynasty in Bangkok. That year James McCarthy, an Irish surveyor, set out with two well-trained Siamese assistants to map the route, through the northwest territory of Siam, along which the government planned to run a telegraph line. This line was to serve Bangkok and Moulmein, in British-occupied Burma, by way of Rahaeng (today Tak province). There was considerable trade between the people of Moulmein and Rahaeng. McCarthy wrote, "The country between Raheng and Maulmein was for the most part hilly, the main watershed being distant in a straight line only about 15 miles. The two towns were in direct communication, the chief path crossing the watershed at an elevation of over 2000 feet, while there were other paths used in the dry and hot weather, as affording better fodder for the cattle employed in transport work."

Holt Hallett, a British engineer who explored the Shan states in the 1870s in search of the best route for a projected railway from Burma to China, noted that "boats from Rahaeng to Bangkok take from 6 to 8 days in the rains, and from 12 to 15 days in the dry season. Returning from Bangkok, boats take 20 days in the rains, and from 30 to 35 days in the dry season. They are longer proceeding up-stream in the dry season than in the rains, owing to the shallowness of the stream, and the numerous sandbanks in its bed."

In the nineteenth century hardly any monks from Rahaeng went to study in Bangkok and none became abbots there. Most abbots of Bangkok monasteries came from villages dotted throughout the Central Plains. Ajan Phu (b. 1830) was an exception. He was born in a village in Rahaeng. Following the local custom, Phu began living in a wat at the age of six when his parents brought him to Ajan Kham of the Monastery of Khae Tree Landing. After living with and serving Ajan Kham as temple boy, Phu was ordained as a novice when he was twelve. Under Ajan Kham's tutelage he learned to read and write Khom, an old Khmer alphabet, so that he could read Pali texts written in Khom script.

In 1850, at the age of twenty, Phu was ordained as a monk at the Monastery of Khoi Tree Landing in Rahaeng. He was given the monastic name Chanthakesaro. Phu spent his first rains retreat, from the full moon of July to the full moon of October, at the wat where he was ordained. For several years, after the rains retreats were over, Phu generally went on thudong with his older brother, Yai, who was also a monk. Eventually the brothers wandered from Rahaeng to Bangkok, a journey that took several months on foot. This was during King Mongkut's reign (1851–68), a time when several of the abbots of Bangkok monasteries were meditation masters.

Phu and Ajan Yai spent the rains retreats at Wat Saket and Wat Chakrawat. Both wats were located outside the Bangkok city wall. Wat Saket was then known for its forest cemetery. There one could routinely see vultures eating corpses and yogis living in huts practicing the meditation on death. At Wat Chakrawat Ajan Phu met a fellow meditation monk, Ma Inthasaro (b. 1837), who was later appointed abbot of the wat.

Wat In, another monastery on the outskirts of Bangkok, had always been known for its meditation tradition. Ajan Kaeo, the first abbot of the wat, was a meditation master from Vientiane. In 1889 Ajan Phu and his brother began spending their rains retreats at this wat. Instead of staying in the resident monks' quarters, Ajan Phu preferred the *pret sala*, a rest-house for corpses and their ghosts, near the warehouse where dead bodies were kept. Here he found the solitude in which to practice meditation. Laypeople did not go near the pret sala for fear of encountering ghosts.

A few years after Ajan Phu first arrived at Wat In, its second abbot died. In 1892, when Ajan Phu was sixty-two and now much respected by local people for his spiritual power, King Chulalongkorn appointed him abbot. Ajan Phu governed Wat In for thirty-one years. When he reached the age of ninety-three, he became abbot emeritus. He died in 1933 at the age of 104 after spending eighty-three years of his life as a monk. His death marked the end of the meditation tradition at Wat In.

Before he became abbot, Ajan Phu had followed the thudong practice of living in the wilderness. Sometimes he walked through forests at night. One night, under a full moon, while he was walking through a forest from one village to the next, he heard the sound *suu, suu, suu.* Mindfully, Phu stopped walking to determine where the sound was coming from. About four meters ahead of him he saw a snake, as big around as his leg, emerging from the thick undergrowth. Its attack was so swift that Phu had no chance to get away. The snake coiled around his ankles and within seconds made its way up to the monk's waist and his chest. Inasmuch as he was skilled in meditation, Phu did not lose his mindfulness; he kept his body still. When the snake waved its head in the air and inflated its hood at Phu's eye level, the monk remained calm and still. In this critical moment Ajan Phu kept (mentally) reciting the mantra *araham, araham, araham.* Gradually, the snake uncoiled itself from the monk's body, slithered to the ground, and disappeared into the darkness of the forest. Ajan Phu continued his walk. He reached the next village at dawn in time for almsround.

It is possible that Ajan Phu had heard an old story about how the mantra *araham* could protect one from a snake attack. This was a story recorded in an old text that Mon monks used to tell when they preached about this protective mantra and big snakes. The story has been retold by Ajan Uttama (b. 1911), the Mon abbot of the Monastery of Solitude Pool in Kanchanaburi, a province northwest of Bangkok.

A local village abbot, so the story begins, observed that children frequently got into fights, yelling and hitting one another. The abbot told the children that when they felt like yelling at their friends, the worst swearword they could use was the word *araham*. The angrier they became, the abbot told them, the more they should shout "*araham*."

Their village was near a forest. In the forest there was a cave, and in the cave lived a huge snake called Lord of the Snakes or the Snake King. One day a snake expert (literally, "snake doctor") came to the village to hunt the big snake. The snake doctor asked the children if there was a giant snake nearby. The children told him that a really big snake lived in a cave not far away. The snake doctor asked the children to take him to the cave, but the children refused. The man got angry and scolded the children, using bad language. This made the children angry, and in retaliation they began shouting "*araham, araham, araham*" at the snake doctor. The snake doctor, who had never heard this Pali word, asked, "What does *araham* mean?" The children told him, "It is the worst swearword. The word can sting and pierce your heart."

According to Ajan Uttama's narrative, the snake doctor then went into the forest by himself and found the cave. At the entrance the doctor recited a mantra that was meant to lure the snake out. The Snake King, who had made a vow to observe the Five Precepts, heard the mantra. He was able to practice patience, but the snake doctor kept reciting the mantra, and gradually the sound began to weaken the snake's resolve. Repetition of the mantra disoriented the snake. Agitated, it could no longer remain still in the cave, so it moved to the entrance, intending to bite the doctor and cause his death. When the snake went after him, the doctor grew so angry that he began shouting "*araham, araham, araham.*" When the Snake King heard the mantra *araham*, he thought to himself, "Although this doctor has committed unwholesome acts by killing snakes, at least he knows the sacred word *araham.*" Thinking thus, the Snake King decided not to kill the snake doctor. This is how the story that Uttama told ended.

The doctor survived because of the merit he made by reciting "*araham.*" One lesson that can be drawn from this story is that, in local Buddhism, a sacred word has power of its own, even when the person who utters the word does not know its meaning.

Ajan Uttama, the teller of this story, is a Mon monk who was born in Ye district in Moulmein, southern Burma. The people and monks of Moulmein generally walked to Tak province to enter Siam, and thudong monks from northern Siam entered Burma through Tak. In 1943 Uttama went to Mandalay to practice meditation under the guidance of the abbot of Wat Palelai in Mandalay. (This forest wat has the same name as the forest wat that Peter Thompson came across in Suphanburi around 1905.) This abbot, Akkawangso, taught the Abhidhamma texts and vipassana meditation. At the end of the 1943 rains retreat Uttama asked the abbot for permission to leave the wat and go on thudong to the forests of Siam before returning to his village wat in Lower Burma.

In the late 1940s, fed up with political unrest and violence, Uttama walked for three days and three nights from Lower Burma over the mountains to the province of Kanchanaburi in western Thailand. (Siam had became Thailand in 1941.) He entered Thailand through Pilok, a subdistrict known for its tungsten mines. At this time Ajan Uttama had been a monk for almost twenty years. In Pilok he met a number of Mon-Thai people who were descendants of nineteenth-century Mon immigrants. They invited the Mon monk to settle in Kanchanaburi.

In 1953 Ajan Uttama spent a rains retreat at Wangkalang, a simple hermitage near a Karen village in Sankhlaburi, a district three hundred kilometers from the provincial town of Kanchanaburi. A large number of Mon as well as Karen people were living in this district. When Uttama decided to expand the Wangkalang hermitage into a monastery, local Mon and Karen villagers helped with the work of construction. The village headman, Suaichong, a Karen fisherman, was very supportive of Uttama and the construction project. When the work was finished, the new monastery was named Wat Wang Wiwek (the Monastery of Solitude Pool). In 1960 Ajan Uttama became its abbot.

One day Ajan Uttama heard that Suaichong, the village headman, had taken sick. The abbot was very concerned and wanted to help him. Ajan Uttama had been invited to give protective chants (*paritta*) at Nitha, a nearby village, that same day. It had been raining since morning, and the weather stayed gloomy all day long. The abbot returned to his wat, and as soon as the rain let up he set out to visit the village headman, whose house was at the edge of a teak forest.

On his way, he walked past the small police station in the village. The station was manned by a police private named Talae, who was very fond of drinking. (Most junior policemen in this area were Karen. Ajan Uttama tells us that Thai policemen did not want to be stationed here in the uplands, because they found the weather too cold.) Talae spotted the abbot and asked him where he was going. Ajan Uttama replied, "I am on my way to see the village headman. Want to come along?" It was early evening and Talae warned the abbot, "It's getting dark. Don't go there. A big cobra in the forest has just killed a cow. The owner of the cow has asked me to find the snake and shoot it." The monk begged Talae not to kill the snake, then continued on his way to visit the sick headman. The sight of the abbot walking alone at dusk caused Talae some concern, so he decided to go along.

When the monk and the policeman reached the teak forest they saw the cobra coiled up right next to the dead cow. The snake was about six meters long, and its girth was that of a man's thigh. Ajan Uttama recalled, "The snake had a pungent smell. When he saw me, he put his head up, uncoiled and stood upright on his coiled tail. He was taller than I am." The abbot stood still and radiated metta to the snake. Talae was nervous and said to the monk, "Radiating loving kindness is not enough. Either we run away or we shoot the snake. To spare its life is harmful to animals and people." Referring to the snake as him, not it, the abbot interrupted Talae with the warning, "Don't ever say you wish to kill him. The snake knows, and he will follow you to your house." Uttama then got Talae out of the snake's way.

When the abbot arrived at the Karen headman's house, he found that Suaichong had been coughing nonstop for a long time. The abbot comforted the headman, who was seventy-nine, by saying, "You are not yet near death." Ajan Uttama asked many questions about the headman's condition, then walked back to his wat. The next morning he returned with an herbal medicine that he himself had prepared. It consisted mainly of the leaves of *ploenton*, a plant that grew along the edges of paddy fields. The monk boiled the leaves, put in some salt, and added some soot from a clay pot. The abbot stayed for a while to administer his remedy. Every time the patient coughed, the monk dipped a chicken feather into the *ploenton* paste and swabbed the inside of the patient's throat with it. After spitting out a lot of phlegm, Suaichong fell asleep peacefully for the first time since he had become sick. Shortly after his treatment the village headman recovered. (He lived for another seven years before dying at the age of eighty-six.)

Three days later a layman came to ask the abbot to heal a sick man at Kalang Pool Village. While walking along the trail to the village, Ajan Uttama heard people talking in several languages at once. It sounded to him like they were arguing. As he came closer, he saw a group of men standing in the middle of a paddy field. From their dress the abbot could tell that they were Mon, Karen, and Lawa. At first Uttama thought they were having a fight, but when he got close he saw that they were standing in a circle trying to hit a big snake with their sticks. It was the same cobra that Ajan Uttama had forbidden Talae to kill only a few days before. The cobra spread its hood and reared up to strike. The villagers told the abbot they did not know whether the snake had come out of a nearby hole or from the forest. They thought it was on its way to the mountain. The abbot asked the villagers, "Well, why don't you let him go then?" One of them replied, "This snake probably weighs many kilos. Its meat must taste good."

Out of compassion for the cobra and to prevent the villagers from breaking the first precept by killing the snake, Ajan Uttama told them, "This snake is the guardian of the forest and mountain. It has been guarding me so that other snakes will not attack me." Hearing that the snake was guarding their beloved abbot, the villagers raised their palms together to pay respect to the reptile. Then they went their separate ways.

Ajan Uttama encountered big snakes so many times that he knew their behavior. He told his pupils that once a snake has shed its skin, which generally happens every year, the snake becomes weak and is unable to hunt. It has to stay inside its hole until it regains its strength. A big snake is able to churn up the earth around its hole and thereby screen itself from view. A small animal that comes near its hole becomes disoriented from the magical power of the snake. The snake then comes out of the hole and takes its victim.

Villagers who lived near the forest always carried machetes to cut tall grass and other things. Like most local abbots, who were repositories of practical knowledge, Ajan Uttama advised his pupils, "If a snake starts attacking you, hold the machete against your body with the sharp edge facing outward. When the snake coils itself around you, the knife will cut the snake." The monk's advice was not to kill. Rather than urge villagers to attack or fight back, what Ajan Uttama proposed was a purely defensive action. Still, it required the mind to be calm and alert, and also called for speed and nerve.

Ajan Uttama was also known for his ability to heal victims of snakebite. The village wat was like a pharmacy. When a villager who said he felt sleepy all the time admitted to having been bitten by a Russell's viper, Uttama kept him awake and administered the herbal medicine that he himself had prepared. The ingredients for snakebite included the roots of seven different plants, found in the forest near the village, that Ajan Uttama had collected and dried out in the sun. He ground the roots into a powder, mixed in some dried bile taken from a snake's gallbladder, and kept the mixture in jars, ready for use. When a patient was brought to the wat, the abbot mixed these medicinal powders with lime juice to make a paste, then spread the paste over the wound. He inserted more paste into the patient's body with a sharp needle used for tattooing. The medicine absorbed the poison, drawing it from the open wound. Once he had administered the medicine to the patient, Ajan Uttama sat in samadhi. With concentrated mind he radiated metta to the patient. Within a day the patient was usually healed. The abbot never accepted money for healing. He said the medicine would no longer be sacred if he charged money for it, meaning it would lose its ability to heal heart and psyche. Like many medicine monks, Uttama knew that metta has powerful healing qualities.

Not all patients were healed, however. Sometimes it took over half a day for relatives to carry the person who had been bitten by a snake all the way to the wat. By the time they arrived, it was sometimes too late. In the 1960s the average village was still far away from the nearest hospital. Most villagers still went to the monasteries to seek medical help until the monks' authority to provide such help was suppressed by the state in the 1970s.

People attacked by a king cobra seldom made it to the wat. The abbot knew that a person bitten by a king cobra dies immediately. "In any case," he added, "it was rare to encounter a king cobra in Kanchanaburi. If you go near a female king cobra, it will attack, especially right after it has laid its eggs. The snake will go after such a threat at a great rate of speed." Uttama's advice to city folks going to rural areas was this: "If you are pursued by a king cobra, immediately take off your shirt or hat and throw it on the ground. The snake will go after the cloth and that will leave you just enough time to get away."

In 1906 Peter Thompson, the British surveyor, wrote, "The ordinary black cobra is at least as anxious to get out of our way as we can be to get out of his, but at the beginning of the rainy season, when the fields are getting wet, he betakes himself to the drier dividing ridges, and we must look carefully where we tread. The great Hamadryad, or King Cobra, alone of all snakes will attack a man unprovoked, and even give chase to him." Thompson described the king cobra as being "so like the colour of the dried grass that sometimes we approach without perceiving him, but when he raises his head and inflates his hood in lusty rage, he is a bold man who would dispute the path with him."

Thompson heard about a local snakebite remedy that was not widely known. "Some Siamese say that they are immune from snake bites, and they will show scars upon their arms which they say were made by the fangs of cobras. To obtain this immunity they eat a drug, made by grinding down from a certain white root a piece about the size of a pea, and mixing with it an equal quantity ground from a black root. The nature of the roots is kept a profound secret and few have even heard of them."

SOURCES

James McCarthy, *Surveying and Exploring in Siam* (1900), pp. 1–2.

Holt S. Hallett, *A Thousand Miles on an Elephant in the Shan States* (1890), p. 413.

For short biographies of Ajan Phu, see *Wat Intharawihan, Bang Khunphrom* (1994), pp. 138–139; and Thepchu Thapthong, *Aphinihan 50 kechi achan* (1984), pp. 116–117. Wat In's official name is Wat Intharaworawihan.

For the story of the snake doctor and an account of the life of Ajan Uttama, see *Luang Pho Uttama 84 pi* (1991), pp. 440–441, 150–154.

P. A. Thompson, *Lotus Land* (1906), pp. 193–195.

25

A TEAK-WALLAH MEETS SNAKES

REGINALD CAMPBELL, the former naval officer hired by a British teak company after the end of World War I, had as much to say about snakes as he did about elephants. Campbell's boss, Orwell, was the senior forest manager in charge of the Anglo-Siam corporation's logging operation in Muang Ngao forest, a four-day hike from the city of Lampang. Orwell had a younger assistant named Smith, whom Campbell later met. When Campbell first arrived his boss told him that Smith had recently "had a miraculous escape from death by cobra-bite" in Muang Ngao. Orwell reported that he and Smith had been walking along a cart track in the jungle "when suddenly [Smith] let out an exclamation and leapt about four feet into the air. He was pretty pale as he came down, and we saw that a cobra was coiled in a rut in the road and had just struck at him, missing him obviously by a matter of inches. Extraordinary thing about it was that Smith didn't know why he'd jumped; some frightful urge made him, he said, which was lucky."

Campbell, a bit older than Smith, was almost thirty. Shortly after he began working in the Muang Ngao jungle he had his first close call with a big snake. "I was resting after tea in my camp chair with my feet up on a camp stool," he tells us, when "suddenly I heard a slithering noise on the ground-sheet below me and to the left, and, turning my head, beheld the tail end of a cobra disappearing under my chair. The slithering noise then stopped abruptly, which told me that the snake had also stopped—right beneath me!"

Living in a tropical jungle compelled the Englishman to learn to deal with the unpredictable on a daily basis. Campbell had to figure out quickly what to do. "For a while I sat, frozen as motionless as a statue in the chair. I longed to bolt incontinently, but in order to do so I should have first to take my feet off the stool and place them on the ground, thus exposing them to the danger of being swiftly struck at by the hidden death."

The suspense must have been chilling. "Seconds passed," Campbell continues, "with neither sound nor movement from either the snake or myself. Then the horrible thought occurred to me that it might be climbing up the back of the chair and that at any moment it might hiss in my ear; at which a great wave of fright seemed to rise up inside me and caused me to perform a feat which I consider to this day a physical impossibility: still in the seated position, and with my legs straight out before me as though they were yet on the stool, I catapulted myself clean out of the chair, over the stool, and out on to the tent verandah, where I landed on my stern. What muscle or muscles supplied the driving power I can't imagine, nor did I pause to ponder thereon; I leapt to my feet and, whirling, saw the cobra emerging from beneath the chair and slithering out by one side of the tent. By the time I had seized a stick only a faint rustle in the fringing jungle told me where it had gone, and I made no attempt to pursue it." The encounter was so frightening, Campbell admitted, that "an hour or so later I had a most violent attack of indigestion, brought on, I presume, purely by nervous shock."

Two weeks later another snake entered Campbell's tent. He was "resting after girdling in exactly the same position" he had been in when he had his first encounter. This time, Campbell wrote, "I was first aware of [the snake] through hearing an unusual rustling in the dead leaves on the ground directly in front of my tent. Being still nervy after the first affair, I looked quickly up over the table, which was between me and the outside, to see a real whopper of a snake, much bigger than the cobra, coming at a fast speed over the clearing straight in my direction. I then sprang out of the chair and dashed out round one side of the table just as the snake came in round the other."

Campbell watched the snake crawl through his tent until, when it reached the back, "it found itself cornered by the 'bathroom,' which came right down to the ground. Rearing itself up on its tail, it began feeling all round for an exit, a most weird and revolting spectacle. And as it did so its scaly skin kept scraping against my tin bath with a sound that set my teeth on edge."

Informed as he was about the snakes of Siam, Campbell "realised almost at once that it was harmless." To inform his readers back home, Campbell explained that "the chief types of poisonous snakes in Siam are the cobra (plus, of course, the king-cobra or hamadryad), . . . banded krait, and Russell's viper, and this chap certainly wasn't one of them. He was long, about ten feet, and of a negative dusty-brown colour, which led me to believe he was a rat-snake." Campbell was overcome by anger and aversion even when the snake was powerless to harm him. "Whether he was harmless or not, . . . a sudden rage seized me: rage at my tent being defiled by this disgusting, stupid reptile. Inside the tent I saw my stick . . . ; seizing it, I sprang through to the 'bathroom' and commenced swiping about in an endeavour to break the snake's back and thus render it easy to kill."

When a Westerner saw a snake his first impulse was to kill it. In Buddhist thinking the intention to kill is born out of aversion or fear. Campbell admitted that "it was I who seemed helpless; I belaboured the canvas, the bath, the ground, but try as I might I couldn't get a real hit home; and all the while the horrible, blind, scaly thing was writhing round my feet and legs." As the snake was trying to get out, "I found myself shrieking for my coolies and raining curses at this thing I could not kill and which could not kill me; then rage gave way to fear, the innate fear a man has of any reptile, and I rushed out of the tent, to meet my coolies hastening up with drawn jungle-knives in their hands." Again, the experience was unnerving. "Somehow the snake escaped before they could get in and dispatch it, and we heard its swishing rustle going up, up, up the jungle-clad slope of ground behind the camp. It seemed ages before the last sound of it died away, and then I realised I was bathed from head to foot in sweat."

Campbell learned that to live in the wilderness he needed to be alert at all times. "These two incidents," he wrote, "left me extremely 'snake-conscious.' Every rustle in the grass outside my tent, whether by day or by night, set me peering about for some possible intruder, and when I got into bed I felt more than grateful for the protection of the mosquito net; otherwise I should have gone to sleep haunted with the fear of waking up with a cold, scaly form alongside me."

Not long after Campbell's second snake encounter his boss, Orwell, came to see how he was getting along with his work. One evening, as the two men were inspecting their working elephants, the mahout of the last elephant to file past them told them he had just seen a big snake. "It hissed at me and my elephant as we passed by it up there," the mahout told them. Orwell thought it might be a python and went into his tent to get his gun. "We began walking up the path, the mahout followed behind on foot and a mob of curious coolies trailing out behind him," Campbell wrote. "After we'd gone a few hundred yards the mahout casually informed us we had reached the spot. He then, together with the coolies, retreated across the bed of the Mae Lah to the safety of the other side, leaving Orwell and me on the path by ourselves. Expecting a python, we looked up at the neighbouring trees, but could make out nothing."

The Lao workers wanted nothing to do with killing. Watching from a safe distance, the mahout warned that the snake was at Campbell's feet. "Glancing down," Campbell noted, "I saw, just within the scrub that bordered the path, an evil head with a flattened hood behind it, and a long blackish body with gray-white marks on the back tapering away into deeper jungle."

Orwell whispered to Campbell that the snake was a hamadryad. Campbell tells us, "I hadn't been in the jungle long, nevertheless I had heard all I wanted to about the hamadryad, or king-cobra. Unlike other snakes, which if not asleep glide away on the approach of humans, the hamadryad will not only not give way; it is more than likely it will attack, especially if its eggs are near, and as its speed is said to rival that of a galloping horse over a short space of ground, and as its bite is deadly poisonous, I knew that Orwell and I were in an unenviable position."

"Keep absolutely still," Orwell told Campbell, "I'm going to shoot."

Campbell stood stock still. "Slowly—maddeningly slowly, it seemed to me—he raised gun to shoulder. And all the time those unblinking, deadly-cold eyes were staring at my legs only a few inches away from them. I believe I silently cursed Orwell for his slowness, and I *know* it was only because I feared the snake might be galvanised into striking, that I did not turn tail and run; but Orwell was an old hand in the jungle and he realised that a sudden movement on his part might cause the thing to rise and strike in a flash."

The two men were frozen in their tracks until Orwell chose the moment to fire. "At last his gun crashed, whereupon we both cast off all caution and fled for our lives. But we needn't have feared; when we gingerly returned to examine the body we found that the horror's head had been blown clean off by the buckshot, though even then we made it thirteen feet six inches long by the tape-measure I used when checking up on the girths of teak trees. Complete with head it must have gone to over fourteen feet, and as fifteen is the outsize limit for a hamadryad, Orwell had shot a pretty specimen."

Campbell had the king cobra skinned and then draped it over the branch of a tree. "It looked quite life-like. So much so that if an unsuspecting villager passed my camp and saw it, he nearly jumped out of his skin. Indeed, the amusement both I and the coolies got out of scaring innocent passers-by lasted us for weeks."

Campbell summed up his three close encounters with the words "snakes are—horror." Lacking the spiritual training of unarmed monks on thudong, whose regard for sentient beings prevented them from seeking to kill any creature, the Westerners relied entirely on their weapons, or those of their paid servants, to protect them. Monks relied on their ability to remain utterly still physically and emotionally, and on the mantras they recited, silently, when in danger—mantras that were intended to help the monk radiate metta to the animal in question.

Unprotected and armed primarily with skills acquired through meditation, thudong monks learned to live with snakes without anxiety or fear. Ajan Khai (1857–1932) provides us with one such example. Ajan Khai was ordained as a monk by a village abbot in Chachoengsao, east of Bangkok. The inhabitants of Chachoengsao were Siamese, Khmer, Lao, and Chinese. The surrounding area teemed with wildlife. Ajan Khai had wandered and lived in the forest for fifteen years. One day he was sitting in meditation in the lotus position under a tree. While Ajan Khai was deep in samadhi a snake crawled over him and coiled itself on his lap. When Ajan Khai came out of samadhi, opened his eyes, and saw the snake, he remained seated in the lotus position, raised his hand slowly, and brushed the snake off. As soon as the monk's hand touched the head of the snake it uncoiled and slithered away. His calm acceptance of the unpredictable indicates that Ajan Khai was an experienced thudong monk.

Ajan Butda, whom we met in "Two Legs Monastery," recalled that he had his first close encounter with a big snake in his early days as a wandering monk. It took place in a cave when he was all by himself. On this occasion Ajan Butda was sitting in meditation with his eyes closed. Then he smelled a pungent odor. Instinct urged him to open his eyes to see what was causing the smell, but he was afraid he might see something horrible. Butda kept his eyes closed. His body broke out in a sweat. It took him a while to regain his mindfulness. Then Butda thought to himself, "Things that have never been seen will be seen. Why be afraid? If it's time [for me] to die, whether my eyes are open or closed, death will come. This cave is very narrow. There is no way to get out alive. With the eyes closed the mind is anxious. Better open the eyes and face whatever it is." As soon as he opened his eyes Ajan Butda froze. Only two meters away, right in front of him, lay a big snake several meters long. "Its head was as big as a coconut. Red eyes. It kept sticking its tongue out!" Ajan Butda sat still trying to figure out what to do. He put his mind under the protective power of the Buddha, the Dhamma, and the Sangha. Then he closed his eyes and made a resolve to give his body to the snake. Once he did so his mind was free from anxiety. Focusing his mind firmly on "Buddho," the thudong monk abandoned attachment to the body. The snake left him alone. The offering of his body as food to the snake shows that Ajan Butda was practicing the perfection of generosity (dana parami).

During this same period a Dutchman named Klaasen, who arrived in Siam in the 1920s, encountered a thudong monk in a cave in the jungle beyond Chiang Mai. Klaasen respected thudong monks and their ability to coexist peacefully with wild animals. In the 1950s, while attempting to find the cave again, Klaasen informed his companion, Ludwig Koch-Isenburg, a young German zoologist, that "this is the main habitat of the most feared snake in Thailand, the king cobra." Alluding to the unpredictability of life in the wild, the Dutchman told the zoologist, "It takes tremendous concentration to anticipate the reactions of so dangerous a snake. But such feats aren't too surprising in this Buddhist world, which devotes itself to composure and absorption. The West is proud of intelligence and activity, but these faculties have more and more degenerated into restlessness and sheer busyness. We Westerners can learn a good deal about inner repose in this country."

SOURCES

Reginald Campbell, *Teak-Wallah: The Adventure of a young Englishman in Thailand in the 1920s* (1935; 1986), pp. 65–71, 230–231.

For a short biography of Ajan Khai Inthasaro, see Sombat Kongsoi, *Kao Phra Ajan* (n.d.), pp. 65–71.

Ajan Butda Thavaro: Chiwit kanngan lae lakdhamma (1994), p. 42.

Ludwig Koch-Isenburg, *Through the Jungle Very Softly: A Quest for Wild Animals in the Far East* (1959; 1963), pp. 170–171.

26

SNAKES, GUNS, AND
GUARDIAN SPIRITS

FROM 1922 to 1927 Frank Exell, a British schoolteacher,
was employed by the Siamese Ministry of Public Education. When his contract with the Siamese government
was not renewed, Exell went to work for Siam Bank, one
of whose branch offices was located in Thung Song, a
railway junction about four hundred miles south of
Bangkok in Nakhon Si Thammarat. The town was on the
doorstep of the tin-mining area. When Exell arrived he
was told by his predecessor that he was about to begin
living "in one of the most cobra-infested areas in the
world." Exell also found out that "there were no roads
and the nearest American Mission Hospital was about a
couple of hours away by train, and there were only two
trains a day, and none after 6 P.M."

At the time Exell was the only European in Thung
Song. The only other nearby Westerner was the manager of a tin mine in Ron Phibun, an adjacent district.
After two years of living in southern Siam, Exell noted,
"When it came to snakes, the north could not compete
with the south. It could have been due to the prolonged
rainy season of seven months which prevailed in the
south. On the other hand, it may have been due to the
vast areas of evergreen jungle. Whatever it was, the north
came a poor second. You came across snakes, of course,
but they were not the everyday occurrence they had been
in Tung Song and Ron Phibun. I did many jungle trips in
the north but I saw few snakes."

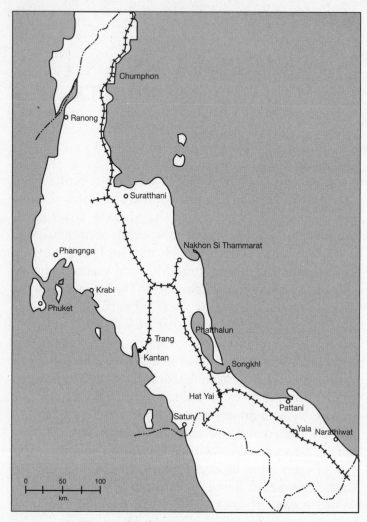

Fig. 27 Southern Peninsula of Thailand

While living in the southern hinterland Exell was puzzled by local people's attitudes toward illness and their lack of faith in the mission hospital. His admiration for local people was apparent, however, when he came to the subject of snakes. "The attitude of the Siamese paddy farmer to snakes was reassuring. He went about barefooted and took not the slightest notice of what might be underfoot. It could have been something to do with Buddhist fatalism but I don't think so. I think it was simply a case of familiarity breeding contempt. The only time I knew them to get a bite was when they were harvesting the rice, but then it was always a harmless water snake. In all the fourteen years I was in Siam I came across only two or three cases of venomous snake bite and two of these were literally 'asked for.' Only one proved fatal and that was an aged Siamese peasant who absolutely refused to have anything done about it. It was too late when they eventually got him to the Mission Hospital at Nakhon Si Thammarat. The older Siamese peasants were often like that about accident or illness. Whatever was to be, was to be. It was their karma and they were prepared to let things take their course."

Living in snake territory compelled local people to observe the habits of the reptiles and learn to coexist with them. From the natives the British bank manager learned that "snakes rarely attacked unless cornered or taken by surprise. They would always move away from you, unless it was a krait, which would literally refuse to move. The Siamese said that it was not because they were lazy but because their habits were nocturnal and they were usually asleep or drowsy during the day time. It was extremely unusual for a snake to come at you. Their one ambition always seemed to be to get away as fast as possible."

Thung Song would have been a paradise for a modern-day herpetologist, but the beauty of some of the snakes that Exell saw failed to move him. Having taken a close look at a variety of snakes, the Englishman admitted the irrationality of his feelings. "I don't really know why I always hated snakes. But I did. I loathed them. I was never one to kill an animal simply for the sake of killing. I either shot for the pot or not at all. But I would kill a snake without the slightest hesitation or remorse. As far as I was concerned they were there to be killed, on principle. It could not have been because they looked vicious. Chameleons, towkay lizards, the praying mantis were all evil looking. But I never had an urge to kill them. What's more, many snakes were things of beauty. Their colourings and markings could be exquisite. There were the steely, blue and black markings of the monster python. The yellowish brown body of the cobras shone with its white and silvery scales. The dreaded hamadryad or king cobra, was black on top, yellow at the throat and glistening white underneath. Most deadly and most beautiful of all were the triangular-shaped Russell's vipers with alternate bands of shining yellow and black and the banded krait with long stripes of the same colours. Yes, they were beautiful. But I loathed them all the same."

With their intense fear of snakes, Exell and his wife instructed their servant never to leave Peter, their two-year-old son, on his own. One afternoon the British couple had their first scare when they caught their son playing with a snake. That day while the parents were having tea in their garden they spotted Peter alone in a far corner. The servant had gone inside the house to get a bath ready for the boy. Exell recalls, "I strolled over to see what he was up to and what he was trying to pick up. He kept toddling forward a few paces and then bending down. When I got there I was scared stiff. He was following a banded krait, saying 'Pretty, pretty.' Each time the snake stopped, he was trying to pick it up before it moved on. It might have ended in tragedy because he was

Fig. 28 Shooting a snake

edging the krait into a corner where it would probably
have turned on him." This experience reminded Exell of
what his predecessor had told him when he first arrived
in Thung Song: "The krait is one of the deadliest snakes
in the world because it is too lazy to move out of your
way."

Exell and A. J. King, who managed the tin mine in Ron
Phibun district, were out one day "climbing the hillside
track to the top dam which was several thousand feet up.
The narrow path was completely ceilinged with trees and
creepers under some of which we almost had to crawl to
get through. Normally you could walk upright but the

terrific monsoon rain had bowed the branches down. The path itself was so slippery with thin mud that we had to pick our steps carefully and were not paying much attention to what might be overhead." From this preoccupied state, Exell wrote, "I suddenly looked up and found my eyes on a level with a huge python which lay along a stout branch. It was on the alert but made no attempt to move. Since we had not gone far up the hill, King went back for his rifle whilst I kept my eye on the snake. Or rather it kept its eye on me. King made a very neat job of it and the skin was a beauty, just over twelve feet."

Whereas villagers might kill a snake for its meat, this Englishman was eager to get a snakeskin for his wife. "I had it cured and it made a handbag, a belt and a pair of shoes for my wife. When we came home on leave she found that imitation snake and lizard skin were the vogue and, at a glance, they looked the real thing. She was so fed up about it that she gave the lot to the charwoman which did not please me very much. The truth was that the imitation stuff was so good and so cheap that there was no market for the real thing and a woman got no satisfaction from having it." Local people no doubt thought it strange that the European would use snakeskin to make shoes, belts, and handbags, accessories for which they had no need. Market forces had not yet created the desire for fashionable clothing, at least not beyond Bangkok. The majority of rural people still went about their daily lives barefoot, and women had not yet picked up the Western habit of carrying leather handbags. They had nothing to put in them.

By the end of his stay in Thung Song, Exell realized, "I survived my two years without a bite and I killed an awful lot of snakes. Admittedly, I shot them at a safe distance." Exell seems to have relished the killing. Many Lao thudong monks believed that *nagas*, the cobra-like snakes that inhabit rivers, had a mythological connection with water, rain, and fertility. Nagas are guardian spirits of the earth who guard treasure. Anybody who dug up the treasures of the earth, like gold or tin, had inevitably to contend with big snakes.

Like the Englishman, the monk La Khempatato (1911–96) was afraid of big snakes. Once, when La was staying in the northeastern region with his teacher, Ajan Man, he admitted his dread of snakes. The forest master responded, "Why be afraid? If you're devoured by a snake, simply brace your feet against its stomach wall." Ajan Man probably meant that then the snake would not be able to swallow the monk all the way down. He was surely joking, but his reply suggests that his meditation training had enabled him to overcome fear. Ajan Man wanted his disciple to understand that encountering a snake need not be a horrible or necessarily fatal experience.

Shortly after his teacher's death in 1949, Ajan La went to Phangnga, a province south of Nakhon Si Thammarat, and here he was able to put Ajan Man's advice to the test. Ajan La was then forty-two. While he was wandering in Phangnga, local villagers guided him to a rock overhang at Turtle Mountain Cave. At the overhang someone had built a platform, raised half a meter off the ground, on which visitors could sit or sleep. Here Ajan La planned to spend a week meditating. "Arrived in the afternoon and lay down for a rest under an overhanging rock." While he was resting, "A big snake came crawling from the north along the cliff to the edge of the platform. Slowly it crept forward and raised its body half a meter off the ground. Its eyes were as big as my thumb. I sat up and crossed my legs on the platform. By now the snake's head was less than an arm's length away. Its body was over four meters long and about ten centimeters in diameter. It looked at me quietly." Ajan La was afraid, yet he observed the snake carefully. Then he waved his hands at the snake and said, "Go away. Go over there. Why suspect me? I send metta to you every day. . . . Not only to you, but to all sentient beings, which I consider fellow beings. . . . May all beings be happy. Go. . . . Go." The snake then crawled toward a nearby spirit shrine and eventually went into a deep hole underneath the rock shelter. "About ten minutes later it came back, approaching the edge of the platform. More mindful this time, I spoke while waving my arm at the snake, 'Go, go, go, go away. Don't you hear me? I'm not here to dig any treasure from the earth or pull one out of the water. Go away.' The snake moved backward one hand's breadth, spun around, and then went back into the hole."

Ajan La thought at first that the snake might be a guardian spirit of a treasure in the area. But after he pondered the incident, the thudong monk decided that the snake was neither a spirit nor a *devata* (deity) in disguise. Ajan La thought that the snake might be connected to him through past karma and wanted to test the extent of his fear by seeing if he would resort to grabbing a stick to hit it. Ajan La believed that he was saved by the power of the Triple Gem (the Buddha, the Dhamma, and the Sangha) and the purity of his heart, which held no harmful intentions toward the animal.

SOURCES

F. K. Exell, *In Siamese Service* [1922–36] (1967), pp. 134–143.

Phra Ajan La Khempatato, *Chiwaprawat Luang Pu La Khempatato* (1989), pp. 238–239, 127.

27

TEMPLE BOY AND SPITTING COBRA

AJAN NGOEN was born in 1890 in the Village of Grandma
Hom's Knoll in Nakhon Pathom, a province about sixty
kilometers west of Bangkok. Ngoen's father was a farmer
and herbal doctor who taught him mantras and medicine
from palm-leaf texts. In 1910 Ngoen (which means "silver")
was ordained as a monk at the Monastery of Grandma
Hom's Knoll (Wat Don Yai Hom). Not long after his
ordination he took up the thudong practice and left the
village. When he returned the villagers asked him to remain, since the current abbot was getting on in years. In
1923, when the village abbot died, Ajan Ngoen was appointed abbot of the wat. He was revered for his compassion, incredible patience, and ability to treat the sick with
medicinal herbs and mantras. During the dry season the
abbot was often invited to other villages to officiate at
ceremonies, such as the shaving of topknots, the ordinations of monks and novices, and chanting at funerals.
Since there were no paved roads connecting his village to
other settlements or nearby towns, he usually traveled on
foot, walking along the low dikes of earth that surrounded
the paddy fields.

On a day in the 1930s Ajan Ngoen was invited to perform a bhikkhu ordination at Wat Takdat, south of
Nakhon Pathom. He took a temple boy named Chuen
along with him. Chuen was not yet ten years old. After
two hours of walking along the dikes in the stifling heat,
Chuen recalled, "The sun got hotter and hotter. My body

was soaked with sweat. I got dizzy from the heat, so I got off the dike." Chuen began walking instead through the tall weeds at the edge of the dike, using his teacher's shadow to shield him from the sun. Chuen recalls: "When Venerable Father stopped, I stopped, too. I was small then. When Luang Pho saw what I was doing, he looked at me with metta. I could tell that he was hot, too. His skin turned as red as a *tamleung* [a fruit]. But he tried to walk in such a way that his shadow always covered me. For the rest of the trip I felt cool."

The monastery to which the two were going was located in a village on high ground above the surrounding paddy fields. As they approached, Chuen recalls, "I continued to walk through the weeds. At the time I did not know that the area in the vicinity of the village was full of snakes, particularly spitting cobras. Many farmers and passersby who had been bitten by the cobras had died. Suddenly I heard a hissing sound *fuuuu*, like the sound a cat makes when it is threatened. Instinctively I began to run, and as I took off I saw a cobra spreading its hood just where my foot left the ground. The snake missed my ankle by only an inch. I could feel it." Once he realized what happened, Chuen became furious with the snake, muttering to himself, "I was walking peacefully and you just wanted to bite me. If you had not missed, I would be dead." Chuen then snatched up a stick from the ground and was about to hit the snake when the abbot stopped him, saying, "Don't harm the snake." Chuen was puzzled, and began wondering, "Why did Revered Father forbid me to hit the snake when the damn snake almost killed me?" Just at the point when the question came into Chuen's mind, the abbot said to him, "Do not take revenge. It is a good thing that the snake missed you. This indicates that in a previous life you did not kill the snake. Do not create a karmic link. Let the snake go. And extend metta to the snake."

The abbot explained Dhamma to Chuen, but the temple boy could not forget that the snake threatened him with its *fuuuu*. "Watch out, you arrogant snake." Chuen thought. "If Revered Father were not here I would have beaten you." In recollecting the event, Chuen said, "I did not know how to extend metta to the snake when I knew it wanted to harm me. I thought if I threatened it with a stick it would go away. Instead it attacked me and made me run up the dike. The damn snake then slithered over toward Luang Pho, but it did not harm him. Instead it went into a hole in the dike."

SOURCE

Chuen Thaksinanukun, *Luang Pho Ngoen: Thephachao of Don Yai Hom* (1962), pp. 286–290. When he was twenty Chuen was ordained as a monk by Ajan Ngoen Chanthasuwanno. After he disrobed, Chuen wrote a biography of his teacher.

28

KILL INSECTS, CLEAN LATRINES

FOR MOST of the nineteenth century Lampang, like other principalities in northern Siam, was ruled by local lords who paid tribute to the royal court at Bangkok. Holt Hallett, a retired British colonial officer and former head of the Tenasserim Division of Burma, visited Lampang in the late 1870s. Hallett reported that the principal exports from Lampang to Bangkok were "teak, sapan-wood, hides, horns, cutch, ivory, and stick-lac." Exports to China included "raw cotton, rhinoceros-horns, soft deer-horns, which are used for medicine, gold-leaf, saltpetre, ivory, and brass tinsel-plates." From neighboring states in the northern region Lampang imported rock-salt from Muang Nan; "cloth, crockery, betel-nuts, and pickled tea" from Chiang Mai; "raw cotton, tobacco, cotton cloth, betel-nut, and cutch" from Muang Phrae; "paddy and rice" from Muang Payao; and "gum-benjamin, stick-lac, raw silk, and fish spawn" from Luang Prabang. Lampang also imported "lead, steel swords, steel ingots, walnuts, lacquered utensils, and opium" from Chiang Tung (Keng Tung) in the Shan states; and from Yunnan in southern China, "opium, bee's wax, walnuts, brass pots, ox-bells, Chinese silk piece-goods, silk jackets and trousers, silk jackets lined with fur, figured cloth, straw hats with waterproof covers." American missionaries who traveled about and lived in the northern principalities noticed that the local languages, religious customs, and practices there were very different from those in Bangkok. Lillian Curtis was the wife of an American Presbyterian missionary; the couple lived in Lampang for four years. In her memoir in 1903 Mrs. Curtis described a religious practice common among monks of the Yuan tradition in Lampang, Lamphun, and Chiang Mai. "All fully-ordained monks would have a rosary. The beads are one hundred and eight in all, each one representing some sacred book or great abbot or the names and merits of Buddha. It is great merit to remember the whole list. The string is made like a Catholic rosary, without the cross."

The missionaries met Buddhist monks who showed them much courtesy and kindness. Curtis wrote, "In some of the *wat luangs* [royal wats] can be found monks who are fairly good Sanscrit and Pali scholars, and who are upright in their lives. These scholar men are always glad to talk with visitors to the wat, especially upon scholarly subjects. They liked nothing better than a visit from the missionaries. Their tastes are refined and scholarly, and they like to learn, though they do not wish to shake off the shackles which bind to the past." The last sentence indicates that these monks had such strong conviction in the local religious tradition passed down from their teachers that they saw no reason to become Christians.

In frustration Curtis noted, "Many warm friendships exist between these rare men, so seldom found, and the missionaries; and great aid is often given by them in translating work done by the mission. If these few men were not Buddhists, they would sway their fellow-countrymen and lead them to a higher and better life. But their faith teaches them that the only way to eradicate the evil in the world is for each individual to cast it out of himself; and if he sees to it that he spends the time in meditation, he has done all that he can do." Western missionaries and their wives met many Buddhist monks who meditated. They were unable to comprehend why monks

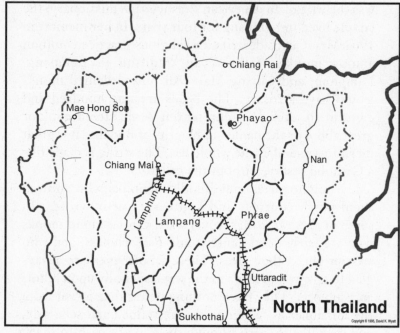

Fig. 29 Northern Thailand

spent so much time doing what to the missionaries seemed
nothing at all. Many Westerners looked down on Buddhist monks, perceiving them as lazy. After decades of
work, the American missionaries succeeded in converting only a few local monks to Christianity, and these were
men who had been ostracized or were facing ostracism
from their own communities.

When the Curtises came to live in Lampang, King
Chulalongkorn (r.1868–1910) had already begun the process of unifying all the principalities into a modern nation-state under Bangkok's rule. From 1893 on, a provincial administrative system, modeled on the colonial
administrations of the Dutch in Java and the British in

Malaya, in which traditional local rulers were kept as figureheads, was implemented throughout the regions that constitute Thailand today. The northern, tribute-paying principalities were incorporated into the new nation and made accountable to the central government in Bangkok and its administrators. The power of the lords of these semi-autonomous neighboring states came to an end; local rulers were superseded by commissioners or governors appointed by Bangkok authorities.

Modernization required the implementation of a secular education system based on Western models. To accomplish this, the many religious traditions that existed had to be brought under the umbrella of the sangha bureaucracy. As a result of the centralization, all abbots became subordinate to the sangha authorities in Bangkok and were required to teach from texts written in the Thai language by Prince Wachirayan, King Chulalongkorn's half brother. From this time on, only those monks who studied Bangkok's new monastic curriculum and passed the state examinations given by Bangkok authorities could be appointed abbots. Local people no longer had the power to choose their abbots. Local abbots no longer had the power to ordain new monks into their lineages.

In northern Siam monks were usually referred to as *khuba* (Thai: *khruba*) instead of *ajan*. Khruba Kasem (b. 1912) was a meditation monk known for his great compassion for all beings. Kasem was born in Kao Muang Village on the Wang River in Lampang. Both parents were descendants of Prince Bunwat, the last local ruler of the principality of Lampang. After Siam became a nation-state and absorbed Lampang and its neighbors, hereditary lords like Kasem's male relatives were given administrative duties and put on fixed salaries. Kasem's father, Nu, was a deputy district officer whose appointment came from Bangkok. Kasem's mother, Chon, opened a jewelry shop.

When Chon was pregnant with her first child, she dreamt one night that the sky was full of rainbows. Chon reached for the rainbows, pulled them toward her and embraced them. Then, just before dawn, she woke up and described the dream to her husband. He explained to her that dreaming of rainbows at dawn meant that a bright jewel will be born. On November 28, 1912, shortly after her dream, Chon gave birth to a boy. He was named Kasem, which means happiness. Kasem was an only son. As a child he was strong, energetic, intelligent, and gentle, although he could be naughty. He attended a government primary school located in a town wat and graduated from that school in 1924. When he was seventeen he was ordained as a novice at Wat Bunyun. The abbot was Khruba Khammoei. Kasem spent the rains retreats at Wat Bunyun. In 1933 he took higher ordination as a monk. He was given the Pali name Khemako, which means one who is secure (in nibbana), but people continued to call him by his original name.

It was one year before Kasem's ordination that the former British schoolteacher, Frank Exell, came to Lampang to work as a bank manager. His description reveals the continued diversity of the population. In the city of Lampang, situated along both banks of the Wang River, Exell reported that "there was a mixed population of somewhere about 50,000 made up of Siamese, Lao, Burmese, Chinese, Indians, Shans and representatives of all the surrounding hill tribes who were always coming and going, Kamus, Karens, Meao, Yao and others. It had, too, its sprinkling of Japs, but, then, every town of any size in Siam had that. Its situation was of considerable strategic importance and it was a strong military centre. The road to the border of old Chiengsen on the bank of the Mekong opened up the way to Burma, the Shan states, Kengtung and Yunnan. It was also one of the busiest smuggling routes for the opium which came from the border country."

In the 1930s, by which time secular education through fourth grade had been made compulsory, primary schools were usually built on land appropriated from the monasteries. As a result of this proximity, children continued, as they had in the past, to play on wat grounds. Na Namfa, a Lampang layman, went to the primary school right next door to Wat Bunyun during the years Phra Kasem lived there as a young monk. He recalled how children used to enjoy playing at the monasteries. "As a boy, I loved to go to Wat Muenkat, Wat Pa Tua, Wat Bunyun, and Wat Chiangman. The last two monasteries were near each other. These were favorites for us kids. I was most familiar with Wat Muenkat and with Wat Bunyun, which was next door to my school. Wat Bunyun was not big, so we kids knew every nook and corner." The children, however, were afraid to go inside the vihara, where the Buddha images were housed. They had heard that there was a big skull in the vihara. Fear of ghosts kept them away. It was said that Khruba Kasem placed a lit candle on top of the skull whenever he practiced kasina meditation inside the vihara.

Like most young monks who were ordained after the passage of the 1902 Sangha Act, Phra Kasem studied Bangkok's new monastic curriculum. He passed the highest level of the Nak-dhamma when he was twenty-four. Although he had studied Pali, Kasem was not interested in taking a Pali exam. As he grew older Phra Kasem preferred meditation practice to reading books. His first meditation teacher was Khruba Kaen, abbot of Wat Prathu Pong in Lampang, who taught him thudong practices.

When Khruba Khammoei died, Khruba Kasem was appointed abbot of Wat Bunyun. Kasem's aunt, his mother's

Fig. 30 A nineteenth-century monk from northern Siam, seated in meditation.

younger sister, had a son named Prawet. The boy was only seven years old when his mother died. Khruba Kasem came to the funeral and adopted Prawet as his son. The boy went to live at Wat Bunyun and was eventually ordained as a novice. Kasem called him Novice Wet, short for Prawet.

The abbot's kuti had a thatched roof, wooden walls, and a bamboo veranda. All over the walls of his kuti Khruba Kasem had pasted Dhammic allegories, proverbs, and verses of his own in Pali with Thai translations. The allegories were in the form of collages that the monk made by clipping images from various sources and pasting them together. Wet recalled that one collage depicted a long wooden barge at sea, fitted with a figurehead of a naga (a serpent with supernatural power). A small castle stood in the middle of the barge. The barge could be said to symbolize a person trying to reach the other shore; the castle perhaps represented *citta* (heart/mind or consciousness). Another image depicted a tiger sitting alone in a forest, the tiger symbolizing the mind and heart of a meditation monk.

Khruba Kasem always slept on the floor of his kuti without a mosquito net. Sometimes he slept outdoors underneath a *kaeo* tree in the wat compound. The abbot was a meditation monk who loved solitude. He preferred being a thudong monk, and usually resided at Wat Bunyun only during the rains retreats. After the passage of the 1902 Sangha Act, all abbots, even those accustomed to going on thudong after the rains retreats, were ordered to stay close to their monasteries at all times. But after the end of each rains retreat, Kasem continued to leave his wat, immediately going to stay in a forest cemetery. He went so far as to see Chaokhun In, the sangha head of Lampang province, in an attempt to resign from his appointment as abbot. The sangha head, not wanting to lose a mature, capable abbot, refused to accept Kasem's resignation. Kasem was then thirty-seven.

In 1949, just before the beginning of that year's rains retreat, Khruba Kasem slipped out of the wat. On every full moon day that marked the beginning of the rains retreat (*vassa*) in July, laypeople came to the wat bringing food offerings to the monks. But this time they found no trace of the abbot except for a letter that he had left on his dhamma seat. In the two-page letter the abbot explained why he could not stay. Prawet recalled only one part of the letter in which Khruba Kasem said to his followers, "Everything I taught you is good. But don't ever think of finding me. I have left everything. Being an abbot is like being the head of a family, with so many responsibilities. The position does not suit me. I want solitude. I will never return."

Certain that they knew where to find their abbot, fifty laypeople went to the forest cemetery at Sala Wangthan. They prostrated themselves before him and begged, "Khruba, we came to invite you back. Today is the first day of the rains retreat. We have strong faith and want to make offerings to you. Please return to the wat." Khruba Kasem sat in silence. He never uttered a word. The laypeople finally gave up and went back to the wat without their abbot. Khruba Kasem spent the entire rains retreat in the forest.

Kasem's mother, whose house was near Wat Bunyun, worried about her son living alone in a forest cemetery. The next day she took her nephew, Novice Wet, with her to visit Kasem at Sala Wangthan and begged her son to return to the wat. The abbot told her, "Mother, I want nothing. I am not suited to be an abbot. I like solitude. I will continue to seek solitude. I will be going to the forest cemetery at Mae Hang Village." His mother left a mosquito net, mat, pillow, and blanket for her son to use.

At the time Khruba Kasem's aspiration must have puzzled many of the young monks and laypeople who had grown up under the influence of the new state Buddhism. Phra Paisal, abbot of Wat Pa Sukhato, has noted that the standard textbooks for monks placed emphasis on morality (*sila*), but nowhere was it stated that the highest goal of Buddha-dhamma is to attain nibbana and to be free from suffering (*dukkha*). Instead, the new textbooks taught that

allegiance to the state and obedience to its rulers constituted a supreme Buddhist value. In the older tradition,
respected abbots had moral influence upon the state in
which they lived; they were more than just being obedi-
ent subjects. Although Phra Kasem had studied the official textbooks, he chose to follow the local khrubas whose
teachings integrated nibbana into ordinary life. Among
lay Buddhists in Lampang the wish to attain nibbana can
be traced as far back as the fifteenth century. An inscription dated 1477 A.D. records that Lord Khampet was appointed to rule Lampang by King Tilokraja of Chiang Mai.
Khampet restored a wat that included a stupa containing
a sacred relic, a vihara and an enclosing wall. He donated
land to the wat along with a number of servants to take
care of the stupa. The inscription reveals that Khampet
made a wish to be reborn a buddha in his next rebirth.

Khruba Kasem's aspiration was to perfect his energy
(viriya) for the final goal. That was why he left his monastery to live at the Wangthan forest cemetery, which lay
under the shade of a great variety of trees. Dead bodies
were placed on top of a brick platform and burnt in the
open. Most people dared not step into the forest cemetery after dark for fear of ghosts. On chilly nights Kasem
hung a mosquito net in the sala and meditated under it.
One night, while Khruba Kasem was sitting in meditation, he heard someone sneak into the sala. Unaware that
the monk was watching, the thief hurriedly tried to untie
the strings of the mosquito net from the corner posts of
the sala. It was pitch dark, and the thief could not see
well. Khruba Kasem got up and quietly helped untie the
strings. Once the mosquito net came down to the floor,
Khruba handed it to the thief, along with his pillow and
blanket. The monk told the thief to get out quickly to
avoid getting caught.

Khruba Kasem was especially sensitive to ants, knowing that however mindful he might try to be, he could easily

sit or step on ants and kill them by accident. Shortly after the mosquito net incident, Novice Wet came to stay at the forest cemetery to attend his teacher. They slept in the same sala. Wet recalled, "At night Venerable Father sat in meditation in the sala while I fell asleep. Sometimes he sat on the floor right next to where I was stretched out. One night it rained very hard, and I could not sleep because a huge army of ants came to the sala to get away from the rain. Since my bed was on the floor, I got bitten. I got up in the middle of the night, looked for a piece of paper, lit it with a match, and roasted the whole army of ants on the floor. Luang Pho opened his eyes from meditation and watched me. He said nothing." In the morning Novice Wet found a note from Khruba Kasem that ordered Wet to "go back to the wat at once and clean all the latrines for fifteen days." This, in the days before indoor plumbing, was considered a harsh punishment.

For Buddhist monks, the intentional killing of animals, no matter how small, is a violation of the first precept. If a monk caught a pupil killing tiny insects, his punishment could be just as harsh as that imposed for killing a large animal. Khruba Kasem gave his novice a harsh punishment to teach him compassion for all sentient beings. When the monk sat in meditation in the forest and was invaded by swarms of mosquitoes, he merely brushed them away. If the mosquitoes refused to leave he would talk to them. "You have sucked up enough of my blood. I'm already thin," he would say.

Referring to the key ingredient, blood, of a soup that Lao people love to eat, Khruba Kasem told his pupils, "We human beings are selfish. We eat animal blood but we don't want mosquitoes to suck our blood. I pity them. They must be hungry too. I can hear them whisper in my ears: hungry, hungry, hungry." His pupils never saw Khruba Kasem kill any insect.

To Khruba Kasem, the bites of mosquitoes, gnats, and gadflies, and the irritation of serious rashes that he endured, were not significant. Living in various forest cemeteries on both banks of the Wang River, Khruba Kasem practiced the perfection of joyous effort, forbearance, loving kindness, and equanimity.

SOURCES

Holt Hallett, *A Thousand Miles on an Elephant in the Shan States* (1890), p. 280.

Lillian Johnson Curtis, *The Laos of North Siam* (1903), pp. 222–223.

For a discussion of the modern administrative system, see Tej Bunnag, *The Provincial Administration of Siam 1892–1915* (1977).

For a detailed discussion of the development of the modern education system in its political, economic, and sociocultural context, see David K. Wyatt, *The Politics of Reform in Thailand: Education in the Reign of King Chulalongkorn* (1969).

F. K. Exell, *Siamese Tapestry* (1936; 1963), pp. 177–178,

For more information on Khruba Kasem's life, see Prawet Na Lampang, ed., *Anuson 80 pi Luang Pho Kasem Khemako* (1991). Toward the close of the twentieth century the Wangthan forest cemetery/charnel ground where Khruba Kasem lived was no longer in an isolated setting. All the big trees had been cut down. The first television station in Lampang was later built on the site where Khruba Kasem once sat in meditation.

For the fifteenth-century inscription of the ruler of Lampang, see Dhida Saraya, "The Development of the Northern Tai States from the 12th to 15th Centuries" (1982), p. 174.

For a discussion of the origin of modern state Buddhism, see Kamala Tiyavanich, *Forest Recollections* (1997), pp. 3–9.

For comments on Prince Wachirayan's texts, see Phra Paisal Visalo, "Buddhism for the Next Century: Toward Renewing a Moral Thai Society" (2003); for a detailed discussion of King Rama VI's nationalistic policies and their impact on Buddhism in Siam, see Phra Paisal Visalo, *Buddhasasana thai nai anakhot* (2003).

29

THE FOREST CEMETERY AT WAT SAKET

WAT SAKET, originally called Wat Sakae (Monastery of the Sakae Trees), was built long before Bangkok was established as the capital of Siam. In 1783 Rama I restored the monastery and had a canal dug around three sides of it that he named Great Serpent Canal. At the time the monastery was given the new name of Wat Saket, the compound, located just outside the city wall of Bangkok, covered many acres. During his reign (1824–51) King Rama III began to build a great stupa, a shrine for relics of the Buddha, on an artificial hill that came to be called the Golden Mountain. This stupa, built close to the city wall, was completed in 1877 during King Chulalongkorn's reign and was for many years the tallest structure in Bangkok. Visitors were drawn to Wat Saket because its Golden Mountain offered a great view of the city and its surroundings. On November 2, 1898, Émile Jottrand, a legal adviser to the Ministry of Justice under King Chulalongkorn, wrote in his journal, "From the hill of Wat Saket, the highest building in Bangkok . . . , the city looks like a forest with a tree-cover through which the many roofs emerge here and there. Towards the countryside, vast rice and sugar cane fields extend, crossed over by buffaloes that walk with a heavy gait and reflect the air of a hippopotamus—mounted behind their necks one sees their keepers seated on their backs."

Throughout the nineteenth century Wat Saket was a center where monks could pursue meditation as well as

Fig. 31 The Golden Mountain at Wat Saket circa 1892

Tipitaka studies. Within the wat compound monks devoted to meditation resided in the *khana nai*, close to the
forested area; monks devoted to study and teaching resided in the *khana nok*, near the wat library and the other
public buildings. Two elders, one a meditation master
and the other a scholar, were appointed as heads of each
of the two khanas. On March 10, 1899 Jottrand described
the monks' quarters in his journal. "Wat Saket is very important. The houses of the monks form a whole colony,
and since they are all single-storey, they occupy a vast
space. Each monk hangs a small lantern in his window; it

218

sways up and down in the wind like the shaving mugs of our barbers."

Wat Saket was also known for its Ghost Gate, the entrance to the forest cremation ground located at one end of the immense wat compound to which dead bodies were brought and where they were laid out in the open air. Lucien Fournereau, a French architect and inspector of art education and museums for the French Ministry of Public Instruction and Arts, visited Wat Saket between 1891 and 1892. He informs us that "Wat Saket, which is in our opinion the greatest scandal of Bangkok, merits a special visit. . . . This monastery has been built by royal order so that the cremations which are prohibited inside the walled city could be done there. Three great subdivisions are distinguished there: the pyre, the mass grave, and the cemetery. The latter, a vast place invaded by the jungle, is the burial place for individuals who died a violent death, by epidemics, by suicide or by accidents. The corpses which are placed there must remain there for three days before being burned; this practice is prescribed in the sacred texts."

When he entered the Ghost Gate, Fournereau encountered "two *saparoe* [men who prepare corpses for cremation] dragging behind them, at the end of a long chain, two corpses which had nothing human left except the hands and the feet, the rest being mutilated, bitten to the bone, the faces swollen, the orbits [eye sockets] rummaged through by the rapacious beaks of anthropophagous vultures."

Anybody could walk in and witness vultures at Wat Saket devouring the flesh and intestines of corpses. The final remains were then cremated. Fournereau tells us that "rest salas for the relatives and the friends of the deceased and niches for the deposit of corpses are placed at the circumference of the mass grave; small square tables

Fig. 32 View of Wat Saket from a canal

are placed there to receive the limbs which are destined for the meal of the vultures."

After "the bones have been adequately stripped of the flesh which covered them," Fournereau continues, "the skeletons are dragged into the courtyard of the mausoleum where the cremations are done. They break the bones with blows of a hatchet, then they are placed on a pyre of bundles of fire wood which rapidly consumes them; during the operation, the *saparoe* covers the unshapely remains with the sarong and the dead man's mat."

Wat Saket, however, was not the only monastery at which commoners could practice generosity after they died by giving their bodies as food to animals. John Crawfurd, the Scottish envoy of the British East India

Company who led a trade mission to Siam in 1822, near the end of Rama II's reign, attended a commoner's funeral, then prohibited from taking place inside Bangkok's city walls. In his journal Crawfurd noted, "[The rite] consists in cutting slices of flesh from the corpse, and with these feeding the birds of prey and dogs, which are seen in numbers about the temples, waiting for their horrid feast. . . . The remains of the body are buried in the usual manner. The only honourable funeral amongst the Siamese consists in burning the body, and the practice is very general. It seems to be viewed as a religious rite, and as a ceremony necessary to assist the passage of the soul to a higher grade in the scale of transmigration, and finally to its extinction or rest."

Crawfurd made it a point to spend time talking with the abbots he met at several royal monasteries in Bangkok. He understood the custom of giving flesh to vultures. "Charity to the lower animals," he wrote, "is considered by the Siamese as a religious virtue of great merit." The Jataka stories that town and village monks drew upon when they preached provided many examples of Buddhist practices in the perfection of *dana* that involve the offering of one's own body as a gift.

In the 1870s Ajan Phu Chanthakesaro (b. 1830), a thudong monk from Tak, came to spend a rains retreat in the forest cemetery of Wat Saket. Many years later, in 1892, Ajan Phu was appointed abbot of Wat Bang Khunphrom. When Ajan Phu died in 1933 the ritual of feeding the body to vultures was still practiced at Wat Saket. Ajan Phu did not leave a detailed record of what he saw at the forest cemetery, perhaps because the rites performed there were so commonplace that the monks of his day saw no need to describe them.

Western visitors, however, could hardly resist describing what they saw in great detail, even though they reacted to the scene with disgust or horror. Carl Bock, the

Fig. 33 A saparoe, corpse, and vultures at Wat Saket

Norwegian natural scientist and travel writer, visited Wat Saket in the early 1880s. As Bock entered the grounds he witnessed two Siamese men carrying a dead body on a bamboo stretcher, followed by a few dozen Siamese laypeople and several bhikkhus, whom Bock, like many other Westerners of his time, erroneously referred to as priests. He described what he called "a sickening spectacle" at the charnel grounds at Wat Saket.

"When the coolies reached the selected spot," Bock writes, "they cast the dead man's body on the ground, and the next moment the air was darkened by . . . ghastly, greedy vultures, as they swooped swiftly down and stood in a semicircle round the body, while the priests and spectators completed the circle. Behind the vultures came a flight of crows, . . . dogs ran round in twos and threes, snapping and snarling at each other and at everything that stood between them and the dead body." When "an official, after sharpening a huge knife, approached the body, the vultures became impatient and impudent, hustling and fighting each other for a front place; once or twice they came quite close to me, and I had to keep them off with my stick."

Bock's grisly account continues: "Then the official already mentioned stooped down and cut the body open, with a long slash down the stomach. The sight of the blood and entrails was too much for the filthy vultures, which began to flap their wings, and to utter their well-known sepulchral scream, jumping about in restless anxiety. . . . The flesh from the thighs, legs, and arms was then cut off, and the chest opened. A priest next advanced and chanted a few words, holding a fan and a pipe in his left hand, and in his right a piece of bamboo with which he touched the body. No sooner had he uttered his last words than the vultures seemed to know their time had come, and, with a frantic rush and a horrible scream, swept forward. . . . Two birds, I noticed, at once picked

the eyes out of the dead man, which, by the way, had remained open all the while, adding to the ghastliness of
the spectacle. . . . The birds tore the body most dread-
fully, sometimes actually lifting it off the ground, and
fighting among themselves as one or another dragged off
a piece of flesh. Once, . . . a dog sneaked in and secured a
morsel, but in a moment two vultures attacked him, one
snatching away his mouthful, and the other giving him a
bite in the neck which sent him away howling. Not more
than ten minutes had been occupied in this horrible feast,
when the vultures retired a few feet, and the human
'butcher' came forward a second time and cut the back
open, followed again by the priest, who performed the
same offices as before, and then there was a second feast
for the birds. By this time some of the vultures seemed
surfeited, and the crows and dogs had a larger share of
what was left of the body. Eight minutes later and little
remained except the head and the bones, which were collected together by the attending friends, whom I left
gathering a few sticks with which to burn them."

Before taking the deceased to a wat, commoners usually kept the corpse at home for perhaps as long as a week.
"Once the coffin arrives at the pagoda where the cremation ceremony will take place," Fournereau reports, "the
family uncovers the dead and gives him to the *saparoe* or
cremator. The latter, before doing anything, introduces
his finger into the mouth of the corpse and extracts the
tical which has been placed there for him, wipes it thoroughly on his sarong and, not having a pocket, places it
in his own mouth: it's his salary."

More calmly than Bock, Fournereau continues: "Then
[the saparoe] washes the face with coconut milk and proceeds to the partial dismembering of the corpse if the
deceased has prescribed that this or that part of his body
will be given as food to the animals. Armed with a large,
sharpened knife, he cuts the flesh in long strips and, turn-

ing them around a moment, launches them as hard he can to the dogs and the vultures which do not leave the temple." In an attempt to place the customs he described in their Buddhist context, Fournereau stated that "this practice is a humiliation which has as objective to acquire merits at the entrance to Nirvana." From the Buddhist perspective, this practice indicates supreme generosity.

After the saparoe finishes stripping the flesh from the body, Fournereau says, "he places the corpse on the pyre made of pieces of wood which each relative or friend has brought with him; the fire is lit and stirred up by the resin which they spread out, high, red flames spring from it; the smoke rises, thick and nauseating, obscuring this diabolical scene."

Westerners like Fournereau were accustomed to seeing the deceased fully dressed, neatly contained in coffins, plain or fancy depending on the wealth of the family. For the Buddhists, the dismembering and burning of bodies in the open air at a forest wat was a normal event, but for the Norwegian writer Bock and the French architect Fournereau, each detail of such a custom was riveting. As the cremation proceeded, Fournereau says that "if the *saparoe* has not taken the precaution to sever the joints of the corpse, the spectacle is even more horrifying; the dead flesh appears to be born again and twitches; the electrified limbs stir, twist and relax; the dead, resurrected, grimaces and atrociously thrashes about on his bed of brands. Oh, horror! an explosion is heard; it is the liquefied brain, dilated by the heat which has broken the wall of the skull and has loudly escaped spraying everything around! The dead then, as if he were exhausted, collapses amidst the oils and fats which flow from his carbonized body and crackles under the kisses of the flame which licks it! The smoke becomes black, stinking, and the wind brings the nauseating miasmas which escape from it at sometimes considerable distances."

After watching the body burn and disintegrate from skin and bones to ashes, Fournereau tells us, "the relatives approach the pyre, collect the main bones, which they place in an urn, and bring them back home; the wind will do the rest and dissipates the last remains of what was a man in the dust."

Like many Western travelers in Siam, Fournereau regarded the Siamese as cowardly because they did not want to risk their lives in what they saw as dangerous situations, such as going into caves to explore the interior, tunneling into the ground to look for ore, or going into a sacred forest, for fear of guardian spirits. However imperfectly, Fournereau at least recognized the influence of Buddhism upon the Siamese when they had to face death. "The Siamese, rather cowardly and fearful when they are doing well, show a rare courage and indifference when they feel that death is going to take them. On this point they are very superior to us who in general do not know how to die: the reason for this resoluteness in their attitude is nothing but the deepness of their religious beliefs, which shines before their eyes the pleasant horizons of the Nirvana."

At Wat Saket there were several huts scattered about in the forest cemetery where visiting monks and yogis could stay to practice meditation. In the nineteenth century ascetic monks and yogis had no difficulty finding dead bodies, in various stages of decomposition, which served as objects of focus for meditation on the impermanent nature of the body and on death. For meditation monks a dead body was a tool, useful to help uproot *kilesa* (defilements) and purge the poison of *upadana*, attachment to the self. Watching a dead body being cremated was a powerful reminder that our living bodies are of the same nature as the dead. In the meditation which focused on a minute inspection of dead bodies, monks saw that the flesh, sinews, and bones of humans and animals were much the same. Every part of the body will decay and rot until it has disintegrated and been dispersed. As meditators watched cremations that did not entail the work of a swordsman, they saw the body disintegrate, the head fall off, an arm break off, then another arm, and a length of leg bone; they were witnesses as internal organs ruptured and burst. Meditators were encouraged to visualize the corpse and the stages of disintegration even when they were not in a charnel ground. As one meditation master taught his disciples, "Repeated investigations [of dead bodies] will steadily deepen your insight until you are able to comprehend clearly and detach yourself from seeing the body as me or mine." The highly skilled meditator, recognizing that the corpse has completely disintegrated and become one with the earth, gradually gives up attachment to body, feelings, thoughts, views, even consciousness itself. At that moment he realizes emptiness.

It was not until after the end of World War II that the first modern crematorium was constructed in Bangkok at Wat Traimit (the Monastery of Three Friends), near Hua Lamphong Railway Station. At the new crematorium charcoal was used instead of wood to burn the dead bodies. Once modern crematoria were established, dead bodies were no longer seen out in the open. Wat Traimit's modern crematorium is the forerunner of the high-tech, gas-powered crematoria that exist in many Bangkok monasteries today.

SOURCES

For a short history of Wat Saket, see *Prawat wat thua ratchanachak* (1982), vol. 1, pp. 90–94.

Émile Jottrand and Mrs. Jottrand, *In Siam: The Diary of a Legal Adviser of King Chulalongkorn's Government* (1905; 1996), p. 133.

Lucien Fournereau, *Bangkok in 1892* (1892; 1998), pp. 147–154.

Carl Bock, *Temples and Elephants* (1884; 1986), pp. 57–60.

John Crawfurd, *Journal of an Embassy from the Governor-General of India to the Courts of Siam and Cochin China* (1828; 1967), p. 321.

For the meditation on death, see Maha Bua Nanasampanno (b. 1914), *To the Last Breath: Dhamma Talks on Living and Dying* (1992), pp. 39–56.

For information on Wat Traimit, see Piyanat Bunnag et al., *Wat Nai Krungthep 1782–1982* (1982), p. 228.

30

CORPSES AND CARRION EATERS

KATHERINE AND George Grindrod arrived in Bangkok in 1892. From 1892 to 1894 the English couple were members of a small group of European teachers hired by the Siamese government to establish a secular school for the children of royalty and the nobility. Shortly after their arrival the newcomers went to Wat Saket and walked up to the top of the Golden Mountain to see the view. From there they saw that the city, buried in tropical foliage, was hardly visible. Katherine Grindrod wrote, "Our view—an ocean of green tree tops for miles around, hiding the river, & all smaller buildings, from view, the wats and minarets of Palace and Temple alone rising above the green." Bangkok was still an integral part of its rural setting.

One afternoon while a "boy" was serving her tea, Katherine Grindrod heard the sound of "a large flock of crows sweeping towards the house." On September 17, 1892, Grindrod wrote in her diary, "The boy & I hurried to the balcony & looked on to the roof—and—horrible sight! There they were a whole ridge full of vultures sitting as close as space would allow with only a crow or two sharing their perch but scores round to share the plunder. I am not yet so accustomed to these foul things as to have them so near & not be disturbed. The boy counted them—25—and more coming till more than 30 were crowded there. The explanation was the presence of a dead dog's body somewhere among the trees. From

Wat Skate [Saket] whither the news had travelled wonder knows how—these birds of dead prey swooped down upon the plantation & they & the crows have had a good time of it—& I a bad one. 'Vultures eat man dead' quoth the boy and I could not but fear that if very hungry they might go as far as to eat other things so I shut up the cake before going out to reconnoitre." In Grindrod's opinion "[the vultures'] existence is a disgrace to Bangkok."

In the early 1920s Reginald Campbell, we may recall, began working for the Anglo-Siamese teak harvesting venture in Muang Ngao forest, a four-day walk from the city of Lampang. Beyond the city virtually all was wild. Tigers and elephants were everywhere in the jungle. Campbell's boss hired Lao and Khamu men to work for him, men who were used to living in the wilderness. It was while living in the wild that Campbell got to observe his men in their element.

One morning Campbell, who was traveling on the Wang River in a boat rowed by two Lao boatmen, spotted a dead buffalo whose "bloated carcass was being torn to pieces by vultures. The scene was loathsome in the extreme, but one couldn't help gazing at it, fascinated. A whole crowd of these filthy birds were pulling at the entrails, flapping their wings and yammering at one another in a sort of high, obscene twitter. New-comers kept soaring down from the heavens, the rush of their sailing pinions sounding most majestical in spite of their disgusting appearance. On alighting they would do a little 'run' at the carcass, then plunge into the ghastly feast. Whilst I watched them from the boat a pariah dog suddenly appeared from nowhere, and started jumping and snapping at the vultures in the vain hopes of driving them off and leaving the body to him. What with the increased yammering of the noisome birds, the drooling and twisting of entrails, the yapping of the flea-bitten pariah and the appalling stench that pervaded the air, I was forced to turn my head away with a shudder. I noticed, however, that, far from being disgusted, my two Lao paddlers were positively enjoying the scene; broad grins were on their dusky faces." When Campbell asked the Lao boatmen if what they saw was funny, their reply, "Very funny, master," disturbed him. The boatmen were amused by the behavior of the dog. Campbell could not see how his Lao workers could find humor in such a disorderly, violent sight.

"I made no comment but hastened the boat on," Campbell wrote. "That evening there came a marvelous sunset; the sky turned from blue to a medley of colour: pink and flame and crimson and saffron and the most delicate green, while ahead of us the river, catching the glow, resembled a Nan scarf of many hues. Again out of curiosity I glanced at my men. How were they taking it? I wondered." To Campbell's surprise, "They weren't taking it. They were ignoring the wonder and the beauty spread out before them."

"See. The sunset." Campbell said to the Lao boatmen. "They twisted their heads round a little towards it" and agreed that "the sun was setting," and then they asked him, "Would master be camping soon?"

"But don't you think it's pretty?" Campbell tells us he "used the Lao word '*ngarm*' for pretty, and the boatmen looked puzzled." Their reaction set him "thinking philosophically." In his memoir Campbell wrote, "These brown men had seen humour where I had seen only horror; yet I had found beauty where they had found nothing at all. Who, therefore, had the advantage? I, the civilised man, or these jungle Laos? It seemed to me we were quits."

For the Lao boatmen, who grew up in a jungle village, nature was not a place to visit. It was their element; it was home. Unless it was raining, they saw beautiful sunrises and sunsets almost every day. The sight of a dead buffalo being devoured by vultures was less familiar. Dead animals did not last long in the jungle. Tigers, for example, would usually drag their victim away to devour it or feed it to their cubs in a secluded place.

As late as the 1930s there were still a considerable number of vultures in Bangkok. Right after the rains retreat ended in November 1932, Phra Nu, a newly ordained village monk from Ubon province, traveled from his village wat to study in Bangkok. In the same year a bloodless coup led by the People's Party toppled the absolute monarchy and replaced it with a constitutional monarchy. Phra Maha Nu (now abbot of Wat Phra Sing in Chiang Mai) recalled that after arriving in the city he stayed with a monk to whom he was related at a monastery in Thonburi. Almost every day he took a boat to Bangkok and walked for half an hour to Wat Thepthida where he pursued his study of pariyatti-dhamma. Phra Nu wished to stay at Wat Thepthida, but he had no connections with monks or laypeople who could help him. Since there was no kuti space available, Phra Nu settled for sleeping on the kitchen floor. He recalled, "Every night before I slept I scrubbed the kitchen floor several times, but I could never get rid of the fishy smell."

The Monastery of the Heavenly Daughter (Wat Thepthida) was a royal wat established in 1836 by Rama III to honor his favorite daughter, Princess Apsonsuda-thep, who served the king efficiently as his secretary. This princess also donated part of her personal fortune for the new buildings, which show the influence of Chinese architecture. Wat Thepthida was on a canal that bore the same name. Here, and at most monasteries built during the reign of Rama III, there were two kinds of monks' quarters: separate kutis for meditation monks at the far edge of the wat compound and a row or more of kutis closer to the wat buildings for monks studying the Tipitaka. The most notable statues at Wat Thepthida are in the vihara, the hall that houses sacred images. A number of statues of bhikkhunis (fully ordained nuns) form a semicircle in front of the main Buddha image.

During the years that Phra Nu studied in Bangkok, the custom of offering dead bodies to vultures continued at Wat Saket, which in the 1930s was no longer separated from the city, since the wall had been taken down. Wat Thepthida was a short walk from Wat Saket, which was still known for its "Ghost Gate," the entrance to the charnel ground where dead bodies were brought to be cremated in the open air. Not long after he took up residence at Wat Thepthida, Phra Nu walked through the Ghost Gate and witnessed the offering of corpses to the vultures. "I saw many corpses being carried into the charnel ground. Perched in the trees were hundreds of vultures, waiting for the corpses. The sky was darkened by these birds circling around the dead bodies. With a sharp knife the saparoe cut the corpses open and took out all the intestines and organs. The flesh from the arms and legs was cut off and the pieces thrown to the vultures. In a short time the birds had eaten all the flesh. The saparoe then burned the bones, using wood found in a nearby swamp. After the bones were cremated the relatives came to collect the ashes. They either scattered the ashes over water, buried them underground, or kept them in a jar at home." In the year 2000 Ajan Maha Nu (b. 1912) recalled this scene, which he had seen almost seventy years before, quite matter-of-factly; it was one that the monks, novices, and temple boys of his day saw frequently. Ajan Maha Nu added an important reminder about the health benefits of such a custom. "The vultures were the nation's cleaning service. Without them our life would have been impossible," he said.

Alexandra David-Neel (b. 1868), a French woman who lived in Tibet during the first and second decades of the twentieth century, witnessed a similar custom called "sky burial" by Tibetans. In Tibet, David-Neel noted, "The body was taken to the top of a mountain, the four limbs cut off with a well-sharpened knife, and the entrails, heart and lungs laid out on the ground to be fed upon by birds, wolves and foxes." Like the Siamese, Tibetan Buddhists believed in the perfection of generosity, and David-Neel reported that Tibetan lamas found in the funerals "a fitting occasion for a supreme act of charity. The dead man wished—or is supposed to have wished—that his body should serve as his last gift, to nourish those tormented by hunger."

By the second half of the twentieth century Bangkok had became a concrete jungle. The vultures had disappeared, along with the forest cemeteries. Modern crematoria have been constructed at Bangkok monasteries. In the 1950s Ajan Maha Nu, who by then had received his Pali degree and become abbot of a monastery in Chiang Mai, went to Bangkok for a visit. He noticed that the vultures were nowhere to be seen. The abbot said that he had no idea where all the vultures had gone; he reasoned they disappeared because vultures need to feed on carrion to survive. Wat Saket, once occupying a large wooded compound, had shrunk in size. It is now located on one of the most congested streets in Bangkok. Those entering the monastery today will see no trace of the big trees in which hundreds of vultures once perched.

SOURCES

Katherine Grindrod, *Diaries of Katherine Grindrod, Siam 1892* (1982), vol. 1, pp. 80–81.

Reginald Campbell, *Teak-Wallah* (1935; 1986), pp. 117–119.

For a short history of Wat Thepthida, see *Prawat wat thua ratchanachak* (1982), vol. 1, pp. 207–211.

Alexandra David-Neel, *Magic and Mystery in Tibet* (1971), pp. 30–31.

Interview with Phra Dhammasiddhachan (Nu Kingkaeo), abbot of Wat Phra Sing, Chiang Mai, January 24, 2000.

THE OLDEST MIDWIFE

AT THE turn of the twentieth century, when the population of Siam consisted mainly of farmers, women participated fully in the food production process and in all aspects of farm labor. In the 1920s Ebbe Kornerup, a Dane, traveled from Moulmein in Lower Burma to central Siam, where most inhabitants were rice farmers or orchard keepers. Whereas some Europeans described the Siamese as lazy in comparison with the Chinese, who were regarded as diligent and hard-working, Kornerup observed that Siamese farmers, men as well as women, worked very hard. "First there is the ploughing with oxen and wooden ploughs, when the earth has to be turned; then the planting-out from beds. People are kept hard at it with their backs bent, briskly putting the young plants in, such a moiling and toiling! The Siamese are very industrious, and that's a fact; just imagine planting out every single ear of corn in Europe—it is truly stupid to say the Siamese are lazy. They are out in the fields long before sunrise; in the middle of the day when the sun is at its zenith, of course, they take a rest; but later in the day they work again. When the planting-out is done, there are still the sluices to look after; there is plenty to attend to. In the places where they sow the rice the work is much less arduous; perhaps they idle there; but would not any peasant all the world over do the same?"

In the 1930s Yu-ee, a Chinese farmer, and his Siamese wife, Num, owned a farm on a bank of Wa Tree Canal in

Damnoen Saduak district, Ratburi province. (Today this area is known among tourists as the Floating Market.) Not far from their farm, at the other end of the canal, was Wat Lak Hok. Like many houses in those days, the wat also faced the canal. The most common way to get around was by rowboat or canoe.

There was no hospital or medical clinic in the area. Married women generally worked on farms or in orchards right up to the day they gave birth. In 1941 Num was pregnant with her third child. On a Saturday in November she was at work in her garden as usual. She watered all the plants, which included several beds of garlic, onions, and peanuts. It was a lot of work for a pregnant woman, and time-consuming. Automatic sprinklers were not yet available. By the time Num finished watering it was dusk. Utterly exhausted, she fell asleep right after supper.

In the middle of the night Num woke up feeling excruciating pain. She urged her husband to get the boat out and go fetch her mother, Tip, a midwife. To get to his mother-in-law's house, Yu-ee had to row two kilometers in the dark. Num was left alone with her two children, a nine-year-old son and a four-year-old daughter. Her older brother, Chui Leng, owned the farm next to hers. His place was quite a long walk away for children, but when the labor pains intensified, Num sent her son out to notify her brother. The boy was too scared to walk alone in the dark, so he took his little sister along. The two children braved the dark, walking along the canal at a child's pace while carrying a bright lamp. As soon as he got the news that Num was about to give birth with no adult around, Chui Leng raced to his sister's house. When he got there, he realized that he had left his little niece and nephew behind. The children eventually walked home on their own. While waiting for the midwife, Chui Leng heated up some water and helped his sister in any way he could to keep her comfortable.

When Yu-ee arrived at the midwife's house, he found that Tip was away attending the village headman's wife, who was also in labor. Until she delivered their baby, Tip could not leave. Because Yu-ee was worried that she might be too late to help, he went to fetch his wife's grandmother, Bun, who was also a midwife. Yu-ee also picked up his own mother and his brother's wife. With the women of three generations on board, he rowed home as fast as he could.

After rowing over four kilometers up and back, Yu-ee finally got home just before dawn on Sunday. Around 7:00 that morning Num gave birth to a baby boy, delivered by his great-grandmother, Bun. At the age of seventy-five, Bun still had the know-how to be a midwife. She used a thin, sharp bamboo stick as a knife to cut the umbilical cord. Num, who had been actively engaged in physical work right up to the last day, had given birth far more easily than most sedentary women.

After the birth Num was given Thai medicine, a bowl of tamarind juice, to drink. The liquid was made of squeezed tamarinds and salt mixed with warm water. It was believed to heal the tissues that were damaged during birth. Yu-ee and Num named their son Wanna, meaning nice complexion. The new baby was surrounded by his mother, his great-grandmother, his paternal grandmother, his father, his uncle (his mother's brother), and his aunt (his father's sister-in-law).

As a child Wanna attended a government school in the compound of Wat Lak Hok. His mother went to the wat regularly. She observed the Five Precepts every day, and on holy days she observed the Eight Precepts. In 1961, when Wanna reached the age of twenty, he was ordained as a monk at Wat Lak Hok and given the monastic name Wanno. He intended to study Dhamma for a few years before disrobing to resume working for his parents on their farm. Twenty years later he was still at the monas-

Fig. 34 Along a canal, 1906

tery and is now its abbot. He has received the ecclesiastical title Phra Khru (Venerable Teacher) Siriwanwiwat
(Skilled in Narrative). People still call him by his original
name, Venerable Teacher Wanna.

Once he became abbot, Ajan Wanna set out to write a
local history in which he interviewed the older people of
the community and described what they did in the old
days. He included an interview with his mother. The information he received about the instant response of everyone in his extended family prior to his birth moved
him deeply. "The minute my mother went into labor my
father went to fetch the midwife. At the tender ages of
nine and four, my brother Charan and my sister Phongsai
had to walk back and forth in the pitch dark to get my
uncle. My great-grandmother had to serve as midwife,

even at the age of seventy-five. From my birth on, my parents and my older brother and sister took care of me under circumstances of considerable hardship until I grew up. As I listened to my mother and realized how much trouble my birth had caused everybody, the tears came out of this abbot's eyes."

Besides giving birth at home, another custom that has largely disappeared is the long recitation of stories at a wake. Ajan Wanna recalled, "During a wake monks used to deliver long chants or recite a story in verse that lasted until late at night. People were afraid of ghosts, and they liked to have the monks around for company. By the time the monks paddled back to their monastery, it might be close to midnight. Today laypeople don't want the monks to deliver long chants at a funeral. They prefer short chants so they can play cards or gamble after the monks leave."

SOURCES

Ebbe Kornerup, *Friendly Siam: Thailand in the 1920s* (1999), p. 215.

Phra Khru Siriwanwiwat (Wanna Wanno), *Namta somphan* (1987), pp. 4–8.

Interview with Phra Khru Wanna, abbot of Wat Lak Hok, Ratburi, April 16, 1989.

32

DHAMMA FROM GRANDMOTHERS

IN THE first half of the twentieth century villages were still occupied by several generations of people. Children lived among their extended family, which included grandparents, uncles, aunts, and cousins. Ajan Panya (b. 1911), whose Pali name is Paññananda, recalled that in his village in Phatthalung, "Although my family spent a lot of time helping neighbors, they never neglected their own children. In fact, the more love they had for their kids, the more love and compassion they extended to other people."

In his formative years Ajan Panya was surrounded by his extended family. When he became abbot of Wat Cholaprathan in Nonthaburi, Ajan Panya credited the elderly relatives who had brought him up for planting in him the seeds of his vocation. "The impetus that turned me to the monastic life came from my family, who raised me according to their custom." Ajan Panya's eyes were said to light up at the memory of the grandmothers, who called him Doggie. "When I was a child, two old women had the most influence on my heart and mind. Yai Nu and Yai Num were sisters. I called them Big Grandma and Little Grandma. Little Grandma was my real grandmother. I was her only grandson. Her older sister, Big Grandma, had no grandson. These two grandmothers lived in the same house. When they slept, they put me in the middle." Every night one of the grandmothers would remind her grandson to put his palms together and bow to his pillow. "Hearing a grandma ask, 'Doggie, did you bow to the pillow yet?' I had to get up and bow before I was allowed to put my head on the pillow. They never explained to me the meaning of the gesture." The Buddhist ritual of focusing one's mind before going to sleep only became clear to Ajan Panya with hindsight. "I did not understand then," he tells us. "After I was ordained, I realized that to bow to the pillow is to pay respect to the Buddha. The ritual helped focus my mind on the Buddha-dhamma."

Venerable Panya's skill as a preacher may have been encouraged in his childhood by the stories his grandmothers told him. "After bowing to the pillow, if I could not fall asleep, the grandmas would tell me old folktales, such as the 'Tale of the Golden Swan' (Suwanahong) and the 'Four Jampa Trees' (Champa-siton). Sometimes they sang me old lullabies that had been passed down for generations. These songs were laced with Dhamma teachings. Although neither grandmother could read, they knew so many stories from the past that they never ran out of Dhamma lessons to teach us. They grew up in a society that was steeped in oral tradition. Women of their generation acquired knowledge not from reading books but from hearing stories told by village monks and elders. They were content with their lives and were able to pass on their wisdom to the grandchildren they helped raise. These two grandmothers instilled a love of Dhamma in me." The stories of the Golden Swan and the Four Jampa Trees were well known in villages throughout the Central Plains, the Northeast, and the South.

Ajan Panya was reared by his devout grandmothers while his mother took care of his younger sister. In the village the young as well as the old got up before sunrise to do chores. At the crack of dawn the monks would walk in single file into the village to receive almsfood. Venerable Panya recalled, "All children got up along with the old folk. Every morning grandmothers got up really early to prepare food to offer to the village monks. I too got up early to wait for the monks to come by for alms."

Farmers normally worked every day except when there was a festival at the wat. The farmers and their buffaloes got a break from work on holy days, which occurred four times a month, in keeping with the phases of the moon. On holy days there were no classes for temple boys, because the monks were busy giving sermons. No fishing or hunting was permitted. The young as well as the old went to listen to the sermons at the wat. Old people who normally followed the Five Precepts would stay overnight in the wat to observe the Eight Precepts and practice meditation. The Eight Precepts require abstention from destroying life, stealing, engaging in sexual activity, telling lies, using intoxicants, eating after midday, dancing, singing, playing musical instruments, watching shows or adorning the body with gold and silver, and using high and luxurious beds or seats. Spending the whole day at the wat gave people a genuine break from their ordinary routines.

On holy days the two grandmothers always took their grandson to the wat to participate in religious activities. Ajan Panya recalled, "I went to the wat so often. The wat was where we held festivals, and it was my playground. Even though children spent a lot of time just running around in the wat compound, it was a good environment for them. Hearing the sermons and the sound of monks' daily chants had a good effect on their minds."

Phra Maha Banyat (b. 1942), abbot of the Monastery of Wheel Well Village (Wat Bolo), grew up in Bolo Village in Chianyai district. The words *bo* and *lo* refer to a dug well whose sides are shored up by the solid wagon wheels used with oxcarts. Wat Bolo was one of the oldest monasteries in Nakhon Si Thammarat province. Originally it was an ashram established by Father Khrua, a brother of the beautiful consort of King Siharat, known (after her death several hundred years ago) as Lady Whiteblood. She was loved and respected as a mother by local people in the Malay Peninsula from Nakhon Si Thammarat to Phatthalung.

Ajan Banyat recalled that when he was a young boy in the 1940s there was no electricity in Bolo Village, no television to watch, no radios to listen to at night. "After dinner young people would go out to visit each other. Small children served their old relatives by walking up and down their backs to relieve them from the aches of all the bending they had to do when they worked in the rice fields. When I was little, I was often called upon to massage the back of my great aunt. To keep me from getting bored my aunt told me all kinds of stories. I was so absorbed in the stories that I forgot how long I had been walking up and down her back." Since Bolo Village has an ancient history, Banyat's great aunt never ran out of stories for him or other children. These stories had been passed on from the elders, who had heard them from their ancestors.

Even in the 1950s, Ajan Banyat tells us, "At night devout Buddhists stayed home to do the chants taught to them by monks. Old people who could not read the Pali texts knew the Buddha's discourses and mantras by heart. My great aunt could remember all the sermons she had ever heard as well as chants and recitations. Along with other old people she chanted aloud every night. Visitors who walked into Bolo Village at night would hear loud chants coming from every house." Chanting, a form of meditation, serves to transform the mind by helping it develop clarity and stability. By repeating a mantra over and over again, it is hoped that the mind will become focused, distracting thoughts will cease to arise, and the devotee will enter into deep meditation. Chanting a mantra or a sutta provided the villagers with security of mind and protection from wild animals or bad spirits. These were skillful ways to engage in the practice of Dhamma.

Frank Exell, the schoolmaster turned bank manager, visited Phatthalung in the early 1930s and noted that "the Siamese had two qualities of which any people can be proud. These were their respect for age and their fondness for their children. Aged parents were an accepted responsibility and there was no pleasanter sight than the smile on the wrinkled face of a grandmother as she watched her grandchildren at play."

Elderly Buddhists often lived an ascetic life, although they did not necessarily become monks or nuns. Ajan Wan Uttamo (b. 1922) recalled that in Hollow Palm Tree Village, where he was born, the Vessantara Jataka festival lasted several days. Elderly people from other Lao villages in Sakon Nakhon often came at that time to stay at his village wat to observe the Eight Precepts and listen to the recitations. These devout elders, women as well as men, were highly respected by villagers.

In the course of his wanderings through the forests of northeastern Siam, Ajan Man occasionally came across women who were highly skilled in meditation. The forest master spent the last five years of his life, from 1945 to 1949, at the forest wat near the Village of Phu Tree Pond (Ban Nong Phu) in Sakon Nakhon. Ban Nong Phu was far away from the nearest gravel road. The only way to reach the village was by walking or riding in an oxcart. The direct route took three or four hours on foot. The indirect route by oxcart took more than eight hours. Ajan Wiriyang, one of the monks who lived at the forest hermitage, recalled, "The village was located in the midst of a dense forest full of hardwood trees. It was in a valley in the Phu Phan Mountains. If one looked at the village setting from the top of a mountain, it was like the inside of a wok. To get to the village one had to cross a small steam that never ran dry."

There were eighty households in the village. The inhabitants, Ajan Wiriyang recalled, were Lao Yo and Phu Thai who "lived in thatched huts. Well-to-do families had wooden houses. People wove their own cloth. They were self-sufficient. The Un River, with its banks lined with bamboo trees, was the lifeline of the village. The people had plenty to eat. Their lives were peaceful." One of the village elders was an eighty-year-old white-robed ascetic. Young monks and novices at the forest wat called her Grandma. When the meditation master Ajan Man met Grandma, he recognized her high attainment and told his disciples that she had surpassed many monks. The discussions that took place at the forest wat between Ajan Man and Grandma about the experiences of meditation fascinated the monks and novices, who believed that Grandma possessed the psychic power to read their minds. They therefore kept up their guard. According to a disciple of Ajan Man, one of the reasons the forest master stayed at this particular wat for such a long time was because of this old white-robed ascetic and her attainment. Unlike all the young monks, who were afraid of Ajan Man, Grandma held her own.

A year after Ajan Man's death in 1949, Maha Bua, one of Ajan Man's attendants, returned to Phu Tree Pond Village to spend the rains retreat at the forest wat there. Grandma was still alive. Using a cane to support herself, she often walked to the wat, which was on higher ground than the village. Even though her house was only four hundred meters from the wat, Maha Bua tells us that Grandma had to stop five times to catch her breath. She came to visit Maha Bua to discuss Dhamma. Monks at the forest wat generally lowered their voices when they spoke. Grandma talked in her normal voice. Ajan Maha Bua recalled, "She talked loudly. Her knowledge came from personal experience. She never went to school. She was not literate. She spoke Dhamma cheerfully. Monks and novices enjoyed hanging around her. Listening to her talk was fascinating."

SOURCES

Phra Maha Chanya Suthiyano, *Chiwit lae ngan khong than Paññananda* (1991), pp. 5–6.

Interview with Phra Maha Banyat, abbot of Wat Bolo, June 29, 2001.

F. K. Exell, *In Siamese Service* [1922–36] (1967), p. 47.

For accounts about the white-robed ascetic, see Phra Maha Bua Nanasampanno, *Prawat Than Phra Ajan Man Bhuridatta Thera* (1971), p. 313; and Maha Bua Nanasampanno, *Yotnam bon baibua* (2000), pp. 178–179.

Phra Wiriyang Sirintharo, "Prawat Phra Ajan Man," in *Prawat Phra Ajan Man chabap sombun* (1978), pp. 137–138.

33

TIGERS AND CROCODILES

IN OLD Siam everyone was familiar with the proverb "Go by land, you meet a tiger; go by river, you meet a crocodile." This old saying conveys something of the difficulties and discomfort people endured when they traveled. Jean-Baptiste Pallegoix, the French bishop who lived in Siam for twenty-four years, described some of the hardships the nineteenth-century Western traveler experienced. "The usual manner to travel is to go by boat on the river and canals; when one is obliged to go on land, since there are neither horses nor carts, one goes on foot or on an elephant or by carts pulled by buffaloes. During these journeys one has to suffer many privations and inconveniences. For example, it happens that one is devoured at night by clouds of mosquitoes sucking blood which do not let you close an eye, or else, during the night legions of ants which are called fire ants (*mot fai*) burst in on your clothes and by their stinging bites quickly force you to move away. One is exposed to various dangers. On the water one must arm against crocodiles; on land one fears the tiger. Snakes sometimes slip under the mat on which you are sleeping. When you put your hand in your pocket, a scorpion stings you with its venomous tail."

Thudong monks normally traveled on foot and spent many nights in forests. An experienced thudong monk knew that in the forest it was not safe to sleep outside his klot. Once, when he neglected his teacher's instruction,

Ajan Phu Chanthakesaro (1830–1933), who escaped
death by snakebite in the story "Lord Buddha and King
Cobra," had a close call with a tiger. Ajan Phu had been
walking through a forest almost nonstop since dawn. In
the afternoon, in need of rest, he laid his klot and
almsbowl on the ground and sat down under the shade of
a huge tree. He was so tired that he fell asleep instantly.
Shortly before dusk Phu had the feeling that somebody
was touching his head. He opened his eyes. With mindfulness he looked up and saw that this somebody was a
tiger licking his shaved head. As soon as Ajan Phu was
fully awake, the tiger walked away. It was a big striped
animal about three and a half meters long. As it turned
away, Ajan Phu could hear the tiger's "ankles" crack. The
thudong monk did not know how long it had been watching him. Being mindful and not making any abrupt moves
probably saved Ajan Phu's life.

On his travels through the hinterlands of Siam, Henri
Mouhot, the French naturalist, often came across crocodiles. In 1859 Mouhot wrote, "Crocodiles are more numerous in the river at Paknam-Ven than in that at
Chantaboun. I continually saw them throw themselves
from the banks into the water; and it has frequently happened that careless fishers, or persons who have impru-
dently fallen asleep on the shore, have become their prey,
or have afterward died of the wounds inflicted by them.
This latter has happened twice during my stay here."

Martha Bassenne, the wife of a French medical doctor,
spent two years in Laos and Siam with her husband. In a
journal entry dated November 9, 1909, Bassenne described what she saw from the stream-powered launch
that was taking the French couple up the Nam Sane to
Vientiane. "At sunset, on the sandy river-banks, crocodiles stretched their long, scaly bodies, the color of dried
mud. One of the attractions of traveling up the Mekong
was to shoot at these large saurians. They testified a pro-

found indifference to our gun-shots when the bullets did not reach them. They did not even lift their heads at the projectile. But, when hit, they instantly dived with supreme skill. At the surface of the water then appeared a large pool of blood and they died at the bottom of the stream where their corpses served as food for their brothers."

It was not unusual for thudong monks on foot in the wildernesses of the Central Plains to encounter both crocodiles and tigers, although not necessarily on the same day. Ajan Phu, who spent decades wandering before he became abbot of Wat In, had another close call, this time with a crocodile in a forest pool. The monk had been walking all morning. Around noon he came across two ponds in the middle of the forest. He looked around and saw two huts not far from one of the ponds. Putting his thudong gear on the ground, Ajan Phu, wearing only his bath sarong, walked toward the nearest pond to bathe. Just before he stepped into the water he heard a villager shout, "Venerable Father, don't go into that pond! Nobody takes a bath there! The crocodiles are ferocious!" The thudong monk ignored the warning and went into the pond. While bathing in a shallow part of the pond he noticed some unusually big bubbles in front of him. Then he spotted a crocodile. It was about six meters away. Its body was in the water, but its mouth was above the surface. There was no chance to get away. As the crocodile swam toward him the monk kept his mind focused so that fear could not enter. He stood still, silently recited the mantra, "*Araham, Araham, Araham.*" When the crocodile reached him, Phu could feel its mouth touch his belly and the sides of his body. For some reason the crocodile did not or could not open its jaws. After nuzzling the monk's body for a few moments, the crocodile turned and swam to the far shore.

As soon as Ajan Phu got out of the pond, and before he could change into a dry lower garment, the villagers from the nearby huts appeared. They prostrated themselves at his feet and requested protective amulets. Ajan Phu made them amulets from whatever materials he found right where he was. Before giving them the amulets that he had blessed, he taught them to overcome their fear by chanting a mantra. To protect the villagers from incurring the karma of violence, Ajan Phu told them to undertake the Five Precepts, the first of which forbids the harming of living beings, including crocodiles. This was Ajan Phu's skillful way of using amulets and mantras as vehicles to teach villagers to practice Dhamma. The thudong monk then continued his journey.

Fig. 35 A crocodile allowing a bird to pick insects from its mouth for food.

SOURCES

Jean-Baptiste Pallegoix, *Description of the Thai Kingdom or Siam: Thailand under King Mongkut* (1854; 2000), p. 414.

Henri Mouhot, *Travels in the Central Parts of Indo-China (Siam), Cambodia and Laos during the Years 1858, 1859, and 1860* (1864), vol. 1, p. 152.

Marthe Bassenne, *In Laos and Siam* (1912; 1995), pp. 22–23.

Ajan Phu Chanthakesaro's story was told by Phra Khru Woraphatkhun, deputy abbot of Wat Intharawihan in Bangkok. See Sombat Kongsoi, *Kao Phra Ajans* (n.d.), pp. 51–58.

34

WHITE-ROBED RENUNCIANTS

AJAN FAN was born in Ban Hai, a Phu Thai village in Sakon Nakhon. His grandfather and granduncles were sons of the Lord of Muang Wang, today in Laos. In 1841 King Rama III (r. 1824–51) sent a Lao official to persuade the people of Muang Wang, on the east bank of the Mekong River, to relocate to the west bank in northeastern Siam. Fan's grandfather and granduncles led a large number of people across the Mekong to the area known today as Sakon Nakhon. They established a new settlement called Muang Phanna. To govern the new muang, the Phu Thai lords relied upon the hereditary political hierarchy. The top positions, in descending order of status, were the Chao Muang, the Upparat, the Ratchawong, and the Ratchabut. Authority over local people and the right to succession were held by local lords who paid annual tribute to Siam. Siam's kings confirmed these appointments; hence, the local nobility retained their influence locally. In 1844 Ajan Fan's grandfather became the Upparat, the second highest position, of the new muang.

One of the many boys who crossed the Mekong to live in the new Phu Thai settlement was Noina, whose name means custard apple. Noina studied the Thai Noi language and later served as an official in the Muang Phanna court. He married a Phu Thai woman. They had one daughter whom they named Dokpi (after a flower). The people of Phanna had to send an annual tribute in gold

Fig. 36 The Northeast of Thailand

to the king of Siam. A considerable amount of gold was required, and the people had to pan for it. Noina was one of the Phanna officials who made the annual trek to Muang Wang, their old home on the other side of the Mekong, in order to gather gold from the river for Siam's king. During the last of these treks Noina realized that he was fed up with living a householder's life. Once he got back to Phanna, he fled into the forests of Phu Phan Mountain without telling anyone. He put on a white robe, kept his long hair tied in a knot on top of his head, lived in a cave at the foot of Phu Phan, and observed Eight Precepts. For the rest of his life Noina was a vegetarian, eating only greens, taro, yams, and pumpkins. He lived the *brahmacariya* life, remaining celibate until he died. Local people believed that he had attained a high level of *abhiñña* (supernormal knowledge). They referred to him as Chao Phukha and regarded him as *saksit* (sacred). The cave in which he lived was called the Chao Phukha Cave.

In 1877, during King Chulalongkorn's reign, Haw brigands from southern China took over Vientiane. The king ordered Lord Suwan of Phanna to conscript the Phu Thai, provide them with weapons and food supplies, and march them to Vientiane to join Siam's troops. The purpose of the military campaign was to eradicate the Haw bandits and protect Siam's tribute interests. Lord Suwan, serving as the troops' general, and accompanied by his deputy and assistant lords, led the local militia to Vientiane. The Haw had a reputation for being fierce, and the Phu Thai were fearful that they might get killed. Before leaving for Vientiane the Phu Thai leaders went to visit Chao Phukha at his cave to ask for his blessing. The holy man, in giving his blessing, reminded the leaders to maintain their moral virtue. He told them not to abuse women and not to take things that were not given to them. The holy man then gave the troop leaders a quantity of sand wrapped in white cloth. He told them to sprinkle this sand on every soldier's head before the fighting began so that they would be able to survive the bullets of the Haw.

Once the Phu Thai troops joined the Bangkok army in Vientiane they built a fortress outside the city. One day Lord Suwan performed a ritual in which he called upon the ancestor spirits, who resided in Muang Phanna, to come and guard them. Lord Suwan also prayed to Chao Phukha for protection: "May the bodies of the Phanna soldiers be soft like the water weed and light like cotton." After the prayer the Phanna leaders sprinkled the holy sand on all the soldiers' heads. The religious ritual empowered the soldiers. With renewed energy, armed only with swords and spears, they attacked the Haw garrison. Haw bullets flew everywhere, but not a single Phanna soldier was hit. Once the Haw had been driven out of Vientiane, the Phanna soldiers were allowed to go home.

Chao Phukha died of old age on December 19, 1884. On the day he died, his daughter, Dokpi, who lived in Egg Mango Village, gave birth to a boy. He was given the name Dham (from Dhamma). Because his birth coincided with the death of his maternal grandfather, local people believed that the boy was Chao Phukha's reincarnation.

Ajan Fan was born fourteen years later, in 1898. By then Rama V had established the colonial system of provincial administration that put all local lords in northeastern Siam under the bureaucratic control of the Bangkok government. Fan's father, a son of the Upparat, had been demoted to mere headman of Egg Mango Village in 1892. Muang Phanna became a district in Sakon Nakhon. In 1899 Bangkok authorities abolished the tribute requirement. The tribute payment was replaced by a four baht head tax that was levied upon every able-bodied man. Between 1901 and 1902, when Fan was only two or three years old, a succession of rebellions led by holy men swept through the northeastern region of Siam and the Lao states. Like the people of Phanna, the Lao in the Northeast looked up to holy men and turned to them for guidance, especially in times of crisis or hardship.

The imposition of the head tax and the harshness of government officials from Bangkok were two of the primary factors that sparked the rebellions. Many of these government officials were contemptuous of the people over whom they ruled and often did not even speak the same language. A succession of poor harvests and increasing poverty also drove villagers to seek the support of local ascetics. Some were former monks who had exchanged the ocher robes for white in order to be able to take action to alleviate the suffering of local people. White-robed ascetics were highly regarded locally as men and women who possessed superior moral qualities. The 1901–02 rebellions, which became armed skirmishes after efforts at negotiation proved useless, were brutally crushed by the Siamese government.

During the first decades of the twentieth century Fan witnessed the suffering his relatives endured under the government officials sent from Bangkok to replace them. When he was still a young boy Fan left his village to study with his brother-in-law, a deputy district official in Khon Kaen. His family wanted Fan to enter the civil service once he grew up, but contact with some senior officials made Fan change his mind. In Khon Kaen the young Fan had the duty of carrying food to convicts. One of the prisoners was the hereditary governor of a muang who had been convicted of murder. Later, when Fan's sister's husband was transferred to Muang Loei and Fan traveled there to visit him, he found that his brother-in-law, too, had been charged with murder. Fan's experiences and those of his relatives convinced him that his chances of obtaining a secure livelihood in the new civil service system were weak at best. He had seen how far many local nobles had fallen. Fan left Loei and, after walking barefoot for ten days, returned to his home village. Discouraged by the dismal prospects of the lay life, Fan took up the ocher robes at the age of ten. In 1918, when he reached twenty, Fan took higher ordination as a monk at a wat in his natal village.

As a young monk Fan learned to practice meditation under the guidance of Aya Khu Dham, the reincarnation of Chao Phukha, who had became abbot of the Monastery of Golden Termite Hill near Bathong Village. People called him Aya Khu, the local term for Venerable Teacher. Village abbots were now expected to stay at their monasteries all year, but Aya Khu continued to spend a good part of each year living in a forest. He enjoyed teaching meditation to his pupils. After the end of each rains retreat, he took Fan and other young monks to live for four months in the wild, where they camped in caves or forest cemeteries to practice meditation. Aya Khu Dham was one of the most revered abbots in Sakon Nakhon. Some years after the Sangha Centralization Act of 1902 was passed, Aya Khu Dham was appointed sangha head of Sakon Nakhon. His administrative duties made it impossible for him to go on thudong to spend the dry season in meditation retreat.

In their wanderings, young thudong monks often encountered yogis, sages, and white-robed ascetics who were highly respected by local people and who often surpassed monks in meditation. In 1933 Ajan Lui (b. 1902) spent a rains retreat in a cave on a mountain in Sakon Nakhon. One day when he went to the Village of Beautiful Termite Hill for almsround, the villagers told him about two white-robed women (*mae khao*), Chan and Yo, who were living at a hermitage near Ban Pa Songkhon, a village in Songkhon Forest. Local people believed that Chan and Yo had supernormal powers. When the rains retreat was over Ajan Lui went to visit the renunciants at their hermitage. In the course of discussing Dhamma with them, he found that they had been practicing *mangkai*, a local term for the meditation on the thirty-two parts of the body. Ajan Lui realized that their understanding of Dhamma, derived from meditation practice, was deeper than his own. He was greatly inspired. Once he got back to his cave, he worked hard, day and night, until he mastered the meditation method that the two renunciants had been practicing.

Holy men and lay renunciants have been around since ancient times. Local histories of muangs or settlements reveal that it was religious persons—either monks, former monks, or men and women who led a different kind of life from the majority of householders—who were the important leaders of a community. In addition to monks, other significant holy men and women—who were not monastics—included *rishi*, hermits who dwelt outside the community and practiced meditation; *chipa khao*, white-robed ascetics; and *mo tham*, former monks who were skilled in healing through mantras and meditation.

Local histories of the Lao in the Northeast, the Yuan in the northern region, and the Mon and Siamese of the Central Plains reveal that holy ascetics were closely associated with a kingdom, principality, or settlement, either as respected founders or as community advisors. The deeds of five rishis have been recorded in three important works, the *Mulasasana*, the *Jinakalamali*, and the *Phongsawadan Yonok*. Rishi Sudeva was the founder of several muangs, one of which was Hariphunchai (Lamphun), first ruled by Queen Camadevi. Rishi Anusisa founded Muang Satchanalai (near Sukhothai); and Rishi Sukadanta founded Muang Lavo (Lopburi) as well as many villages. Rishis were also associated with mountains: Buddhajatila with Doi Pa Tai, near Lamphun; Subrahma with Doi Ngam, also near Lamphun; and Sudeva (Thai: Suthep) with Doi Suthep near Chiang Mai. These hermits were ordained as Buddhist monks in their youth and then disrobed to live as householders. In time they became dissatisfied with lay life, and it is then that they became rishis. Through living an ascetic life and practicing meditation they attained the five higher knowledges: psychic power, divine hearing, telepathy, recollection of previous births, and divine eye.

In Lao traditions local people called male elders Pho Yai, which means Great Father. Pho Yai Khamma (1891–

1990) was a lay ascetic who lived into the last decade of the twentieth century. He was a former monk and master artist. Most of the exquisite works of art in monasteries in Roi Et and other provinces in the northeastern region were created by him and his pupils. Because he could create such beautiful work out of ordinary materials, many people believed that he was a deity reborn as a master artist. In an interview Pho Yai Khamma said that before the imposition of state Buddhism, lay renunciants were often highly influential; that many holy men, sages, and lay ascetics, women as well as men, were prominent figures in local communities. When asked, in 1989, why then have we not heard much about lay renunciants, their influence, and their contributions to local communities, the ninety-eight-year-old Pho Yai replied, "Who is going to believe us?"

SOURCES

For the story of the founding of Muang Phanna and the Haw bandits, see Toem Wiphakphotchakit, *Prawatsat Isan* (1999), pp. 254–262, 222–223.

The story about Chao Phukha and Aya Khu Dham was told by Ajan Fan Acharo in Suphon Nachom, *Chiwaprawat lae patipatha Phra Ajan Fan Acharo* (1977), pp. 255–259, 10–11, 147–148.

For accounts of the holy men's rebellion, see John B. Murdoch, "The 1901–1902 'Holy Men's' Rebellion" (1974), pp. 47–66; Charles Keyes, "Millennialism, Theravada Buddhism, and Thai Society" (1977), pp. 283–302; and Tej Bunnag, *Kabot R.S. 121* (1987).

For Ajan Lui's account, see Suriphan, *Chiwaprawat Luang Pu Lui Chanthasaro* (1990), p. 45.

The discussion of the role of holy men in early history is from

Constance M. Wilson, "The Holy Man in the History of Thailand and Laos" (1997), pp. 345–364.

In *The End of the Absolute Monarchy in Siam* (1986), p. 12, historian Benjamin A. Batson writes that "the late nineteenth-century Thai government, with its goals of technological development, rationalization of the administration, and expansion of central government control to areas remote from the center, was in many aspects similar to colonial regimes in neighboring countries, and the Thai official sent from Bangkok to supervise the administration in Chiang Mai or Ubon was only somewhat less 'foreign' than the British district officer in Malaya or the French resident in Indochina."

For a discussion of the Mulasasana, the Jinakalamali, and Phongsawadan Yonok, see Dhida Saraya, "The Development of the Northern Tai States from the Twelfth to Fifteenth Centuries" (1982); and Donald K. Swearer, "Myth, Legend and History in the Northern Thai Chronicles" (1974), pp. 67–88.

Interview with Pho Yai Khamma Saeng-ngam, June 24, 1989. I am grateful to Ajan Arkhom Worachinda, director of Isan Studies, University of Maha Sarakham, for taking me to Ban Khamin in Roi Et to interview Pho Yai at his home.

35

TAP TAO CAVE

IN THE early ninth century, after the city of Hariphunchai (Lamphun) was built, a group of rishis invited
Princess Camadevi to come from Lavo (Lopburi) and establish her dynastic lineage there. Rishi Sudeva, the
founder of Hariphunchai, is believed to have been the
progenitor of the Lawa people and the protective spirit
of Chiang Mai. Today the Lawa are a distinct minority,
but chronicles reveal that around the time of the founding of Lopburi, the Lawa in the Chiang Mai region were
well established before the arrival of Tai Yuan people.
Palm-leaf records show that the Lawa were city builders,
expert metalworkers, and designers of irrigation systems.

The custom of making pilgrimages was established by
Buddhists in Siam as far back as the fourteenth century.
A Sukhothai inscription from this period indicates that a
senior monk, Mahathera Si Sattha, undertook pilgrimages to Hariphunchai Stupa and to other sacred shrines
containing relics of the Buddha. Throughout the nineteenth century monks and laypeople of all local traditions
in Siam continued to follow the custom of going on pilgrimage on foot, for it provided pilgrims with an opportunity to use the difficulties they experienced as a means
to purify their minds and to accumulate merit. Paintings
on the walls of the ordination halls in many monasteries
often depict monks and laypeople of all classes on their
way to sacred sites. The Buddha's Footprint in Saraburi
was the nearest pilgrimage site for people who lived in

Bangkok and other parts of the Central Plains. For the Lao, the Yuan, and the Shan of the northern principalities, the destinations were stupas—shrines holding sacred relics. People from Chiang Mai went to the stupa on Doi Suthep; the people of Lamphun went to Hariphunchai Stupa; and people from Mae Hong Son went to Kongmu Stupa on Kongmu Mountain. Some pilgrims made the effort to travel far from their villages to practice meditation in caves that contained Buddha images. One of the most celebrated of these caves was Tap Tao Cave. This was the nearest pilgrimage site for the people of Muang Fang, today a district in Chiang Mai province.

Making a pilgrimage required considerable preparation, commitment, and effort on the part of laypeople. The pilgrims had to carry food for the entire journey. Monks, white-robed ascetics, and laypeople camped overnight in the woods. The rich traveled by elephant and took their servants with them. In spite of the hardships, many lay Buddhists were eager to go on a pilgrimage. The trip provided women, who rarely got a chance to travel, with a big break from their responsibilities at home, and the difficult journey was joyful because people went in groups.

The relatively few Westerners who traveled extensively throughout Siam and the Lao states in the nineteenth century reported having seen white-robed women (*mae chi*) inside the monasteries they visited. Sometimes called "nuns," these were, and still are, women who have taken the Eight or Ten Precepts and live an ascetic religious life. One Westerner was understandably surprised to encounter white-robed women, out in the middle of nowhere, on the way to Tap Tao Cave.

Between 1881 and 1893 James McCarthy, superintendent of surveys for the Siamese government, criss-crossed the North with his assistants, carrying on the work of surveying for the purpose of obtaining accurate information

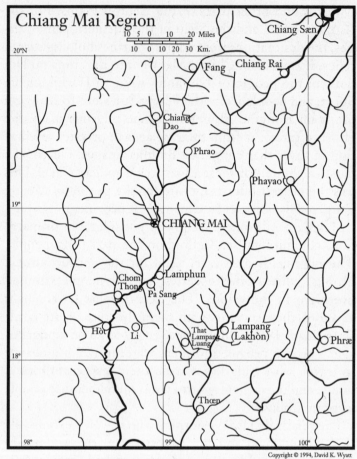

Copyright © 1994, David K. Wyatt

Fig. 37 Chiang Mai and surrounding region

for maps and with a view toward potential telegraph and railway routes. On one of his journeys in the month of February during the dry season, McCarthy arrived at Chiang Dao, "an irregularly shaped village, surrounded by a rickety palisade," on a mountain that he ascertained was 7,160 feet above sea level. As he was leaving Chiang Dao (today a district in Chiang Mai), the Irish surveyor saw a small group of elderly white-robed women travel-

ing without men. The ascetics were carrying their be-
longings and had been camping out, much like wandering monks. They had already walked from a village in
Lampang to Chiang Mai.

"Leaving Chiang Dao, I met four old ladies on a pilgrimage to Taptao Cave," McCarthy wrote. "The youngest one was over sixty. Dressed in white, in a habit like a
nun's, they had walked from Lakawn [Lampang], and had
been to Prabat Si Roi [the Buddha's Footprint at Si Roi].
They told me they would not be sorry if they died when
making their pilgrimage. To lighten their burdens, I undertook the care of some few things they were carrying,
and promised to have them safely delivered at the cave.
The fact of these ladies traveling about the country, and
camping out, sometimes in the jungle, far from any village, shows that the regularly beaten tracks are free, at
least, from the danger of wild animals." Relatively free,
one might add.

McCarthy had been told that Tap Tao Cave was the
abode of terrible spirits. When he got there he "handed
over the lady-pilgrims' property, and entered the sacred
cave, which was far from inviting. It contained numerous
statues of Buddha, and dark recesses said to lead to all
sorts of fabulous places."

In the nineteenth century Tap Tao Cave was not easy
to get to. Although McCarthy, accustomed to strenuous
hiking himself, did not describe the effort it took to get
to the cave, another Western traveler did. In the early
1880s, Carl Bock, the Norwegian travel book writer who
was exploring northern Siam, came to Muang Fang.
While waiting for his supplies to arrive, Bock's boredom
was broken by the sight of "a group of pilgrims from the
Ngiou [Shan] country, . . . accompanied by a yellow-
robed priest or two, on their way to the famous cave of
Tam tap tao, there to offer their devotions and gifts to
the great Buddha."

Fig. 38 The view from Muang Fang

Seeing the pilgrims inspired Bock to go visit the pilgrimage site himself. In March, the dry season, Bock and his party of six men, led by a native guide, set out with three elephants. Bock wrote, "The road lay all day across the plain surrounding Muang Fang, sometimes through thin forest and bamboo-groves, but mostly through long, rank jungle-grass which the Laosians cut for roofing their huts. At several places the grass had taken fire, through the intense heat of the last few days, and at one spot the flames were so fierce and the smoke so dense that we had to make a detour through the forest, the elephants being afraid of fire." In the forest Bock met another group of Shan pilgrims. "Here we came to a camp of twenty-five or thirty Ngious [Shan], men, women, and children, returning from a visit to Tam tap tao, where they had offered their gifts of cloth, wax tapers, and gold leaves. We camped close by, and left again early next morning, arriving at the cavern about noon."

It took Bock and his men a day and a half to get to the cave from Muang Fang. Describing the famous cavern, Bock wrote, "The entrance to the cave itself is between seventy and eighty feet up the steep side of a limestone hill some 300 feet high, rising suddenly from the plateau, which is itself 600 feet above sea-level. The footway up the hill is very difficult to traverse, starting at first in water, and gradually rising along the sharp edges of fractured rock, which neither time nor weather nor the traffic of centuries of pilgrimages had smoothed away, till it leads at last along the top of a precipice down which one false step would throw the traveller to certain death among huge boulders, tree-trunks, and pools of water. The cavern itself," Bock continues, "was of interesting formation, the roof being a fantastic array of stalactites of various forms. High up in the centre of the roof, which was probably sixty feet in height, was a natural skylight, through which a dusky beam of light fell on the head of a gigantic recumbent figure of the Buddha, in as the leg-end runs, his 'dying attitude,' lying on an elevated plat-form in the centre of the cave: but this light from above only made the rest of the great cave appear darker by comparison, so I lighted my lamp in order thoroughly to explore the interior."

Inside Tap Tao Cave Bock saw traces of the wandering monks who had been there. "All around the central god [the main Buddha image] was an assemblage of figures, half life-size, of the same material as the great Buddha, representing disciples of the great Master, sitting and praying or listening, with uplifted folded hands. Every one of these smaller figures was covered with a great number of yellow rags and skull-caps on their heads, left by the priests as token of their devotion."

In 1880 Holt Hallett, a British engineer, went to see Tap Tao Cave in the company of an American mission-ary, the Reverend Daniel McGilvary, and another com-panion named Martin. McGilvary spoke local languages fluently and served as interpreter for Hallett. "On dis-mounting at the foot of the hill," Hallett writes, "we camped for breakfast, and then started on foot to the cave amidst a heavy shower of rain. Before we had proceeded 50 feet, we found that we should have to wade nearly up to our waists in the icy water flowing out of the face of the hill, and therefore returned to rearrange our toilets." The Westerners supplemented their own attire with vari-ous pieces of native clothing and, like the locals, went barefoot. "I put on a Burmese Shan costume, topped by a waterproof coat; Mr. Martin wore a flannel shirt under a coat, and a Siamese *panoung* [sarong] or petticoat; whilst Dr. McGilvary draped himself in a gossamer waterproof, and carried a pair of sleeping-drawers to put on when he reached the cave. None of us wore shoes or stockings, and the sharp fragments of limestone in the path made us walk very gingerly."

From Hallett's report we can imagine what it must have been like for the four elderly women ascetics to climb up to the cave. Hallett continues, "After leaving the brook, we scrambled up a slope of shattered limestone and great blocks that had tumbled down from the cliff until the path lay up the face of the precipice, when it became so difficult as to make me rather dread the return journey. On reaching the entrance, we found it ornamented with stuccoed figures of spirits, having bird bodies, and elephant tusks and trunk in lieu of a beak."

Inside, Hallett reports, "was a lofty cavern lighted by a natural skylight. On a raised platform in the cave was a great reclining image of Buddha, some 30 feet long, and around it a number of figures representing his disciples. Numerous small wooden and stone images of Buddha had been placed by pious pilgrims about the platform. Pillows, mattresses, robes, yellow drapery, flags, water-bottles, rice-bowls, fans, dolls, images of temples, . . . houses for the spirits, and all sorts of trumpery, were lying together, with fresh and faded flowers that had been offered to the images, and were strewn in front of them. A steep ladder led up to niches near the roof of the cave, in which other images were enshrined."

Hallett did not explore the cave, but his friends did. "My companions, who were full of ardour, determined to explore the inner recesses of the cave, and accordingly lighted their torches and proceeded farther into the bowels of the earth, whilst I enjoyed a quiet smoke amongst the gods. Down they went creeping through narrow low passages, over rocks, and along ledges, with chasms and pits lining their path as the cave expanded, bottomless as far as they could judge by the faint light of their torches, but really not more than 20 or 30 feet deep, until they could get no farther, and had to return, having proceeded about an eighth of a mile."

Westerners approached the interior of the cave with a

sense of adventure and to show that the local belief in guardian spirits was silly. The pilgrims believed that before they entered the caves they needed to purify themselves by strictly observing sila: Five Precepts for laypeople and Eight or Ten Precepts for lay ascetics. Once they entered the cave they had to maintain their mindfulness; otherwise, if the spirits wished to punish them, they could become disoriented and not get out alive. The faith of the pilgrims did not need proof. If the cave was said to be holy, they believed it. Local people did not undertake a pilgrimage lightly. The average commoner had to face the prospect of losing his or her life on the way to or from the cave. The threat of attack by tigers, elephants, or snakes was omnipresent, and people also feared ghosts. For these reasons pilgrims generally went in groups, preferably with a monk, because it was believed that monks were capable of providing them with protection from anything that might menace them on the way. The fact that the four elderly women traveled by themselves indicates that they had great faith in their spiritual practice.

As recently as the 1950s many caves like Tap Tao were still far from the beaten path. Wandering monks continued to travel to Tap Tao Cave on foot, and some stayed at the cave to meditate for weeks on end. Total ease of access, provided in the late twentieth century, has diminished the purpose of the pilgrimage, which was to use the difficulty of getting to the site as a way to purify the mind so that the pilgrim could have a clearer idea of the difficulties and joys of the bodhisat practice.

SOURCES

For information on the Lawa, see *Inter-Ethnic Relations in the Making of Mainland Southeast Asia and Southwestern China* (2000), p. ix.

For the Sukhothai inscription and information on Rishi Sudeva, see Dhida Saraya, "The Development of the Northern Tai States from the Twelfth to Fifteenth Centuries" (1982), pp. 133–134.

James McCarthy, *Surveying and Exploring in Siam* (1900), pp. 126–127.

Carl Bock, *Temples and Elephants* (1884; 1986), pp. 288–290.

Holt S. Hallett, *A Thousand Miles on an Elephant in the Shan States* (1890), pp. 343–344.

For the legend of Camadevi, composed by Mahathera Bodhiramsi in the early fifteenth century, see *The Legend of Queen Cama* (1998), translated by Donald Swearer and Sommai Premchit.

For an account of how local Buddhists purified themselves before going on a pilgrimage to a sacred cave, see Phra Maha Sathit Tikakhayano, *Prawat tham luang Chiang Dao* (n.d).

36

FALLING MINDFULLY

IN OLD Siam the monastery was a repository for all kinds of knowledge. Monks were trained in a variety of arts and crafts, such as sculpture, painting, masonry, carpentry, and wood carving. In their travels Westerners often saw village monks engaged in physical labor. During their stay in Bangkok in 1822, John Crawfurd and George Finlayson, British envoys, explored many monasteries on the banks of the Chao Phraya River. In one monastery the visitors saw monks at work painting and sculpting. Carl Bock, the Norwegian travel writer who came to Siam in the early 1880s, noted that monks "spend their leisure time in painting and decorating the temples, while during the dry seasons they perform pilgrimages to caves." In the 1890s H. Warrington Smyth spent a night at a monastery in Paknam Pho (Nakhon Sawan province) "where the monks were busy rebuilding the landings and the *sala*, or rest-house."

When Siam was still sparsely populated, village monks and novices constructed most of the buildings in their monasteries and kept them in good repair. Laymen either were too busy with their own work in the paddy fields and orchards to help much or were away from the village working for their overlords. Sometimes village men came to help the monks once they were freed from their own work. But there were two tasks that villagers, young monks, and novices were afraid of: restoring the stupa and repairing the roof of the uposatha or vihara. To be on the roof meant being above the Buddha image inside the hall. This was considered disrespectful and brought demerit. These tasks were therefore always left to the abbot, because people believed he had superior spiritual power. When villagers came to the monasteries to ask their abbots for help with one thing or another they often found the elderly abbots up on the roof of the ordination hall or vihara, making repairs.

Ajan Chang (b. 1848) was abbot of Wat Khiankhet, a Mon monastery in Thanyaburi (today in Prathum Thani, a province on the outskirts of Bangkok). We met Ajan Chang, whose given name means "elephant," in the story "Tending Water Buffaloes." Chang grew up in a Mon village whose inhabitants had migrated to Siam from Martaban in Lower Burma. From the time he was a boy Chang helped the adults and became very good at construction work. As abbot he built most of the new buildings at the wat, including monks' quarters, a chanting hall, and the ordination hall. The Mon villagers came to help the monks. In 1906 Ajan Chang began building a two-story ordination hall. He was then fifty-seven years old. On one occasion, as he was climbing onto the roof, the abbot slipped and fell to the ground. The laypeople who were working with him at the construction site were horrified, but to their great surprise, the abbot got up as though nothing had happened. He then walked to his kuti to rest. There was no apparent injury to any part of his body.

Ajan Fan (1898–1977), whom we met in "White-Robed Renunciants," was a forest monk known for his skills in constructing salas and kutis and sculpting Buddha images. These skills, along with meditation practice, were taught to Fan by Aya Khu Dham, a Phu Thai abbot who was believed to be the reincarnation of a holy man. Ajan Fan was known for his ingenuity. He built a forest hermitage, consisting of kutis and a preaching sala, on the uneven rocky ground of a mountain slope, a feat villagers thought was impossible.

In March 1950, during the dry season, Ajan Fan took two disciples, a monk and a novice, to the heavily for- ested Ox Mountain in Nongkhai province, where he hoped to spend the upcoming rains retreat. The monks and novice had to spend a night in the open. In the morn- ing seven men from nearby villages brought in food sup- plies for the monks and guided them to the top of the mountain. As they walked along an elephant path in the jungle they noticed old as well as fresh tiger tracks. Ac- cording to Phra Suphon, the accompanying monk who later disrobed and wrote Ajan Fan's life story, it took the men and monks more than half a day to reach the Bud- dha Cave on the hilltop where Ajan Fan wanted to stay. The villagers spent the night on the hill, observed the Eight Precepts, listened to Ajan Fan's sermon, and medi- tated with the monks and novice until the early hours of the morning. The next day the villagers offered food to the monks and novice and cut some wood for them to use to repair the kutis. In the middle of the afternoon the village folk walked back down the mountain and returned to their homes. Throughout the dry months that the thudong monks and novice stayed on the mountain, they depended on the forest villagers for alms.

Well before the onset of the rainy season unusually heavy rains pounded the area for a day and night. A group of men from two forest villages, who had gone to visit the monks, were compelled to stay overnight at the cave because of the inclement weather. The next day Ajan Fan asked the villagers to escort him around the mountain so that he could look for medicinal herbs. The two men led the way, followed by Ajan Fan and the young monk. The novice did not go with them. At one point, the monks and laymen had to leave the track, which followed a stream, and climb a steep hill along a rocky path made slick with wet moss. The monk who accompanied Ajan Fan recalled, "The two villagers had already climbed up the slippery rock, and Ajan Fan was only one step behind. As the Ajan was about to cross the small creek, he slipped, fell down, and hit his head on the flat rock. The impact was so loud that it sounded like someone had cracked a coconut. His body began rolling downhill, head first." The young monk was shaking with fear. All he could do was watch in horror as his teacher slid past him. He could hardly keep his own balance. Ajan Fan slid downhill head first for over eighteen meters, but then his body slowed briefly in a shallow bed of moss, long enough to cause the Ajan's body to turn around before it continued to slide downhill, now feet first. The young monk thought, "There is a crevice ahead of the ajan, wide enough for a man's body to go through. The water of the stream pours through this crevice. If the ajan slides down through the crevice he will most certainly be killed."

Just before his body reached the crevice Ajan Fan suddenly got up and resumed walking as though nothing had happened. The young monk was very concerned; he asked his teacher to seek another path. Ajan Fan refused, saying, "Since the body fell on this path, it must go back to where it came down." He then went on retracing his steps up the slippery slope until he reached the villagers. Except for a few bruises on his elbows, Ajan Fan showed no sign of injury.

The thudong monks returned to the hermitage in the evening. They washed themselves clean and boiled water to drink. Then Ajan Fan did his usual walking meditation. At night, while attending his teacher, the young monk asked the ajan how he felt when his head struck the rock so hard. Ajan Fan replied, "It felt like a cotton ball hit the rock."

That accident in Ajan Fan's thudong life occurred when he was fifty-two years old. The monk telling this story in the 1970s explained that Ajan Fan did not lose mindfulness when he fell. "When Ajan Fan slipped, he was able to attain one-pointed mind within seconds before his head hit the rock. It did not hurt because in samadhi his body was as light as a cotton ball. Indeed, Ajan often taught us to be mindful at all times whether standing, walking, sitting, or sleeping."

Ajan Fan was long remembered for his compassion and healing powers. On his thudong wanderings he encountered many sick people whom he was able to heal with herbal medicines and mantras. In the early 1940s, when Ajan Fan was living in a forest near Surin and Burirum, the villagers called him "Chao Phu Mibun," a local expression for Bodhisat.

Khantipalo (b. 1932), an Englishman who was ordained as a bhikkhu in 1961 and lived in Thailand for eleven years, went to practice meditation under Ajan Fan at his forest wat. "Ajan Fan, who often spoke Phu Thai, was like everyone's idea of a favourite grandfather but an immensely powerful one. He was compassionate and tried to understand the workings of troubled 'Western' minds." Commenting on the spiritual power of Buddhist masters, Ajan Khantipalo has pointed out that "great teachers have no problems as they have seen the Four Great Elements—earth, water, fire, air—in the light of emptiness and are able to treat them as interchangeable. A fall from a high place need not wound a body if it was an 'air-body' rather than a predominantly earth-and-water body."

SOURCES

George Finlayson, *The Mission to Siam and Hue, 1821–1822* (1988), p. 220.

Carl Bock, *Temples and Elephants* (1884; 1986), p. 212.

H. Warrington Smyth, *Five Years in Siam, from 1891 to 1896* (1898), vol. 1, p. 86.

For a brief biography of Ajan Chang Dhammachoto, see *Aphinihan 59 kechi ajans* (1984), pp. 28–30.

For information about Aya Khu Dham and Ajan Fan, see Suphon Nachom, *Chiwaprawat lae patipatha Phra Ajan Fan Acharo* (1977), pp. 255–259, 10–11, 147–148.

Ajan Khantipalo (Laurence Mills), personal communication, September 19, 1997. In 1978 Khantipalo established Wat Buddha Dhamma in Wisemans Ferry, Australia, where he taught for fourteen years. He is the cofounder of the Bodhi Citta Buddhist Centre, a nonsectarian place of practice in Queensland.

37

MEETING THE TIGER IN SILENCE

IN THE 1920s Hermann Norden, fellow of the Royal Geographical Society of Great Britain, fellow of the American Geographical Society, and professional writer of travel memoirs, was touring in northern Lao territory then occupied by the French. Norden stopped at Chiang Khong, the old capital of a Lao kingdom on the high plateau, now an important village in Tran Ninh. The French administrator there provided an Annamite soldier, who had lived in Laos and spoke both the local dialect and rudimentary French, to accompany Norden to Muang You. Norden called his new assistant "Three-sixty-three," which was his military identification number.

Muang You, formerly a frontier post of Luang Prabang, was on the Khan River, a tributary of the Mekong. To get to the Khan River, Norden, his Annamite assistant, and the Lao bearers had first to travel on horseback for two days across Tran Ninh province. The party started out at dawn. Moved by the natural scene, Norden wrote, "We had the trails to ourselves; beautiful trails very rarely travelled by any European. Sometimes we skirted ravines, and often we passed through jungles of vegetation: palms with fronds like huge feathers; great clumps of trees grown together out of which orchids sprouted. I saw other flowers of brilliant hues—hibiscus, rhododendrons, azaleas."

The men stopped for lunch at a telegraph station that consisted of two bamboo huts at the edge of a clearing.

Norden reports, "From here our trail climbed and twisted. We spent the night near the crest of the ridge in a *sala* surrounded by a bamboo palisade. This barricade was six feet high and had been built to protect against tigers. Tran Ninh, so rich in mineral wealth, is also rich in ferocious animal life. Not long before my visit a young administrator who passed the night in this *sala* was amazed to find in the morning that one of his horses had disappeared. The remains, partly devoured, were found a short distance beyond the enclosure; convincing evidence that a tiger had cleared the bamboo fence and, with another prodigious leap, had carried away the strangled horse. The men in the *sala*, good sleepers all, had heard nothing."

While his assistant went looking for the chief of a nearby Hmong village, Norden thought about the tiger. Having a gun gave him a sense of security. "The fence was bent from his last visit; this time he need not jump so high. I kept my rifle in hand hoping that he would come while I was ready and waiting for him."

That night, Norden continued, "the men shared the *sala* with me; they in one room, I in the other. The danger from tigers was too great to allow anyone to sleep outside. In the night I heard the animal's triple call— bwaak . . . bwaak . . . bwaak."

Norden and his men continued their journey in the morning. "After Kone Kene our trail pitched downwards and then began a sharp climb." At noon they stopped for lunch near a place called the Hut of the Furrow. After the meal Norden told his men to take a rest while he went for a walk in the forest. "I left my gun and camera, and with only a bamboo stick set out. A little while alone in the wilderness was the experience I most desired; a chance to think and sense my surroundings undistracted by others. I had no hesitation about the trail. The one over which we had come across, a rocky stretch, climbed on before me, outlined with telegraph poles. A short way behind our resting-place I had seen the beginning of another trail which led downward. That it must be the trail to a Meo village I knew from my experience in Tong-King; I was proud of having become so jungle wise. My chosen path was in places almost obliterated by limestone, and the vegetation became sparser as I proceeded. But the telegraph poles were evidence that I was on the right road, and anyway the *commissaire* at Xieng Kouang had told me that there was only one road to Moung You. I walked rapidly on, happy in my solitude."

As Norden recalled, "The silence was heavenly, but suddenly it was broken. Bwaak . . . bwaak . . . bwaak . . . bwaak came from the distance. Came faintly at first; then louder." Norden confessed, "I had always wanted—or had thought that I wanted—to see a tiger without having to perch in a tree as the guest of an Indian maharajah, or to trap him with a goat, or go out with an electric light. I now discovered I wanted nothing of the sort. I turned and ran back as fast as I could go. When my breath gave out and I had to stop I looked at my watch. Two hours had passed since I left the men. They must have gone to sleep over their opium pipes, I thought, and I blew my hunting whistle. There was no answer. I was thoroughly frightened, but for the moment I could run no further. I dropped down on a fallen tree-trunk to gain strength for another spurt. The men must come this way sooner or later, and I tried to make it sooner by blowing the hunting whistle again and again. Finally an answer came, and after another eternity Three-sixty-three himself arrived with the horses and the coolies."

As it turned out, when the Annamite soldier failed to find Norden, he sent the Lao bearers out to search for him. Then the Annamite heard the whistle. Relieved to find Norden, a nervous Three-sixty-three advised, "Tigers are here. Let us go quickly."

"We did." Norden acknowledged, "In my desire for exercise in self-communion I had walked into the most notorious trap in all Tran Ninh. This road, lined with telegraph poles, had been abandoned because of the tiger danger. The new route travelled to Muong You was the Meo [Hmong] trail I had noticed near the Hut of the Furrow." Traveling through the wilderness in a group was frightening enough. Imagine how much more terrified Norden would have been if he had been completely alone with no chance of being rescued.

About this same time, in 1926, a young novice named Bunnak went wandering along the lower Mekong River by himself. The youngest child in his family, Bunnak was born in 1912 in a Lao village in Ubon Ratchathani in northeastern Siam. He had demonstrated a desire for the monastic life from the time he was six years old. Bunnak was so persistent that his mother finally took him to the wat and gave him to the village abbot, with whom he lived as a temple boy.

Bunnak first experienced living away from home and hiking through a forest when, before the rains retreat officially began on the day of the full moon in July, the abbot took the temple boys to a forest wat far away. It took three days and three nights for them to reach their destination.

When Bunnak was nine years old he was ordained as a novice. As a novice the boy observed the Ten Precepts. Killing animals, no matter how small, was a violation of the first precept. The village abbot was skilled in both insight and concentration meditations. Under his abbot's tutelage, Bunnak practiced the satipatthana (the Four Foundations of Mindfulness) and kasina (visualization) meditations.

When he turned fifteen, an age most villagers regarded as that of a young adult, Bunnak felt the need to test his practice. One morning the novice asked the abbot for permission to go on a thudong by himself. The abbot refused on the grounds that Bunnak was too young to go alone. After pleading with the abbot, Bunnak confessed, "I already made up my mind last night," and said that he would go. The novice placed a ceremonial tray of flowers in front of the abbot and prostrated himself at his teacher's feet to beg forgiveness. Bunnak then left the wat to wander alone in the forests along the Mekong, equipped only with his klot and the meditation methods that his teacher had taught him.

Nine days after leaving his village wat, Bunnak crossed the Mekong into territory under French colonial rule. While walking in the foothills he came to a pond in which various kinds of lotus were blooming. Bunnak described the scene. "The edges of the pond were steep and high. I found five paths that went down to the water. All kinds of animals in the area—tigers, wild elephants, bears, wild gaurs, and monkeys—came to this pond for water." The novice decided to stay. "The water here is so clean, and the forest is refreshing. This is a suitable place to stay to practice meditation." As Bunnak walked around the pond he spotted a big Mysore fig tree about four hundred meters from the edge of the pond. He pitched his klot there under the shade of the fig tree.

At dusk Bunnak heard the call of tigers—aoo euu, aoo euu, aoo euu, aoo euu—coming from the other side of the mountain. This was the first time in his life that he had ever been alone in the forest, and he was stricken with terror. "The sound became louder; it seemed that the tigers were coming to the pond for water. Then the growling came from all four directions. I was terrified." Still, Bunnak thought to himself, "I have brought my life into the midst of danger in order to test my meditation practice." Thinking thus, his resolve strengthened. He observed how his body reacted when the sounds made by the tiger came in contact with his ears. "I got goosebumps.

It was amazing that the hair on both my arms stood up straight. The growling got nearer and nearer, one tiger coming from each of the four directions. My chest got tighter, my neck got stiff, tears came streaming down my cheeks. I took my robe out of the almsbowl and covered myself from head to toe. Sat in the lotus position. Could not think of anything else because my chest was so tight and my neck was still stiff. Tears kept falling from my eyes."

On the tenth day after he had left the village wat Bunnak was still consumed with fear. He kept having the thought of going home, but he was afraid his fellow monastics would laugh at him if he came back so soon. He began to ponder the Buddha's teaching: notice where the misery lies, observe how the fear starts, and determine how it can be eradicated. Bunnak realized that he must change the habit pattern of his mind in order not to react to the sound with fear. He had to go to the root of the misery and figure out how to eliminate the cause of suffering by striking at its origin. Bunnak observed what he experienced within his own body. "In the evening the tigers on the hill growled as usual. My chest got tight. I began to think, I have put up with this fear for ten days. It has not gone away. This is dukkha. . . . It is better to be eaten by a tiger than to face fear day in and day out. If the tiger kills me today there will be no one to be afraid any more. No more dukkha. It is better to suffer for a few hours while being eaten by a tiger than to suffer from fear every day with no end."

Once he made up his mind to conquer his fear, Bunnak put on his robe, walked to the edge of the pond at the spot where the tigers came to drink water, and sat down at that very spot in the lotus position. He made up his mind to face fear head on. "When the tiger comes to eat me, it will bite my neck first. I will die shortly. I will no longer have to suffer terror for days on end." The novice then asked for a determination *(adhitthana):* "If I should die here, may the fruit of my practice, such as observing the precepts, send me to the next birth in heaven."

Continuing to sit with his eyes closed, Bunnak remained mindful. "Some time later a tiger came by. I could hear his breath and his grunt, 'kuk huu, kuk huu.' I opened my eyes and saw a huge tiger right in front of me. I looked at his front paws; they were as big around as my neck! Suddenly my chest got tight again and large teardrops rolled down my cheeks." Bunnak lowered his head and body into a prostration position and prepared to be eaten. "The grunting—'kuk huu, kuk huu'—became louder, and the tiger pawed the ground. I could feel bits of dirt hit my head a few times. Then the tiger sprang up onto higher ground. His growling—'aoo euu, aoo euu, aoo euu'—began to fade away." Bunnak, lifting up his face, was surprised and elated. "The tiger did not eat me! The danger did not come to me!" The young novice got up immediately and began walking along the rim of the pond, following the tiger. He was about twenty meters behind it. "When the tiger saw me, he leaped toward me, and I walked toward him. There were only two steps between me and the tiger. But then the tiger turned around and bounded toward the hillside. And I began to walk back to my spot under the fig tree."

While walking back to his seat, Bunnak thought, "It is difficult to obtain birth as a human being. To be born a human is to have acquired the most merit. Whether we live or die is beyond our control, it's up to the karma." This was wisdom gained by personal experience. The novice sat on the flat rock where he always sat and reflected more about the incident. "A while ago I wished to die, so I lay down in front of the tiger; yet the tiger did not kill me. It was not my karma to die yet. A man could be safely in his hut surrounded by his relatives who do not want him to die, and yet death comes to him. Whether we survive or get killed is not up to us. It is our karma that has control over us." Having experienced the truth directly, the novice lost his fear.

That night Bunnak grew sleepy very early. It had only just turned dark when he lay down on the flat rock and gazed at the bright stars in the sky. The change in him was evident. "I felt at ease. When I heard the tigers call nearby—'aoo euu aoo euu'—I thought, having realized that I am not the owner of my life, I appealed to the Lord of Life: 'Dear Karma, the tiger is now approaching me. Do whatever you think is right.' Then I fell asleep."

The following day Bunnak got up early and hiked across two hills. It was noon when he came to a thick forest called Taboeng Nang. Feeling thirsty, he stopped by a stream in the middle of the forest. "When I reached the water, I saw a tiger eating a man. The tiger was gnawing on the man's right thigh." Watching the tiger, the novice thought, "Dear Karma, have I ever done this? If I have killed a tiger in a previous life, let it kill me. If I am not karmically linked to the tiger, let me survive so I can work for the Dhamma. Let there be no obstacles on my path."

After he said his prayer the novice calmly knelt down to drink water. "The tiger leaped over the dead man's head and came to the edge of the stream. After I drank the water, I walked along the stream following the tiger. When the tiger saw me, it ran on ahead of me. Then, less than a kilometer away, it stopped to lie down. When I finally caught up with the tiger, it raised its forepaws as if it intended to grab me." While focusing his mind, Bunnak again asked for a determination (*adhitthana*). "If the two of us were karmically linked in the past, let it be so. If I never killed you in the past, may you not harm me." With the resolve to attain realization, the novice calmly walked toward the tiger. He was a few meters away from it when the tiger suddenly sprang into the forest. Fortified with the power of adhitthana parami, the fifteen-year-old novice then continued his journey.

SOURCES

Hermann Norden, *A Wanderer in Indochina: The Chronicle of A Journey through Annam, Tong-King, Laos, and Cambodia with Some Account of Their People* (1931), pp. 202–211.

Phra Ajan Nak Khoso, *Samanera Bunnak thieo kammathan* (1992). During the course of his wandering Bunnak met several thudong monks who were disciples of Ajan Man (1870–1949). In 1932 Bunnak was ordained as a monk at Wat Boromniwat in Bangkok. He was given the monastic name Khoso. People called him Ajan Nak. At the request of a laywoman who supported his bhikkhu ordination, Ajan Nak wrote his life story after he became a monk. Ajan Nak continued to live a thudong life and wander in the Northeast until his disappearance, the date of which is unknown. In 1979 Amaro Bhikkhu of Wat Kalayanamit in Thonburi wrote, "Some people think that Ajan Nak Khoso died in the jungle." See *Kan Thudong Phua Nibbana* (1979), p. 87.

38

SISTERHOOD OF THE YELLOW ROBE

BETWEEN 1895 and 1899 Lillian Curtis, married to L. W. Curtis, an American Presbyterian minister, lived in Lampang in northern Siam. The Curtises had taken on the Presbyterian mission at Lampang that had already been established by Daniel McGilvary. Protestant and Roman Catholic missionaries made it a point to be informed about the customs, character, and social rankings of the people among whom they worked. Curtis was especially interested in the status of women. From her own experiences in Lampang and its vicinity, Curtis wrote, "The wife and daughters always form part of the family circle upon the veranda; and, in brief, it may be said that they form a part of all the life of the land, save the monastic life of the temple." Except for white-robed ascetics, (*mae chis*), Curtis must not have seen women monastics; otherwise she would not have claimed the exclusion of women from the monastic life. But she did not travel to the most remote villages in Siam and the Lao territories.

When Hermann Norden, with his Annamite assistant Three-sixty-three, was traveling from Chiang Khong to Luang Prabang in northern Laos, he had to go through Muang You on the Khan River. From Muang You it would take Norden another four days of rowing downstream on the Khan River (called the Nam Kan by Norden) to get to the Mekong and Luang Prabang.

After Norden discovered, from personal experience, that the old road, which had recently been lined with

Fig. 39 Map of Laos showing Luang Prabang and Siang Khwang
(Chiang Khong)

telegraph poles, had been abandoned because of the danger of tigers, he took the safer route to Muang You, which, he was told, was along a Meo [Hmong] trail. "We followed the climbing trail. From the crest of the ridge I caught a glimpse of water shining in the distance. The Nam Kan and Muong You were now not far away; there remained only a fifteen-mile stretch of road through a bamboo forest which gave grateful shade after the scorching sun of the fire-cleared district. . . . Beyond the bamboo we came to the Nam Kan's embankment. Muong You was on the other side of the river, and we crossed in the smallest ferry I have ever seen. The little boat could accommodate two or three men, but the horses had to be taken over one at a time. All the river men's skill was required to get them on board and to keep them there."

In the nineteenth century a small muang was usually comprised of clusters of villages ruled by a petty chief. Muang You, a frontier station of Luang Prabang, had once been a much bigger place before it was raided in 1887–88 by Haw bandits from Yunnan. Norden and Three-sixty-three did not know what to expect before they arrived there, but "Muong You proved to be a village of about two dozen huts, a *bonzerie* [monastery] and a custom house. All the honourables of the village were on the shore to meet me. The master of the port offered me hospitality but I chose to stay in the bungalow near the river's bank. The host there presented me with a fan made of peacock feathers. He brought it on a tray with a few jasmine and hyacinth blossoms. Soon the village chief arrived, gorgeous in rose-coloured *sampot* [sarong] and a black jacket with gold buttons. He also brought an offering of flowers, two jasmines in a silver bowl. I took the flowers and dropped a piastre into the receptacle. From the reluctance with which the chief accepted the money I saw that these charming attentions were not offered with the expectation of payment."

The chief and Norden's Annamite interpreter escorted him through the main village. Norden commented on the friendliness of the Lao people. "Each little bamboo house had a veranda from which people smiled down and said, '*Sembai baoh*,' which is good-day." When he arrived at the monastery Norden noticed, with surprise, a group of female monastics in the yard. "At the *bonzerie* I was astonished to see young women in yellow robes and with shaven heads; a Buddhist sisterhood. They were busily sweeping an already tidy yard; an older woman superintended the work."

It appears that there were female novices or nuns in existence, at least at the northernmost border of Siam, in French-occupied Lao territory. According to conventional belief in Thailand today, only old women take up the monastic life. This account suggests that such was not always the case.

The women Norden saw could have been bhikkhunis. The younger ones, if they were under twenty years old, are likely to have been samaneris. A female novice observes Ten Precepts; a bhikkhuni, the fully ordained female equivalent of a monk, observes 311 rules. The women in Norden's account wore robes of the same ocher color as those of Theravada monks. Considering the high social status of Lao and Shan women at the time, it is entirely likely that in some local traditions women who pursued religious lives would have received the same social support as men. Since villagers did not write down their local histories, we have no written records of their local religious customs.

Norden described Muang You, whose custom must have allowed women to don the yellow robes, as idyllic. The people made him feel honored and welcome. "More flowers were waiting for me when I returned to the bungalow. This time they were scarlet hibicus. There was no doubt that I was among a gracious and beauty-loving people."

On the day he was to leave Muang You, Norden got up at dawn, curious to see what kind of boats the chief had provided for him and his party to get to Muang Gloom. "Daylight found me on the beach eagerly eyeing my pirogues. They were two, one for myself and one for my outfit; each had three paddlers. About thirty feet long, very narrow and with a sharp keel, the boats were like those I had seen taking the rapids of the Black Water [River]. A bamboo hood at one end provided shade, but one must take that comfort lying down; the hood was too low to admit of a sitting posture." Soon "the village chief . . . and the boatmaster, some *bonzes* [monks] whose yellow robes made pleasant patches of colour, and a dozen children" came to see Norden off. Here Norden parted with his Annamite guide, who returned to his family in Chiang Khong. From here to Muang Gloom Norden traveled with no interpreter. It took two days of rough going to get there, and Norden was grateful that "the paddlers were expert" and that "their eyes were jungle-trained."

Norden came to appreciate the skills of his men. "Every season lives are lost on the Nam Kan. Fragments of wrecked pirogues are not uncommon sights floating on the water or harboured on bank or boulder. In rocky spots of many whirlpools I was always put ashore and the men carried the pirogues. Their lithe stripped bodies, tattooed from waist to knee, were beautiful to see as they pulled and tugged at the boats. There were points where cliffs narrowed the river channel, and the water boiled through in torrents. Here the men must pilot the boats through, but first I would be landed. Always as I walked on to meet the men on the other side of the danger point I was apprehensive that they would not get through to meet me: that this time the peril was too great. We were apprehensive that our pirogue was now in pieces and the gallant boatmen drowned. I no longer doubted the

Frenchman in Hanoi who had said 'the trip down the Nam Kan is no journey for a *poule mouillée*,' which is to say, milksop."

Toward dusk on that first day, Norden wrote, "We landed near a point where several empty pirogues were beached. Laden with baggage, the boatmen led the way along a winding trail to a settlement. They stopped in front of a large hut flanked by banyan trees." This was where Norden was to spend the night. "A little group of men and boys collected while the boatmen carried my things up the pole with cross-pieces which served for a ladder to enter the hut. One glance told me that it was not a sala for general travellers. This was a *bonzerie* [monastery], a shelter for monks both of the village and itinerant." When he entered the hut Norden saw half a dozen monks on the floor. "My entrance had a strange effect. The sleepers were wakened and, without a word, all left the hut." The monks left in order to give the space to the traveler.

As at Muang You, the village chief here, wearing a mix of local and Western garments, greeted the European visitor with flowers. Norden wrote, "Soon the village chief arrived in blue *sampot*, black vest and campaign hat. He brought orchids. Though he spoke no French somehow he made me understand that I was invited to come to his house. . . . But I was too tired to move on, especially when moving meant to go down that entrance pole and up another as difficult, or perhaps worse. I wanted nothing so much as to strip off my clothes, wet from many drenchings with showers of spray." A village boy brought him boiling water so that he could make tea. Norden ate the cold chicken that he had brought from Muang You and fell asleep in spite of the insects.

When he got up the next morning Norden saw a group of monastics, men and women, who were waiting for alms. "A dozen *bonzes* and old women, all with begging bowls, were squatted on the grass in front of the hut when I went down the pole at daybreak." Norden did not say what color robes the monastic women wore. Here in this village (Norden may never have learned its name) it seems that monastics waited to receive alms in front of a sala that appears to have been reserved for their use, whereas in the Central Plains of Siam, before roads were built, monks typically paddled boats on almsround and received food on the boats. Here Norden is sensitive and respectful. Although he was not Buddhist, he politely followed the local custom of offering food to the monastics. "Even so early their bowls contained some rice and fruit. I was not the first that day to profit by the chance to win merit. The gift exacts no gratitude from the receiver. The opportunity to give is the conferred privilege."

Later that same day Norden arrived at Muang Gloom. The Lao chief of the muang, who had come up the river to meet Norden "wearing a purple *sampot*," showed Norden around. "Three dozen or more substantial huts showed that Moung Gloom was an important village." During the two days that Norden stayed in Muang Gloom he went hunting, and on one occasion he lent his gun to the chief's son. The chief and his son returned from the hunt with three deer. "One was a *mundjok* which they had captured alive. I had already made the acquaintance of that tiny deer, which looks like a kid except for its reddish pelt. French colonial children have them for pets, and I observed that the little Laotians also accepted the graceful creature as a playmate." Today the tiny *mundjok* is on the endangered species list.

Norden was touched by the hospitality of the village chief and his wife, who invited him to spend the night in their house and to eat with them and their children. He stayed in Muang Gloom for three nights. As he explored the village, he observed a few women at their tasks. One was a girl who quickly "paced up and down, winding thread from a ball in her hands around poles set at either end of the veranda. Some older women were busy at weaving fish nets. But for the most part the veranda life was luxuriously idle. Men and women fondled babies. Old men lay in the corners puffing at opium pipes."

Speaking of opium, H. Warrington Smyth (introduced in "Paddle Your Own Canoe"), who served as Siam's director of the Department of Mines from 1891 to 1896, points out that "one cannot condemn Indo-Chinese mountaineers for smoking opium, for it is, in moderation, the best antidote that exists to the terrible fever bred in these hills by long marches, varying temperatures, and empty stomachs. At the same time, the Nan men [in northern Siam] do without it, and they are almost the only people in Indo-China of whom it can be said."

At Muang Gloom Norden parted company with the Lao boatmen who had risked their lives to get him there safely. He was given several new boatmen who were to take him to his next destination.

Looking back, writing in 1931, Norden realized that of all his experiences in the Lao states his trip on the Khan River, with its beautiful birds, wilderness, and dangerous rapids, was among the most memorable. Norden's encounters with the local Buddhists, who revealed their gentleness and warm hospitality, and the camaraderie and companionship of the admirable boatmen associated with the image of this wild stream, led him to write, "I was too sad in the realisation that the trip on the Nam Kan was over. I love that river. Later on the Mekong, and yet later on the China Sea, I remembered with a thrill of pleasure that some of that water had belonged to the Nam Kan."

SOURCES

Lillian Johnson Curtis, *The Laos of North Siam* (1903), pp. 106–107.

Hermann Norden, *A Wanderer in Indochina* (1931), pp. 211–230.

H. Warrington Smyth, *Five Years in Siam* (1898), p. 194.

39

JESUS AND THE FUTURE BUDDHA

IN 1910 William Clifton Dodd, a minister representing the American Presbyterian Mission in northern Siam, embarked on what he called an "exploring tour" that took him from Chiang Mai to Sipsong Panna in Yunnan in southwestern China. His goal was to reach "regions where no missionary had ever preceded." Muang La, a two-day hike north of Chiang Rung, was inhabited by the Lue, who were devout Buddhists. At a monastery in Muang La, Dodd showed a throng of curious villagers illustrations of Christian themes. "Tired as we all were, I had hung up the picture roll out in the court of the monastery where we were stopping. By the time I had finished my bath, the Lue were making all sorts of wild guesses about those wonderful pictures. At first they meant nothing sacred to them. Indeed, if you could have heard and understood their comments you would have concluded that they meant nothing to them but entertainment. When their curiosity had been somewhat sated, I explained the pictures. It was a fine sight to see their mirth change to reverence, then to deepest interest. The message was absolutely new to them, and many of them lifted their hands in adoration. As the adoration was directed neither to me nor the picture, but to 'The Coming One' whom I was heralding, I did not forbid."

When a Lue man in the audience asked Dodd, "'Is this Yesu (Jesus) he whom we call Ariya Metteya?'" the Christian minister replied, "'Yes, because Ariya in Sanskrit means Aryan, high-born, and Metteya [in Pali] means merciful.'" Dodd continues, "I then proceeded to show that Jesus is highest-born of all who ever came to earth, and that he is all-merciful." Hearing this, the Lue Buddhist said sadly, "'And so the Coming One has already come, and we did not see Him.'" Dodd put two and two together. "At once I understood the man's sorrowful reception of what ought to have been the best news he ever heard. Buddhist books teach that Ariya Metteya, the next Buddha, or self-illumined one, will deliver from the otherwise ceaseless round of re-births all who are alive on this earth at that time and who have accumulated a sufficient stock of merit and have become sufficiently pure so that they can see him; for only the pure can see him, even when he is incarnate." The missionary was able to use the local belief in the future Buddha Metteyya (Sanskrit: Maitreya) to his advantage, both to explain the historical Jesus as well as the Second Coming. "In all the countless

Fig. 40 From Chiang Mai to Sipsong Panna

ages, this is the one chance for salvation; and the poor man's first thought was that he and all the rest of them had missed that one chance. But quick as a flash from heaven came a light into his face, a reflection, I doubt not, of the illumination of the Spirit in his heart." To the missionary's delight, the worried Lue villager who mistook Jesus for Metteyya declared, "We did not see Him with our eyes; but we see pictures of Him. We see His book, we hear His message, we are here when His religion comes, and that is enough." Dodd concludes, "I believe fully that he accepted the message."

In 1876 the American missionary Daniel McGilvary toured through four muangs in the vicinity of Chiang Mai, trying to convert local people to Christianity. In Muang Ken, McGilvary wrote, when he asked people to worship Jesus, "Most of them" replied that they " would consider it. Some would go further and say that they worshipped Jesus under the name of their promised Buddha Metraya, yet to come."

It is not surprising that the Lue Buddhists mistook Jesus for Metteyya. The coming of Metteyya and the beginning of a new, entirely just social order had long been prophesied in local palm-leaf manuscripts kept in monasteries in every region and recited to the villagers by monks and local scholars. The belief in Metteyya was deeply rooted in local Buddhist traditions in the lands known collectively after World War II as Southeast Asia. The worship of Metteyya can be traced at least as far back as the reign of King Luthai of Sukhothai in the mid-fourteenth century. An inscription from King Luthai's reign mentions Metteyya and ten other bodhisats.

King Chulalongkorn (Rama V), who created the modern Thai state, believed there was only one Buddha. The following incident, reported in the *Daily Record of Royal Activities*, illustrates the difference between the worldviews of a modern ruler and his subjects. In November 1883

Rama V traveled by royal boat to Lopburi. Local people who lived in the vicinity of Wat Mani Cholakhan in Phrommat subdistrict worshipped Metteyya. Knowing that the king was coming to visit, they placed a statue upon the altar. When the king arrived he offered robes to the ten monks who held honorific titles. After the monks put on the new robes and the king turned to the altar to light candles, he saw that the only image present was that of Metteyya. The king immediately ordered an image of the Buddha to be brought to the altar so that he could perform his prostrations before the monks began chanting their blessing. According to the *Record*, the king said to the monks, "People should not take refuge in Metteyya. Metteyya is not part of the Triple Gem: the Buddha, Dhamma, and Sangha. The king donated money to restore this Metteyya statue and came to celebrate the festival with local people, but not because he shares their foolish belief in the coming of Metteyya." *The Record* also reported that the king turned to Phra Yanrakkhit, the monk with the highest title, and asked him, "Do you prostrate yourself before the Metteyya image?" The Dhammayut monk replied, "No, I do not."

SOURCES

William Clifton Dodd, *The Tai Race: Elder Brother of the Chinese* (1923; 1996), pp. 66–68.

Daniel McGilvary, *A Half Century among the Siamese and the Lao* (1912; 2001), p. 171.

For the inscription written during King Luthai's reign, see Prasert Na Nagara, *Ngan charuk lae prawatsat* (1991), p. 45.

The record of King Chulalongkorn's visit to Wat Mani Cholakhan, reported in *Phra ratchakit rai wan* (The Daily Record of Royal Activities) in November 1883, is cited in S. Plainoi, *Klet borankhadi prapheni thai* (1969), pp. 369–370.

40

THE COMPASSIONATE
ARAHANT

IN 1910, while the American Presbyterian minister William Clifton Dodd was showing pictures of Jesus to the Lue villagers in Sipsong Panna, Pun Punnasiri (1897–1973) was a temple boy living at Wat Song Phinong in Suphanburi in the central region of Siam. Like the Lue villagers, Pun's parents and his teachers also believed in the coming of Metteyya. Somdet Pun, who became the abbot of Bodhi Monastery in Bangkok in 1947, recalled, "After we temple boys learned to read and write the Khmer alphabet, our ajan gave us a Phra Malai text to read. The story of Phra Malai was written in the Khmer script. Two or three pupils who were at the same level in their study of Khmer shared one book, and we read the story together. Those who were beginners read the story aloud with the older pupils. Eventually we were able to read Phra Malai on our own."

It was through the legend of Phra Malai that the belief in the coming of Metteyya was disseminated among the Tai people. Phra Malai was an arahant known for his great compassion who lived many ages ago in the human realm on the island of Lanka in Jambudipa. One morning, when he was out on almsround, he came upon a poor man carrying eight lotus blossoms gathered from the pond in which the man had just bathed. He was on his way to the market to sell the beautiful flowers. Instead, the man presented the lotuses to Phra Malai, and as he did so, he expressed the hope that as a result of this act of merit he might never be born poor again. As Phra Malai accepted the offering, he told the poor man that his wish would be granted.

On another occasion, Phra Malai went to a realm of hell to alleviate some of the suffering there. The beings in hell begged him to find their relatives when he got back to Jambudipa and ask them to make merit on their behalf. Phra Malai did so, and once the relatives performed acts of merit, the hungry ghosts were reborn in heaven.

Phra Malai also ascended to Tavatimsa Heaven to worship at the Culamani Stupa in which relics of hair and a tooth of the Buddha are enshrined. After presenting the eight lotuses he had received from the poor man, Phra Malai began conversing with Indra, the deity presiding over this realm. Phra Malai asked Indra why he had built the stupa. Indra replied that he did so to provide the deities in heaven with a means of continuing to make merit; otherwise their next birth might be in a lower state.

When Phra Malai next asked Indra when Sri Ariya Metteyya would leave Tusita Heaven where he made his home to come and pay respect at the stupa, Indra replied that Metteyya would arrive soon, for he came to Tavatimsa Heaven regularly, on each uposatha day (the days of the new and full moon, which are observed as holy days by monks and devout laypeople on earth).

While Phra Malai and Indra were conversing, a deity with a retinue of a hundred celestial beings arrived to worship at the stupa. When Phra Malai asked Indra what the deity had done in the past to merit such a reward, Indra replied that the deity had once been a poor man whose compassion led him to give his meager meal to a starving crow. As more deities with increasingly large retinues continued to arrive, Indra explained how each deity made merit—generally through practicing generosity, observing the precepts, and having faith.

When Metteyya finally arrived, Phra Malai saw that he was surrounded by countless celestial gods and goddesses. Indra told the arahant that Metteyya had accumulated vast merit by practicing the Ten Spiritual Perfections for countless numbers of years. Metteyya also performed the Five Great Sacrifices, which meant giving up material possessions, wealth, children, wife, and even his own life.

After paying respect at the stupa, Metteyya greeted Phra Malai and asked him where he had come from. When he heard that Phra Malai had come from the human realm, Metteyya asked what the beings there were like. Phra Malai told him that some people were rich, but most were poor; some were handsome, but most were plain. Some, he said, lived to be old, but many died young. A few did good deeds, but the majority were quite bad.

Metteyya next asked how the people of the human realm made merit. Phra Malai explained that some listened to sermons, some made offerings, some had Buddha images cast, some built wat buildings and residences for monks, some provided robes and other requisites for monks, and some dug ponds and wells. People performed these good deeds primarily because they hoped to meet Metteyya in the future.

Metteyya then gave Phra Malai a message to take to the people of the human realm. Those who wished to meet him, he said, should listen to all one thousand verses of the entire Vessantara Jataka, which were to be recited over the course of one day and one night. People were to bring one thousand candles, a thousand sticks of incense, flowers, and other appropriate gifts as offerings to the monastery. (In order to meet this last requirement village people had to cooperate to get one thousand candles and incense sticks made by hand. Making merit was communal. The Vessantara Jataka festival thus served as a way to get villagers to do things together that would benefit the whole community.)

Fig. 41 Hungry ghosts

Before returning to Tusita Heaven, Metteyya told Phra Malai that after Gotama Buddha's teachings have been on this earth for five thousand years, the religion will deteriorate. Humans will degenerate both physically and morally. Incest, promiscuity, chaos, and violence will be ubiquitous. After much terrible fighting, virtually everyone will die. Only a small number of wise people who will have retreated to the forest and hidden themselves in caves will survive. These are the people who will create a new human society, one committed to the moral way and based on mutual goodwill.

Throughout Burma, Laos, and Thailand many different versions of the Phra Malai legend were recited at the Vessantara Jataka festival or performed at funeral services. Scenes from the story have been depicted in murals at monasteries in every region of Thailand. Throughout the nineteenth century, and even in the early decades of the twentieth, Phra Malai texts could be found in practically every wat in central and southern Siam. People commissioned artists and calligraphers to make new copies of the manuscripts and presented them to the monasteries as a way of making merit.

The legend of Phra Malai was written and spoken in poetic form. Although royal versions do not describe the realms of hell in graphic detail, the chanted verse version of the legend enabled local preachers to embellish the basic text with earthy, usually humorous images drawn from everyday experience. Many of the misdeeds described in the variations created by local preachers reflected the social conditions of premodern Siam and often poked fun at pompous or foolish individuals. One such variation describes the karmic retribution that awaits unjust rulers: "Those rulers who are corrupt or who rule unjustly are born with huge decayed, foulsmelling testicles that hang down to the ground." In another example, a corrupt government official who exploited peasants received retribution by being reborn as a hungry ghost. "He had testicles that were as huge as water jugs. They hung way down to the ground like a shoulder bag. Rotten and putrid, bloated, and stinking, they were like slimy snails. Whenever he wanted to go somewhere [the hungry ghost would] fling his testicles over his shoulder, stagger under their weight, and reel from side to side. When he wanted to sit down, they'd get pinched between his legs, and he'd have to stand up, and then sit down on top of them." Killers of animals, liars, cheats, greedy people, the disloyal, and the self-serving met with similarly loathsome fates. Some were covered with festering sores; others were boiled in cauldrons, pecked endlessly by birds, got acid poured down their throats, or were made to live in burning buildings.

For children of Somdet Pun's generation, the Phra Malai legend was central to their education because it provided the basic groundwork for the development of morality *(sila)*, moral shame *(hiri)*, and intelligent fear of consequences *(ottapa)*. Somdet Pun recalled, "I enjoyed reading the Phra Malai story in verse. I gained so much benefit. The poetic story sank deep roots in my heart. This book taught me to understand the meaning of gratitude *(bunkhun)*. While I was growing up, the teachings of Phra Malai in verse remained at the back of my mind and affected every decision I made, every step I took. In the Phra Malai book there were paintings illustrating the realms of hell and heaven and depicting the people and their environment after Metteyya's arrival on Earth. I was proud that I could read the text. The elders [laypeople as well as monks] were immensely pleased that we children had mastered the recitation of the Phra Malai text. They all assured us that we would not go to hell; after we die, they said, we would go to heaven. Hearing the elders' praise made me feel happy. I felt as if my body were floating on air. Their simple praise made me feel that I was a good person."

The Phra Malai story is generally devoid of action; thus each poet who retold the story in verse would make use of his repertoire of poetic tricks and techniques to add variety and interest to the legend. Children and adults enjoyed reading or listening to the Phra Malai story because of the aesthetic quality of pleasant sound. One of the reasons villagers looked forward to the festivals when they could hear the monks and novices recite the Phra Malai and Vessantara Jataka stories was because the language was so musical and euphonious. The listeners felt as if they had been transported into different realms. A gifted preacher was able to make his message both meaningful and melodious.

The Phra Malai legend—recited, sung, and dramatized—served as a way to impart moral principles and provide lessons in karma for villagers throughout the land. The Phra Malai and Vessantara stories were meant to be read out loud to a crowd. Part of the enjoyment for preachers came from the fun they had finding expressive words capable of painting a picture and in creating pleasing sounds through rhyme patterns, alliteration, and play with vowels and syllables. These devices also made the texts easier to remember. Recalling his experience as a temple boy in the second decade of the twentieth century, Somdet Pun wrote, "We had fun reading Phra Malai. We recited the verses together out loud. The poetic words made them easy to memorize. Some temple boys who had learned Phra Malai by heart teased the younger ones by mimicking them. Sometimes we got into a free-for-all. When our recitation practice got out of hand, our ajan told us to stop playing around."

In 1892, five years before Pun was born, King Chulalongkorn decreed that boys and girls were to be educated in elementary schools established by his gov-

Fig. 42 Novice Pun in 1912

ernment. The curricula and methods of teaching, based upon Western models, were adapted to the needs of the Thai state. These educational reforms could be implemented far more rapidly in Bangkok than in the remote hinterlands of Siam. In the interest of promoting Western rationalism, teachers were not permitted to introduce material that encouraged "superstition" or dealt with subjects that could not be verified by science. This meant that the Jataka and Phra Malai stories, through which basic Buddhist teachings had been made comprehensible to laypeople in Siam for hundreds of years, had to be discredited. What was needed was a convincing argument.

A Western scholar of Buddhism, T. W. Rhys Davids, inadvertently provided the king with the evidence he needed to redefine the role of the Jataka stories. Relying heavily on the scholarship of Rhys Davids, Rama V published an essay in 1904 in which he explained that Jatakas were more properly studied within a purely historical context in which the stories were to be seen as examples of ancient, even pre-Buddhist folklore. Copies of the king's essay were widely distributed. In the climate for rational Buddhism that was being created, the belief in rebirth and in the realms of heaven and hell could no longer be defended. Those monks, lay ascetics, and laypeople living far from the capital who clung to the old stories for their value in teaching morality and the bodhisat way of life could now be dismissed as simpleminded.

Somdet Pun, whose traditional early training was rooted in the lessons contained within the Phra Malai legend, was well aware that it was being discredited and its champions regarded as fools. He argued that it is better to be a moral fool than an immoral smart person. "The Phra Malai story instills in us many wholesome feelings. Some modern people say that the story fools timid children. I think it is better to be a fool who does not violate sila-dhamma or who is too afraid to do misdeeds. A fool who is kind and generous and does no harm to anybody is a good person. He is better off than a person who is clever at committing misdeeds, who is selfish for lack of loving kindness and goodwill."

In response to criticism leveled against the teaching of the Phra Malai story to children, Somdet Pun explained how the story served as a vehicle for religious and moral instruction for the young. As an example, the abbot pointed to the episode of the poor man who presented lotuses to Phra Malai, showing how it could be expanded. "The Elder tells us about a poor man who makes a living by picking vegetables in the forest and carrying firewood to sell. The money he earned he spent on taking care of his parents. He never neglected his parents. One day he picked a handful of lotus flowers in a pond. On his way to the market to sell the lotuses, he saw Phra Malai approaching from the opposite direction. The poor man had nothing to give the monk. Wanting to make merit, he offered Phra Malai the bunch of lotuses. They were the only thing he had. The poor man took care of his parents out of deeply felt gratitude. Because of this merit, after he died he was reborn in a heaven realm." The teaching of *bunkhun*, Somdet Pun, concludes, "is the wisdom that ancient people planted in the mind of every child."

Ostensibly to protect children, modern Thai critics condemned the graphic evocation of the horrible fates of the beings in hell described in the Phra Malai story. Hell seems largely to have disappeared from the modern religious imagination in Bangkok. The horrifying parts of the story were sanitized. The irony of all this is that images just as grotesque, just as horrible, if not more so, are available at cinemas and on TV throughout Thailand where the young flock to watch murder and violence in Western- and Thai-made movies and television programs. In the early decades of the twentieth century children were afraid of the realms of hell, but they do not appear to have suffered any trauma because of listening to graphic depictions of the agonies and punishments there.

Until they reached an age when they were able to understand the intentions and volitions (*cetana*) in the mind that compel people to act in certain ways, grimly graphic descriptions of the realms of hell had the power to deter children from acting blindly according to their moods, feelings, and habits. In Somdet Pun's recollection, "The depiction of the hell realm was really scary. It made my body hair stand up. While I recited the story, my voice became quiet when I came to the part about Phra Malai going down to visit the beings in hell. I had to pause and reflect on my own actions."

Furthermore, the story taught that the actions of body, speech, and mind—how we engage with the world around us—make a difference in the end. According to Phra Malai, anyone who hits or harms a parent will be reborn as a hungry ghost. His or her hands will be as big as palm leaves. A person who yells at his parents or scolds those who raised him will be reborn as a hungry ghost with a mouth as tiny as the eye of a needle. "When I read this episode," Somdet Pun recalled, "I asked myself if I had done anything like this in my own past. If I had, I regretted it. Whenever one of my friends saw any of us kids being stubborn or talking back to our parents, he would threaten us saying, 'Your mouth will be as tiny as a needle hole! Your hands will be as big as palm leaves!' I will never forget his mocking. That stopped us from committing misdeeds. In the old days people who read the Phra Malai story were deeply influenced by Phra Malai's teachings. If you think they were fools, then they were good fools. They brought no harm to anybody; they did good deeds; and they were full of gratitude. They were honest people." Somdet Pun's message to modern critics is that our actions have results, and if what we do now makes no final difference, then all moral purpose has been done away with.

As a temple boy at his village wat in Suphanburi, Pun was known for his imagination. He was also fond of reading. Pun came to Bangkok in 1912 to live with a relative, a monk then in residence at Great Relic Monastery. A year later, at the age of sixteen, Pun was ordained as a novice and moved to Bodhi Monastery where he lived with his uncle, Ajan Sot (1884–1959), a meditation monk. Novice Pun passed the third level of the Pali Studies exam and was called by the title "maha" even before he became a monk.

In 1917, in order to please his mother, who could not come to Bangkok, Novice Pun returned to his natal village to be ordained as a monk. The ceremony took place at Wat Song Phinong in Suphanburi. Maha Pun then went back to Bangkok and became a teacher at Bodhi Monastery. Later on he passed level 6 of the Pali exam. For twenty-five years Maha Pun was content teaching Pali, and he had a large number of pupils. In 1941 he was given a royal title and became one of the assistants to Somdet Wannarat (Phuen), abbot of Bodhi Monastery. Since the wat was the largest monastery in Bangkok, there were seven other resident monks besides Maha Pun who were given royal titles at that time.

Although Maha Pun was known among his fellow monks for his language skills, at first he did little with his gift. However, when his mother died in 1941, Maha Pun wrote a book called *Letters from Song Phinong*, which was distributed at his mother's funeral. The book was so interesting and well-written that soon monks from other monasteries in Bangkok asked Maha Pun to write cremation volumes for the funerals of senior monks. In 1947 Somdet Phuen, the abbot of Bodhi Monastery, died. Ajan Pun was appointed to succeed the abbot, who had been his teacher. Ajan Pun, then fifty years old, did not really want to govern a monastery, especially the largest one in Bangkok, but he had no choice. He had to accept the appointment.

A few years after he became abbot, Maha Pun became gravely ill with an intestinal disorder that nearly killed him. While he was recuperating, he stayed in the vihara in which the Palelai Buddha image was housed. This Buddha image, about four meters tall, is a small replica of the gigantic Palelai Buddha in Suphanburi. Created when Bodhi Monastery was restored during Rama I's reign (1782–1809), this small Palelai Buddha image was the main Buddha in the northern vihara of the wat compound. As a native of Suphanburi, Maha Pun gained strength just from being near the Palelai image. One day while he was looking at the Palelai Buddha, an idea came to his mind. He resolved to channel his creative energies into writing novels in order to reach a wider audience. The favorable reaction to his previous books, coming from people whose judgment he trusted, led him to believe that the Dhamma, if expressed in domestic, middle-class fiction, might be meaningful to those people who were scornful of stories about hungry ghosts and animals that speak.

In 1949, not long after his recovery, Maha Pun, writing under the pen name Santiwan (Peaceful Forest), published the first of many novels. Those who enjoyed reading the first novel had no idea that the author was a monk. When readers found out, they were amazed, for they did not think that a town monk with a royal title could be so down-to-earth and perceptive about the everyday struggles and problems of married couples, parents, and children. Maha Pun's books, fiction as well as nonfiction, were widely read by men and women because they engaged the emotions as well as the intellect.

As abbot of Bodhi Monastery, Maha Pun became known as a preacher and prolific writer. After he received the title Somdet Wanarat in 1961, laypeople as well as monks began calling him, affectionately, Somdet Pa (the equivalent of Cardinal Father). In 1972, when the Dhammayut Sangharaja, Chuan Utthayi, died unexpectedly in a car accident, the king appointed Somdet Pun to take his place. Somdet Pun, who had been in poor health, died in 1973 only a year after becoming sangharaja. He was then seventy-six years old. By the time of his death, state Buddhism was being overwhelmed by the forces of consumerism.

A loose network of "development monks," called Phra Sekhiyadhamma, emerged in the 1980s with the aim of returning sangha leadership to monks responsible to their local communities and local people's needs. This network is the Thai monastic version of nongovernmental organizations (NGOs). Phra Sekhiyadhamma includes many monks dedicated to community development, environmental issues, and traditional healing work at the village, district, and provincial levels. They respond to the problems and abuses of modernization with creative adaptations of old skills, Buddhist teachings, and approaches learned from NGOs. Also included in the group are more scholarly monks who support the grassroots work of their colleagues through writing and social analysis. Most of the pioneers are now seventy years old, while the second wave is a generation younger. A new generation is coming along, too, with both rural and urban roots.

Phra Paisal, an abbot and a member of the executive committee of Phra Sekhiyadhamma, shares Somdet Pun's opinion that belief in heaven and hell, long relegated to the realm of superstition, can play an important role in strengthening people's sense of morality. "It is apparent that in the past hundred years, Buddhism has been transformed to fit with modernity. Ironically, while superstition was supposedly removed from Buddhism in the process of purification, western rationality, scientism, and nationalism replaced it, resulting in the removal of transcendental and ultimate aspects. In other words, traditional superstition was replaced by modern, foreign superstition."

Phra Paisal, whose writings in the 1990s focus on the need to reform the current Thai sangha, notes, "Despite its emphasis on morality, official Buddhism has failed to strengthen the actual morality of Thai society." One explanation this Buddhist thinker offers is that rationalistic Buddhism lacks "the sacred." Phra Paisal continues, "The sacred (*saksit*) here refers to that which is beyond the five physical senses, and is inaccessible and unexplainable by mere rationality, but which, nonetheless, can be attained or realized by the mind. It has a quality or power that those who access it can receive and benefit from. It is a refuge or security for those who believe. Its dynamism is beyond social codes and is incomprehensible to the untrained mind. The ways to realize it are diverse, just as there are many ways of conceiving of it."

In his assessment of rationalistic Buddhism, whose beginnings reach back a decade or so before the middle of the nineteenth century, Phra Paisal writes, "Once Buddhism was reformed to be more scientific, there were no tangible sacred things to take the place of deities, heaven, spirits, and the like. Even the Buddha was demystified to be made more human. Nibbana, or the ultimate is, in fact, another form of the sacred, the unconditioned aspect (*asankhata*). Yet it, too, was removed from official Buddhism." As a result of stripping the sacred from the moral code of state Buddhism, Phra Paisal points out, "People are expected to practice morality through the sheer force of intellect and rationalization; but intellect alone is not effective enough to develop a moral life. Morality has to be deepened to the spiritual level. Faith or fear of sacred power, experience of inner peace, and connection with the ultimate through meditation, are all necessary spiritual conditions for maintaining one's morality. With the absence of the sacred, the moral code of official Buddhism no longer has any spiritual support or meaning."

SOURCES

Somdet Pun's life story can be found in his diaries, published in *Banthuk Somdet Pa* (1984); see especially pp. 20–21.

The legend of Phra Malai and Metteyya and examples from the chanted verse *(klon suat)* version have been excerpted from Bonnie Pacala Brereton, *Thai Tellings of Phra Malai* (1995), pp. 203–226.

For a penetrating discussion of King Chulalongkorn's 1904 essay and the changing view of Jataka stories among the Thai elite, see Patrick Jory, "Thai and Western Buddhist Scholarship in the Age of Colonialism: King Chulalongkorn Redefines the Jatakas" (2002), pp. 891–918.

For a clear exposition of the principles that underlie morality, see Pasanno Bhikkhu, "The Foundations of Virtue and Right View" (2002), pp. 1–5.

Phra Paisal Visalo, "Buddhism for the Next Century: Toward Renewing a Moral Thai Society" (2003), p. 4; and *Buddhasasana thai nai anakhot* (2003).

For accounts of the monks, nuns, and local people who follow the principles of Phra Sekhiyadhamma, see Sanitsuda Ekachai, *Seeds of Hope* (1994).

41

AJAN INKHONG, MASTER PAINTER

IN BUDDHIST monasteries in Siam the interior walls of important buildings were traditionally decorated with murals painted by monks or lay artists. These paintings generally depict the Buddha's life story, Jataka stories about the past lives of Gotama Buddha, and other stories from religious texts. Proverbs, old sayings, and Dhammic allegories were also often incorporated into the paintings. Although religious subjects were important, mural artists often included vignettes of people engaged in daily routines: villagers planting rice, collecting honey, and fishing with bamboo traps, children flying kites, Chinese merchants opening their shops, farmers constructing houses, couples making love, soldiers fighting in war. One painting on the wall of the ordination hall at Wat Devasangharam in Kanchanaburi depicts a woman, in a squatting position, about to deliver a baby. She is being assisted by a midwife and her husband. Usually at this critical moment the woman would be holding on to a piece of cloth hung from a crossbeam, but in this painting the artist added a touch of humor by showing the woman holding on to her husband's bald head.

Mural artists took keen interest in the striking features of foreigners, and they tried to portray them as realistically as they could. Representations of people of many nationalities, such as Persians, Indians, and Chinese, can be found almost everywhere. Europeans, with their light skin and extraordinary costumes, often created a sensation among local people and were a delightful subject for local painters.

In the nineteenth century there were monks all over Siam who were skilled artists and craftsmen. They passed on their knowledge to younger monks and novices. Buddhist artists did not sign their work, since they considered their efforts a religious service. Personal fame was inconceivable to them. We only know those whose names were written down in wat records or remembered by elders.

Lay and monastic artists trained by serving as apprentices to master artists living in a monastery. Carl Bock, the Norwegian travel book writer, saw many monks at work as artists and artisans. When he was traveling in Siam between 1881 and 1882, Bock noted, "If the Wat is near the river, the priests build their own boats, and all of them spend their leisure time in painting and decorating the temples, while during the dry seasons they perform pilgrimages to caves and temples of hallowed memories such as the famous limestone cavern of Tam tap tau, the temple Doi sua tape at Chiengmai, or the Wat Phra Bat near Lakon, with its footprint of Buddha."

In 1853, soon after Mongkut became king, he decreed that the names of all artisans throughout Siam were to be kept on file with the Department of Ecclesiastical Affairs in the event the king needed to provide artisans already attached to the court with additional help on extensive projects. The list shows that a great many painters, sculptors, glass workers, goldsmiths, silversmiths, blacksmiths, metal casters, tinsmiths, jade carvers, bronze workers, wood carvers, furniture makers, experts in working with mother-of-pearl, and masons were monks.

One of the best known of Bangkok's nineteenth-century artists was Ajan Inkhong, a contemporary of Somdet To. King Mongkut called these two Buddhist masters "Khrua Inkhong" and "Khrua To." *Khrua* was a local term

for monks who had special skills and who were also regarded as somewhat eccentric. The mural master's original name was In. Because he was the oldest novice in his
wat, he was given the nickname Novice Khong ("Grown").
Inkhong came from Bang Chan, a village in Phetburi, an
old principality known for having produced many prominent artists. Though he must have been born in the late
eighteenth century, his birth and death dates were not
recorded. Inkhong took higher ordination as a monk at
Wat Liap in Bangkok when he was in his twenties.

In 1822, during the last decade of the reign of Rama II,
a new monastery was established in Paknam by Phraya
Phetphichai, an engineer who supervised the construction of a new muang, Nakhon Khuankhan, and the dig-
ging of a canal leading to the new settlement. After the
monastery was completed, it was given the name Wat
Protketchetharam. Local people called it Wat Pakhlong,
meaning Monastery at the Mouth of the Canal.
Throughout the nineteenth century every abbot of Wat
Pakhlong was a meditation teacher. There were several
Buddha images in the wat's buildings, including a statue
of Metteyya. Ajan Inkhong painted the mural in the ordination hall.

Mongkut had known Ajan Inkhong from the time when
the prince was still a monk. After he became king,
Mongkut frequently demanded Ajan Inkhong's services.
Whenever he built or restored a wat, the king usually ordered Inkhong to paint the murals in it. Mongkut commissioned Inkhong to paint the interior of two pavilions,
the Royal Mausoleum and Rajakoramanuson Hall, located in the compound of the Emerald Buddha Temple.
Inkhong's paintings in these two halls depict historical
events, including a war between Ayutthaya and the kingdom of Burma. The murals show various stages of warfare: preparations before battle, soldiers on the march,
offensive and defensive moves, King Naresuan com-

manding the Siamese army at the front, royal palaces and temples being destroyed by fire, and the combat on elephant-back between the Siamese king and the Burmese prince. Inkhong also painted scenes of ordinary people during wartime: refugees fleeing their homes, local people rising up in defense of their land, and women with swords in both hands fighting the enemy alongside the men. Inkhong's paintings, particularly the scenes of hand-to-hand combat between kings or princes mounted on elephants, were so lively that viewers said they felt as if they were on the battlefield themselves.

When Mongkut had a new palace built on a hill in Phetburi he also restored an old wat on the same hillside. The king called his new palace Phra Nakhon Kiri and renamed the monastery Wat Mahasamanaram. Local people simply called the hill Khao Wang (Palace Hill) and the restored monastery Wat Khao Wang. Ajan Inkhong painted the murals on the walls of the ordination hall. Of the surviving works of the great artist, they are the only ones painted in his hometown.

Inkhong's paintings on the walls of the ordination hall at Wat Khao Wang depict monks and laypeople of all classes making pilgrimages to the Buddha's Footprint north of Saraburi, the Great Stupa in Nakhon Pathom, the Stupa of the Buddha's Relic in Nakhon Si Thammarat, and Wat Khao Wang in Phetburi.

Ajan Inkhong's paintings also show his awareness of Western art in the way he uses atmospheric and linear perspective. What is most remarkable, however, is that his scenes include Western men and women and Western-inspired architecture, novelties in Thai mural art. Ajan Inkhong witnessed a time when Bangkok was just beginning to show the influence that Europeans and Americans were having in and around the capital.

The king also commissioned Inkhong to paint murals in the ordination halls of two Dhammayut monasteries in Bangkok, Wat Bowonniwet and Wat Boromniwat. The murals at these two monasteries express Dhamma teachings in strikingly atypical pictures. These include scenes of people watching a horse race, a physician removing cataracts from patients' eyes, ships sailing across the sea, and a crowd looking at a gigantic lotus in a pond. Again, the extraordinary thing about these works is the fact that all of the people depicted are Westerners.

Ajan Inkhong painted two quite different versions of the giant lotus for each of the Dhammayut wats. Though the details vary considerably, both paintings show Westerners at the edge of a pond, gazing out at an exceptionally large lotus blossom perched on a tall stalk, the height of a two-story building. Other Siamese muralists painted gigantic lotus blossoms, too, but in their work the flower is always shown with a Buddha seated upon it. In Ajan Inkhong's murals there is no Buddha to be seen.

By depicting Westerners and adopting three-dimensional illusionism, Ajan Inkhong was considered highly innovative by his monastic contemporaries. Up to this time—the 1850s and 1860s—very few Siamese had ever traveled to the West. Inkhong's source materials were the Westerners who were living in Bangkok and his own imagination. Through his royal patrons, the artist got to see prints and paintings from Western countries that diplomats, missionaries, and others had brought as gifts for the king and members of his court. He must have seen the collection of photographs of America which President Pierce sent to King Mongkut in 1856. Among these were pictures of New York City, Boston, Philadelphia, West Point, New Orleans, and a locomotive.

Henri Alabaster, who worked as the interpreter for the British consul-general in Siam during Mongkut's reign, saw Ajan Inkhong's murals at Wat Bowonniwet. "By compounding native and European drawings of different dates," he wrote, "the artist has introduced us to a scene of ladies and gentlemen of the time of Louis XIV, having a picnic and dance on a hill, under which is a railway tunnel with a train about to enter it; and not far off a contemplative Buddha is pondering on the mutability of human affairs, or, perhaps, on the change of fashions."

During the dry season Bangkok monks who were not abbots of royal monasteries usually went away on a thudong. Master artists commissioned by the king had to remain in Bangkok. In order to prevent visitors from interrupting his concentration while he was planning the murals for the ordination halls, Ajan Inkhong is said to have locked himself up in his kuti at Wat Liap. He put a padlock on his door to give the impression that he was out. He entered and left his kuti through a back window. This way he could find the solitude he needed. Ajan Inkhong made many sketches of figures such as demons and monkeys in books made of *khoi* paper. One of his sketchbooks has survived and is preserved in the National Library in Bangkok.

Ajan Inkhong remained a monk for life. Many monks and former monks who apprenticed under him became master artists in their own right, among them Ajan Kasina-sangwon, abbot of Wat Thong Nophakhun in Thonburi, and Ajan Rit (1837–1921) of Wat Phrasong in Phetburi. Ajan Kasina painted the murals of the ordination hall in his monastery. His paintings also included Dhammic allegories.

After Ajan Inkhong's death, the next generation began to puzzle over the allegories that he painted in the murals of Wat Bowonniwet and Wat Boromniwat. In a letter that King Chulalongkorn wrote to Prince Wachirayan, his half brother, the king expressed his perplexity over the murals. "I felt deprived of religious knowledge," the king wrote, "and could not possibly figure out the meaning of the Dhamma in the murals." The king believed that Ajan Inkhong's paintings were significant. He wanted very much to learn the meaning of the metaphors hidden there.

The mural paintings that Ajan Inkhong painted for his own monastery, Wat Liap, have not survived. During World War II American pilots bombed the Rama I Bridge, built in 1932, and the electrical works near the bridge. Wat Liap was in the heart of this strategic area. The wat buildings, its records, and Ajan Inkhong's paintings were destroyed. Had it not been for the enormous effort of a small number of resident monks, who loved Wat Liap, the monastery would have disappeared.

SOURCES

For information on the subjects depicted in mural paintings, see Ponroj Angsanakul, "Phap sathon sangkhom thai nai kitchakam faphanang," in *Borankhadi* (1983), pp. 256–260.

Carl Bock, *Temples and Elephants* (1884; 1986), p. 212.

For photographs and detailed descriptions of some of Ajan Inkhong's mural paintings, see Wirada Thongmitr, *Khrua Inkhong's Westernized School of Thai Painting* (1979); for other mural paintings in Ajan Inkhong's day, see Apinan Poshyananda, *Modern Art in Thailand: Nineteenth and Twentieth Centuries* (1992), pp. 3–7.

For a short history of Wat Protketchetharam (Wat Pakhlong), see *Prawat wat thua ratchanachak* (1982), vol. 1, pp. 369–372.

Henry Alabaster, *The Wheel of the Law* (1871), p. 283.

The story of Ajan Inkhong working in his kuti was told by Prince Narit and cited in N. Na Paknam [Prayun Uluchada], *Beauty in Thai Art* (1967), p. 232.

King Chulalongkorn's comment is cited in Sombat Plainoi, *Mural Paintings* (n.d.), p. 5.

For a detailed discussion of Wat Liap and the monks' plight during World War II, see *Prawat Wat Rajaburana* (1995). The monastery's official name is Wat Rajaburana but laypeople and monks still refer to it by its original name, Wat Liap.

42

MEDICINE MONKS

DURING HIS reign (1824–51) King Rama III ordered an extensive renovation of Bodhi Monastery. He wished to turn the monastery into an encyclopedia of all traditional arts and sciences. The renovation took sixteen years to complete. Inscriptions and paintings at the wat dealt not only with the lives of the Buddha but also illustrated themes in astrology, botany, medicine, Thai massage, and yoga. Rama III ordered the systematic compilation of traditional pharmacological recipes from various sources. The inner walls of the wat were inscribed with recipes for 1,110 herbal remedies. Visitors were welcome to walk into the wat compound and copy medicinal recipes from the walls free of charge.

During their stay in Bangkok in 1822, John Crawfurd and George Finlayson, representatives of a British trade mission, toured many monasteries on the banks of the Chao Phraya River. The largest that the Scotsmen visited was Bodhi Monastery. As they examined one building after another in the compound, the Westerners took in the wall paintings and other remarkable features, later recording what they saw in their journals. On April 12, 1822, Crawfurd wrote that in one building there was a long arcade in which no three-dimensional images were evident, "but on the walls . . . were daubed many human figures, thrown into attitudes the most whimsical, distorted, and unnatural that can well be conceived. Under these figures were inscriptions in the vernacular language, giving directions how to assume the attitudes in question, and recommending them as infallible remedies for the cure of certain diseases. In many of the cases which we saw, the remedy, if practicable, would certainly be worse than the disease, whatever that might be." Had he known anything about yoga asanas or Thai massage positions, Crawfurd might not have found the illustrations of these postures quite so absurd.

During the 1880s, Maxwell Sommerville, an American professor from the University of Pennsylvania, visited Siam. He was an expert in glyptology, the study of carvings and engravings, particularly on gems. Sommerville, who spent much of his time visiting monasteries and studying inscriptions, noticed that "copies of the principal Pharmacopoeia of Siam are in the possession of the bonzes [monks] in the temples. It comprises several volumes, and is considered sacred by them. It is said to have been compiled by the Aesculapius of the Buddhist sect in their country. In his youth he was their god of convalescence, their Telesphorus. He lived in the time of Buddha, and was adored by his disciples. His work has always been revered by his co-religionists. To him were made known all the medical properties of plants, bones and tissues of animals, reptiles, etc. The legend records that the information came to him in a miraculous way: he having understood the language of plants, they made known to him their errand in this world." This "Aesculapius of the Buddhist sect" was most likely Jivaka, the Buddha's physician. It is interesting that Sommerville drew a comparison between Jivaka and Aesculapius, the legendary Greek god of medicine, who transmitted knowledge of medicinal plants and the curing of diseases to humans.

In old Siam there were no hospitals as we know them; the monasteries served as hospitals in time of need. The Reverend Dr. D. B. Bradley, an American physician and Presbyterian missionary, arrived in Siam in 1835 and

Fig. 43 Nineteenth-century engraved marble panels at Wat Pho (Bodhi Monastery) in Bangkok illustrating specific pressure points used in Thai bodywork treatments of persons suffering from ailments caused by an imbalance of the wind element.

practiced medicine in Bangkok for many years. Bradley wrote a long article on the Siamese theory and practice of medicine that was published in the *Bangkok Calendar* in 1865. Lengthy excerpts of Dr. Bradley's article were included in a memoir written by the Reverend Noah A. McDonald, an American who arrived in Siam in 1860.

Bradley wrote, "The Siamese believe the human system to be composed of four elements—water, air, fire, and earth, and that disease is simply a derangement in the proportions of these elements. They believe also that all nature is constituted in the same way, and that the elements without are continually operating upon the elements within the body, producing health or disease. For instance, if fire from without enters the body in undue proportions, it will derange the healthy equilibrium of the same element within, and will produce one or more of the diseases into which fire enters, such as fevers, measles, smallpox, etc. Each element is supposed to have its season of influence to produce, just as the fruits of the earth have their seasons. Their medicinal books, and common parlance, both say that in such and such months, wind produces most disease, and in such and such other months, fire produces most, and so with all the other elements. The internal elements are also supposed at certain times to become deranged from causes wholly internal. For instance, one of their theories in regard to apoplexy is, that the internal wind blows from all parts of the body upon the heart, and with such force that it is often ruptured, and death immediately ensues. The other theory is, that the wind has fled, and left a vacuum in the upper storey, and it must be forced back again, if a cure is to be effected."

According to Bradley's report, "All diseases are produced either from an excess or diminution of one or more of the four elements; and, according to their [Siamese] theory, wind produces more diseases than any, or all of the other elements combined. If you ask any Siamese what is the matter with him, in nine cases out of ten, he will answer, 'Pen lom'—it is wind, or disease produced by wind."

Dr. Bradley noted that Siamese theory "also teaches that all vital motions of the body are primarily produced by wind taken into the system by inhalation, as wind enters a bellows, and proceeds to the heart, and the heart by its expansions, invites it into the body, and then, by its own power it passes to all parts, and is the approximate cause of all internal circulation." The missionary doctor explained that "there are two grand divisions of internal wind, viz., that above, and that below the diaphragm. Strictures in the chest, headache, epilepsy, and apoplexy, are produced by wind beating upward. Colic, flatulency, inflammation of the bowels, etc., are caused by wind from above beating downward."

Holt Hallett, the British engineer who traveled in northern Siam in the 1880s, learned from Dr. Bradley that to combat disease the physicians in Siam "depend more upon a large combination of ingredients in a prescription than upon the power of any one or two of the same. Hence they often have scores of components in a single dose. One hundred and seventy-four ingredients were counted by Reverend Bradley in one prescription, which was ordered to be taken in three doses."

From the medical missionary Hallett also learned that doctors in Siam usually "employ their vegetable combinations chiefly in the state of decoction or infusion. A common way of speaking of the quantity of medicine which a person has taken is to say that he has swallowed three, five, or more pots of it—each pot containing from two to four quarts. And a common way of paying the doctor is by the potful, from 30 to 60 cents each. The form of pills is esteemed a more select mode of administering their vegetable medicines; but as these are more expensive and troublesome to prepare, patients are charged more highly for them."

Hallett also wrote that "a Siamese doctor, according to an account given by [Dr. Bradley], is distinguished from other folk by his medicine-box, wrapped in a piece of figured muslin or some silken or woolen fabric, holding half a bushel, more or less, of pills and powders, carried under his arm or in his little skiff, or in the arms of a single servant. As the customs of the country require physicians to remain day and night with their patients while suffering under grave diseases, it is impossible for them to attend upon many persons at a time. Doctors are therefore far from being in the possession of a lucrative practice, and few are lucky enough to be able to save sufficient to enable them to acquire a teak house surrounded by an orchard." Being a doctor in old Siam was not a way to get rich. Healing was not a livelihood.

Khruba La (1898–1993), abbot of Wat Pa Tung in San Kamphaeng district, Chiang Mai, was highly respected as a healer as well as an artist. Khruba La often made house calls on foot to visit patients in his community. If the sick person lived alone, the abbot would urge neighbors to look after the patient. In 1989 Bunloet Pochita, principal of Wat Pa Tung School, recalled, "When I was a child, I came down with smallpox and I almost died. Venerable Grandfather La was able to heal me. He saved my life."

Khruba La was also known for his oratorical skills. A gifted storyteller, his descriptive sermons about nature and wildlife drew large crowds, and when he preached, the whole sala came alive with his dramatic voices and the laughter and cheers of the audience. He was also a craftsman and blacksmith. In any farming community a blacksmith was a most important artisan because he made farm implements. Besides having built a traditional Dhamma pulpit made of carved wood, Khruba La painted, sculpted Buddha images, made furniture, built oxcarts, and repaired buildings in the wat. Many temple boys and novices who lived at the monastery apprenticed with Khruba La and learned useful skills.

Like his contemporary, Khruba La, Ajan Sawai Dhammasaro (1887–1979) of the Monastery of Krang Village in Suphanburi had many skills. Besides being a gifted preacher, Ajan Sawai was also an expert in herbal medicine. He is said to have been able to heal people who became ill from black magic. The abbot was also revered for his skills in making clay votive tablets by hand. The process of making such amulets was communal and time consuming. The ingredients had to be collected from the soils of many sacred sites. The laypeople who helped the monks and novices stamp the votive tablets were required to observe the Five Precepts and to practice meditation by reciting the mantra "Namo Buddhaya." Ajan Sawai, who distributed the potent votive tablets to laypeople free of charge, attracted many people to the wat and gave them the medicine of Dhamma.

In the early 1880s the Norwegian Carl Bock observed that Buddhist monks, "who also are the medical practitioners of the country, have always in stock a great number of medicinal plants."

When their children got sick, parents usually turned to the monks at the village wat. Ajan Panya (Pan), abbot of Wat Cholaprathan in Nonthaburi, recalled that when he was a temple boy living at Wat Nanglat, the monastery of his ancestors in Phatthalung in the southern peninsula, he was not in good health. Pan suffered epileptic seizures several times a month. In 1918 his father went to Wat Khuha-sawan in Phatthalung to consult his mother's cousin, Ajan Phum, a physician monk highly skilled in herbal medicine. Shortly thereafter, Pan's father moved Pan to Wat Khuha to live with Ajan Phum. Ajan Panya recalled, "Venerable Uncle gave me a pot of boiled medicine to drink. It was so bitter that I could not swallow it without eating honey or sugar right away. After three months of drinking several pots of bitter medicine, my epilepsy gradually disappeared." Like Ajan Sawai, Ajan Phum used mantras to cure people who were possessed by evil spirits.

People had regular access to physician monks, and they paid no fees. Ajan Panya points out that Ajan Phum "saved hundreds of lives with his medicinal knowledge. The great bulk of his medicines were vegetal: barks, roots, leaves, stems, fruits, and herbs. Sometimes he used animal parts, such as pulverized deer antler, which were boiled with the herbs. Venerable Uncle was known for his ability to remove the poisons of snakebites. He also used mantras as part of the healing process. He could cure people who were possessed by ghosts or who had become ill from black magic." Ajan Panya adds, "Venerable Uncle was full of compassion. If the sick could not come to his wat, he would walk to their huts to visit the patients, provided that they did not live too far from his wat. Often he had to spend the night at their houses."

Ajan Buddhadasa (1906–93), the best-known forest master in the southern peninsula, established Suan Mokkhabalarama (Grove of the Powers of Liberation) in 1932. Ajan Buddhadasa's original name was Nguam. He grew up in Phum Riang, Suratthani province, six hundred kilometers south of Bangkok. At the age of ten he became a temple boy and lived at Wat Nok in Phum Riang for the next three years. As a temple boy he collected herbs for the abbot. He learned to identify a great many plants and knew their healing properties. Ajan Buddhadasa retained this knowledge all his life, used it personally, and occasionally advised others. He recalled that during the first three decades of the twentieth century, two of the most revered abbots in Chaiya were meditators and physician monks. Both abbots knew Ajan Buddhadasa's parents well. According to Ajan Buddhadasa, Ajan Thum Inthachoto, abbot of Wat Nok, "was a skilled meditator who lived an ascetic life. Before he became abbot he was a thudong monk. The ajan allowed a young relative who had leprosy to live with him. The boy's duty was to heat the water for the old monk to drink. Although others feared to be in such close contact with lepers, the ajan's attitude was that if there were any germs they probably were killed by the boiling water. He had real compassion for the unfortunate." Ajan Thum died in the 1930s, not long after Buddhadasa established Suan Mokkh.

Ajan Sak Dhammarakhito, abbot of Wat Hua Khu, was also known for his compassion. As Ajan Buddhadasa described him, "Venerable Teacher Sak was unselfish. Local people, Buddhists as well as Muslims, always turned to him in time of illness. In critical cases they woke him up in the middle of the night. The abbot got up and went to their houses to attend to the relatives who were sick." Ajan Sak died in 1930. By then the young Ajan Buddhadasa had gone to Bangkok to study Pali.

Both Ajan Sak and Ajan Thum were contemporaries of Ajan Khai (1857–1932), the medicine monk whom we met in "Venerable Grandfather Egg." Ajan Khai administered to the Siamese Buddhists, Indian Sikhs, and Chinese who lived in Bangkok near Wat Tinlen, where the ajan was a resident. These Buddhist masters never sought to convert their non-Buddhist patients; they used their skills in herbal medicine to treat the sick out of compassion. The physician monks realized that the Muslims in southern Siam, the Chinese who migrated from mainland China, and the Indian Sikhs in Bangkok had their own religious beliefs and practices. As one Buddhist teacher put it, to impose Buddhism on people who happened to live near the monasteries "would run counter to the spirit of nonharming exemplified by the Buddha."

Some abbots learned to practice medicine and prepare remedies from their fathers if the latter happened to have been village doctors. Ajan Uttama (b. 1911) of the Monastery of Solitude Pool in Kanchanaburi, a province west of Bangkok, learned herbal medicine from his father, who lived in Moulmein in Burma. After he was ordained as a monk in 1932, Uttama spent the rains retreat at Wat Kesala in Ye district with his preceptor, Venerable Ketmala, a Pali scholar and a master of esoteric knowledge. The abbot later recalled, "Under the guidance of my preceptor I practiced meditation, studied medicinal texts, mantras for keeping ghosts away, and mantras to heal various kinds of diseases."

When he was a young monk, Uttama studied at Big Pagoda Monastery (Wat Phae Jai) in Lower Burma. On one occasion he went to stay at Wat Matsaya to help the monks there build their kutis. One evening Uttama went to practice walking meditation in a forest cemetery. There he saw a boy, about eight years old, with smallpox pustules all over his body and a very high fever. The villagers had left the boy there to die; both of his parents had already died of the disease. In those days it was the custom to confine those who had smallpox to a forest cemetery to prevent the disease from spreading.

When he saw that the boy was still alive, Uttama wrapped the child in his robe and carried him to his kuti, where he prepared an herbal remedy. Uttama boiled neem leaves and got the boy to drink the liquid. He bathed the boy with the same medicinal water. After ten days of drinking and washing with this preparation the boy recovered.

Uttama named the boy "Bakhin." In the past, babies and young children were not given formal names. Parents called their children by endearments like "Little Doggie" or "Little Mouse" or by words that captured something of a young child's appearance or behavior. When a boy was ordained as a novice, usually at the age of twelve or thirteen, the ordaining abbot then gave him a monastic name. Uttama brought Bakhin to the abbot of Matsaya Monastery to be a temple boy. When Bakhin turned thirteen, the abbot ordained him as a novice.

Missionaries and most Western travelers were aware of the local people's belief that spirits could produce a multitude of physical ailments and other disorders. Dr. Bradley addressed this belief in his article in the *Bangkok Calendar*. "They [the Siamese] also believe that spirits, good and evil, have great power over the elements, and have much to do in producing disease. They are consequently held in continued dread of them and use every means to propitiate them. They never start on a journey, or enter a forest where fevers prevail, without first making an offering to the spirits." The disorders people suffered from then correspond to what we regard as nervous and psychological disorders today. Local doctors knew that medicinal herbs and prayer could help.

Dr. Bradley noted that the Siamese "believe that medicine has the power to counteract the deranged elements, and restore them to a healthy equilibrium. The origin and practice of medicine they believe to have been supernatural. Their medicinal books," Bradley wrote, "declare that the father of medicine was so privileged, that wherever he went, every individual member of the vegeto-medical kingdom was sure to summon his attention, and speak out, revealing its name and medical properties; and since the days of miracles have passed away, the science is only now to be acquired by following closely the original medical books."

In 1888 the first modern hospital, Sirirat Hospital, was built on the west bank of the Chao Phraya in Thonburi. At first most of the drugs used in this hospital were derived from medicinal plants, but as the number of Western-educated physicians increased, so did the use of modern Western drugs. This trend was to continue until local herbal remedies were ultimately replaced entirely by Western drugs in hospitals and health centers all around the country. By the end of the twentieth century, a great many of the forests in Thailand had been destroyed and many primary sources for herbal medicines had disappeared. In 1992 the National Identity Board, a government agency, finally admitted that the establishment of the first modern hospital marked the beginning of the decline in the use of herbal medicines in Siam. Nevertheless, herbal remedies are still preferred by some monks and laypeople, especially those from rural areas. Interest in herbal medicine has made something of a comeback in the last decade of the twentieth century, both in Thailand and in the West.

SOURCES

John Crawfurd, *Journal of an Embassy from the Governor-General of India to the Courts of Siam and Cochin China* (1967), pp. 111–112, 40.

Maxwell Sommerville, *Siam on the Meinam from the Gulf to Ayuthia* (1897), pp. 140–141.

Dr. Bradley's comments on spirits and medical texts, which appeared in the *Bangkok Calendar*, are cited in Rev. N. A. McDonald, *A Missionary in Siam (1860–1870)* (1871; 1999), pp. 75–82.

Holt S. Hallett, *A Thousand Miles on an Elephant in the Shan States* (1890), pp. 272–274.

Information about Khruba La Chantho is from Withaya Chupan, *Kamson Luang Pu La* (1989), and from interviews with Phra Palat Kasem Khemacharo, assistant abbot of Wat Pa Tung, and Bunloet Pochita, principal of Wat Pa Tung School, August 11, 1989.

For a biography of Ajan Sawai Dhammasaro, see *Luang Pho pua wat pua ban* (1999).

Carl Bock, *Temples and Elephants* (1884; 1986), p. 212.

Paññananda (Ajan Panya), *Chiwit khong khappachao* (1983), p. 9.

Interview with Ajan Panya (Paññananda Bhikkhu), abbot of Wat Cholaprathan, January 17, 2001.

For Buddhadasa's recollections about Ajan Thum and Ajan Sak, see *Lao wai mua wai sondhaya attachiwaprawat khong than Buddhadasa* (1986), pp. 60–65.

The quotation on the spirit of nonharming in Buddhism is from Laurence Khantipalo Mills, *Noble Friendship: Travels of a Buddhist Monk* (2002), p. 51.

For the story of Ajan Uttama, see *Luang Pho Uttama 84 pi* (1991), pp. 56, 65.

For information on Sirirat Hospital, see *Medicinal Plants of Thailand: Past and Present* (1992). For a discussion of traditional medicine in Siam, see Jean Mulholland, "Thai Traditional Medicine: Ancient Thought and Practice in a Thai Context" (1979), pp. 80–115.

43

BACKWARD OR ENLIGHTENED?

THOSE NINETEENTH-CENTURY Western travelers in Siam who had also been to India, China, or Japan were particularly struck by the high social status of women in the regions that are now known collectively as mainland Southeast Asia. Bishop Bigandet, a French Roman Catholic priest, lived for forty years during the first half of the nineteenth century in the Shan states, a mountainous region that became known as Upper Burma. In a remarkable passage, translated and cited by English-speaking Westerners familiar with his writings, Bishop Bigandet not only testified to the high position held by women in the nineteenth century, he credited Buddhism with providing the conditions for the high degree of equality that was evident between the sexes. "In Burmah and Siam," the bishop wrote, "the doctrines of Buddhism have produced a striking, and to the lover of true civilization a most interesting result—viz., the almost complete equality of the condition of women with that of men. In these countries, women are not so universally confined in the interior of their houses, without the remotest chance of ever appearing in public. They are seen circulating freely in the streets; they preside at the *comptoir* [store counters], and hold an almost exclusive possession of the bazaars. Their social position is more elevated, in every respect, than that of the persons of their sex in the regions where Buddhism is not the predominating creed. They may be said to be men's com-

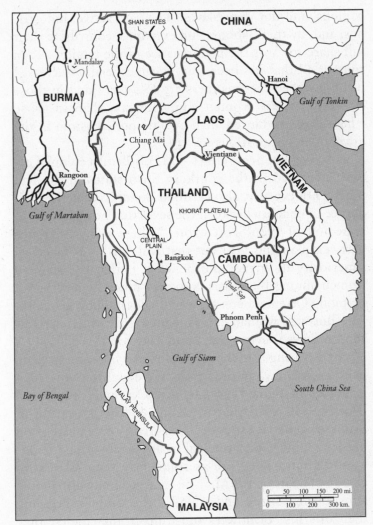

Fig. 44 Mainland Southeast Asia

panions, and not their slaves. They are active, industrious, and, by their labours and exertions, contribute their full share towards the maintenance of the family. . . . In spite of all that has been said by superficial observers, I feel convinced that manners are less corrupted in those countries where women enjoy liberty, than in those where they are buried alive by a despotic custom in the grave of an opprobrious slavery."

James George Scott (1851–1935), a British colonial officer stationed in the southern Shan states in the late nineteenth century, also credited Buddhism for the high degree of equality between the sexes that he observed. In a memoir of 1926 Scott wrote, "There is no difference between man and man but that which is established by superiority in virtue; and hence it is that the state of women among Buddhists is so very much higher than it is among Oriental peoples, who do not hold by that faith. The Burmese woman enjoys many rights which her European sister is even now clamouring for."

John Bowring, the British diplomat who came to Siam in 1855, wrote, "On the whole, the condition of women is better in Siam than in most Oriental countries." Bowring observed that in Bangkok "the education of Siamese women is little advanced. Many of them are good musicians, but their principal business is to attend to domestic affairs; they are as frequently seen as men in charge of boats on the Menam; they generally distributed alms to the bonzes, and attended the temples, bringing their offerings of flowers and fruit. In the country they are busied with agricultural pursuits."

Travelers often found women engaged in work that required hard physical exertion. In 1822 John Crawfurd noted that women "perform every description of outdoor and field labour, such as carrying burdens, rowing, ploughing, sowing and harrowing." Crawfurd understood that in nineteenth-century Siam "these labours fall naturally to their share, and are the necessary consequence of corvée labour," a system of labor procurement that required all able-bodied men between the ages of eighteen and sixty to give their labor to the state for approximately four months of the year. Crawfurd noted, "The call of the Government for the service of the men necessarily throws an unusual share of toil upon the women. They were constantly to be seen occupied in such descriptions of labour as are the exclusive province of the male sex in other countries. They are, for example, employed in the heaviest field labour, and on the Menam [Chao Phraya River] are more frequently seen than the men rowing and navigating the different descriptions of craft, either employed in fishing or in [trading]. Little concealment or seclusion is observed with respect to women of any rank."

H. Warrington Smyth, the geologist who lived in Siam from 1891 to 1896, observed that "the women are the workers of the country; no sowing or reaping can be done without them; no bargain can be driven if the good wife or the clear-headed daughter be away; nothing can be undertaken without their counsel." Rural women performed many of the same tasks as men, though there was of course some reasonable division of labor. The one task that women did not engage in was hunting.

In the 1920s Ebbe Kornerup, a Danish traveler, and his local assistants were rowed across the Mae Ping River to Rahaeng by a woman. "The Meping was very wide now after the rains, but so shallow that we had to wade out a long distance before the water came up to our knees," Kornerup wrote. "We splashed our way out to a canoe in company with a plump and pleasant woman with short hair; she was wearing trousers and a Siamese *panung*, and the betel and tea-leaves she chewed had made her lips both smeared and crimson. But how she chortled as the water splashed up over her trousers! This was the ferrywoman who was going to take us across. The canoe was soon full of travellers and their luggage; there were plenty of dogs, chickens, and pigeons in cages, not to mention a cat in a basket. The ferrywoman and another stout body, who sat flat on the bottom so as not to tip the boat up, talked nineteen to the dozen all the time."

In 1881 the Norwegian writer, Carl Bock, observed, "The women do all the really hard work which falls to the lot of the Laosians. They plant the rice, they gather the harvest, they husk and clean it." Bock further noted, "While the women are engaged in these duties, or the

Fig. 45 A mature Shan woman

similar ones of drying fish, weaving, and making clothes, the men now and then go into the forest with their cattle and elephants, cut wood, collect bamboo, or gather grass for roofing, never forgetting before going to work to make their offerings in the nearest temple."

While traveling through Phrae, a Lao muang north of Sukhothai, Ernest Satow, the British consul-general, also witnessed women doing the bulk of the farmwork. "A little before sunset I went out for a walk, and on returning through the town met a number of women coming back from their labour in the fields. As the men are obliged to work for the chief, they are in a great measure prevented from looking after their crops, and the proportion of men to women as agricultural labourers is as one to two, according to what Phya Chai Racha [the governor] told us." Satow lived in Siam from 1885 to 1888. On the basis of his observations, culled both from his travels in the north as well as his experience of life in and beyond Bangkok, the British diplomat concluded, "I do not know of any country where the female sex enjoys so much independence as in the Laos, and their morals are certainly no worse than those of Asiatic women who are confined in Zenanas [a secluded part of a house, inaccessible to men]."

The Reverend Daniel McGilvary (1828–1911), whose Presbyterian mission was in Chiang Mai, lived in Siam for fifty years. He noted that "the Lao have a proud preeminence among non-Christian races in the position accorded to woman. In the family, woman's authority is universally recognized. At the time we speak of it was much the same in the government also. The influence of women in affairs of state was doubtless greatly increased during the previous reign [in Chiang Mai], when there being no sons in the royal household, the daughters naturally became more prominent. They were trained to understand and to deal with public business."

We may recall that in 1880 Holt Hallett, a British engineer, undertook an expedition into northern Siam to search out a route for a railway that would connect Moulmein in British Burma with Chiang Mai. For part of the trip Hallett's guide was Daniel McGilvary. Hallett, who shared McGilvary's views, wrote that "women were very well treated amongst the Shans, quite as well as amongst the Burmese, and this is particularly noticeable in cases proffered by women against men in the courts; the women's word being taken as indisputable evidence. Child marriage is unknown in the country; divorces are very rare; marriage is a matter of choice and not of trade; and the aged are respected by their relations and cared for."

American missionaries frequently drew crowds at markets, where they often preached, showed pictures, played portable organs, and sang hymns. William C. Dodd (1857–1919), the Presbyterian minister who lived for over thirty years among Tai people in Siam, the Shan states, and Yunnan, wrote, "It makes all the difference imaginable in the status of women as a race, and in the future position of the bride that she does not go to be practically a drudge and a slave in the household of her husband, like her Chinese sister; on the contrary, her husband comes to live in her household."

In the nineteenth century, Jews and Christians tended to prefer sons over daughters. Upon marriage, a son could expect to carry on his family's name, whereas a daughter was expected to change her name to that of her husband. Western women of the time, accustomed to the preference for male offspring, might have felt a twinge of envy after reading a passage like that written by the Reverend Dodd in which he indicates how happy the Tai were to produce female offspring: "Her very birth was welcome because she would bring this son-in-law into the family. If a Tai woman has no daughter she is left alone in her old age. The little daughter in a Tai home is the pet of her father and the darling of her mother's heart." Whereas European women were laced into layers of cumbersome clothing and bound by a strict code of conduct, Dodd noted that a woman in Siam "has as much outing, has the privilege of wearing as few clothes and has as much freedom in every day as her brother."

In a predominantly agricultural society like that of Siam, literacy was not considered necessary for survival. Archibald Ross Colquhoun, a Scotsman who explored the northern region in the 1880s, wrote, "The girls are kept at home under the immediate supervision of their mothers, who teach them to be industrious; and train them, from their infancy, in the acquirement of common sense. . . . Nearly before they have left the breast, they seem to become far-sighted little women of the world. Walk through any village or town, and you will see damsels squatted on the floor of the verandah with diminutive, or sometimes large, stalls in front of them, covered with vegetables, fruit, betel-nut, cigars, and other articles. However numerous they may be, the price of everything is known to them, and such is their idea of probity, that pilfering is quite unknown amongst them." Colquhoun observed, "They are entirely trusted by their parents from their earliest years; even when they blossom into young women, chaperons are never a necessity; yet immorality is far less customary amongst them, I am led to believe, than in any country in Europe."

In the late nineteenth century when the Reverend L. W. Curtis and his wife, Lillian, took on the Presbyterian mission at Lampang that had already been established by Daniel McGilvary, they made it a point to be informed about the customs, character, and social rankings of the people among whom they lived and worked. Both husband and wife would have read much, if not most, of the literature available in English on Siam and the Lao states, and they had opportunities to speak with explorers and other missionaries, all of whom gathered information. Lillian Curtis knew about the high social status of Shan women. "It is a well known fact," she wrote, "that among all Shans, women are allowed a freedom of movement in the village and markets, keeping stalls, transacting business, holding property, and in many respects the equal of man." According to Curtis, who lived among the Lao and Shan in Lampang, "It is among the Laos and Shans that we find woman holding more nearly her true place in the home and community than with any other non-Christian people upon the globe."

Unlike Bishop Bigandet, Lillian Curtis attributed the high social status of Lao and Shan women to their indigenous cultural roots, not to Buddhism. "We know from the mythical chronicles of the Shans that woman held the place she now occupies for ages before Buddhist missionaries ever came to the country. That the chronicles are mainly myths does not weaken the conclusion that woman held her present position at that time, for myths would prove that as conclusively as facts. Also there are many tribes among the Laos that have never been converted to Buddhism, and among these tribes woman's position is the same as among the Buddhist Laos. So upon investigation one necessarily concludes that woman's position is due to a high racial development, instead of to the influence of Buddhism."

On the subject of marriage, Curtis wrote that among the Lao "usually a maiden is free to marry the man of her choice." There was no religious ceremony. "The groom," Curtis wrote, "has left his father's house in the full sense of the word. If he has sisters he cannot inherit a single fruit grove nor rice field. He becomes a son to his parents-in-law, and his earnings for several years go toward the general family support. He also changes his former liege lord and becomes a serf to the lord of the family of his wife."

Curtis learned to speak Lao and had ample opportunity to talk with Lao women, both commoner and elite. Missionaries were actively involved with the local people in the communities in which they made their homes. When she reports that "the vast majority of the property is in the hands of the women, and they manage it, too," Curtis is speaking from firsthand knowledge. "A man would not dare sell a buffalo or rice plain without first obtaining his wife's consent. In fact, he would seldom care to trust his own judgment in the matter, but would prefer a consultation with his wife. The wife also holds the purse and is business manager for the family."

In sharp contrast to the stigma attached to divorce in nineteenth-century Europe and America, Curtis noted that among the Lao "divorce is easy, and the laws are in favor of the women. . . . If a man wishes to be divorced from his wife, he cannot bid her go, for the property is hers, so he must needs creep away. . . . Though divorce is so easy, there is less of it than in most heathen countries. A man or woman does not as a rule lightly break the bond of the happy home life." Curtis adds, "These customs are existent throughout the length and breadth of the land of the Laos, but in the various provinces there are shades of differences and they must be slightly modified for the officials and princely classes."

In 1885 Colquhoun wrote that in Chiang Mai "divorce is the most simple and unceremonious affair; as both husbands and wives have separate property, they simply divide partnership, the wife taking her goods and chattels with her. If only the husband wishes for the divorce, and his wife has done no wrong, he has to give her twenty-four rupees, and hand over half the property and the custody of the children. Should she have misbehaved, she can claim nothing whatever. In the same way, should the husband take to drinking, or otherwise misconduct himself, the woman has the right to turn him adrift, and to retain all the goods and money of the partnership." Colquhoun observed that the women "will put up with a very great deal before they take such strong measures with a man they have once been fond and proud of."

In 1904 A. Cecil Carter reported that "the position of women is high in Siam. They enjoy, both in business matters and social life, a great independence." In 1905 Peter Thompson, the English surveyor, wrote that in Siam "the marriage tie can be dissolved as easily as it is formed, and polygamy is permitted, but the ordinary peasant contents himself with one wife and to her he remains very faithful. Women do not occupy at all an inferior position in Siam, and they enjoy at least as much freedom as in European countries." Travelers in rural Siam noticed that women generally relied on their own resources and not on the aid, or validation, of men. Unlike in Europe, Siamese children grew up seeing their mothers manage the family finances, not their fathers.

In the second decade of the twentieth century the king of Siam, wishing to adopt a Western custom, urged his subjects to attach surnames to their personal names. Married women were required to take on their husbands' new last names; children were given the surnames of their fathers. Lucien Hanks, an American anthropologist who went to Thailand after the end of World War II to study the village way of life, noted, "In Thailand, a family line is missing, though Rama VI (r. 1910–25), after years of schooling in England, proclaimed that each family in his kingdom should take a patrilineal surname. People sought out names by one or another means, yet the plan succeeded only in part because children often changed the family name, obliterating the connection between generations. Sons, moreover, may move to the bride's household when they marry, so that continuity of generations can run more consistently between mother and daughter than between father and son. At death a man

Fig. 46 Lao women in Siam

tends to dissipate the body of his estate by dividing it among his daughters as well as sons. In the household of a cultivator there is a precedent for giving the house to the youngest daughter along with a portion of the cultivated fields, for she with her husband may have cared for the old man or woman through the final years."

Hanks's comments reveal that the patrilineal system, which took many years to establish, did not make sense to people who had no need for such a policy. Given the

349

freedom to choose which surname to adopt, many people took their village's name as their family name. To add to the confusion, it was not unusual for unmarried sisters and brothers to adopt different surnames.

Many of the missionaries who came to Siam in the nineteenth century, delighted to have an opportunity to learn the languages and customs of the men and women among whom they worked, were surprised by the degree of equality they observed between the sexes. Equally surprising, and extremely disappointing to them, was the fact that they made so little progress in converting local Buddhists to Christianity. Archibald Ross Colquhoun, cited above, traveled in the north of Siam and knew the missionaries well. In 1879 he wrote, "It is the experience of both Protestant and Roman Catholic missionaries that it is very difficult to convert a Buddhist."

While living in northern Siam in the late 1890s, Lillian Curtis observed that "the church [the sangha] and the people [local Buddhists] are one. The Sacred Order is so dovetailed into the social life that it cannot be separated from it."

Frank Exell, who lived in Siam from 1922 to 1936, noted that "for the Siamese, especially in the provinces, the temple was almost a part of their daily life." While he was working for the Ministry of Education in Bangkok, Exell often visited Buddhist temples in the company of his Siamese language teacher. The English schoolmaster observed that the temples were better attended than England's churches. "A place of worship in England is just about dead on weekdays. But not so a Buddhist temple. Apart from the swarms of yellow-robed priests, there was the constant coming and going of Siamese of all ages. They entered silently, laid some small gifts at the feet of their Buddha, and then engaged in silent prayer. Some apparently came daily for the comfort it gave them. Others brought their personal problems with a simple faith that bore no grudge if prayers remained unanswered. If they did not get what they prayed for then no blame would be attached to Buddha."

Noting that the Siamese generally believed in the law of karma and rebirth, Exell wrote, "It seemed to me that our missionaries were beaten before they even started. What had they to offer these simple folk in whose own religion there was always that 'second chance', the opportunity to atone in a fresh existence and make their way step by step to their nirvana?"

Between 1850 and 1930 Western visitors who traveled about in Siam encountered two kinds of Buddhism. One embraced the local forms of Buddhism practiced by the majority of the people, including local aristocracies, who lived in muangs throughout the regions claimed by Siam. The other was the Buddhism founded by Prince Mongkut, whose followers were mostly members of the royal family, the upper class, and government officials who lived in Bangkok. By the end of the nineteenth century, the Buddhism favored by the elite became the standard for state Buddhism. By the middle of the twentieth century, Mongkut's scientific Buddhism had been transformed into a bureaucratized religion. The strength of local traditions had by then been greatly undermined.

Although the old forms of Buddhism varied from place to place, they did share common features. In local traditions Buddhists did not separate the religious from the worldly life. Monks, whether they lived in villages or towns, had close relationships with the people in their communities. Boys were generally brought up and educated by monks, who taught secular as well as religious subjects. In local Buddhism, however, monks made no distinction between Dhamma and the knowledge required to practice arts, crafts, and medicine. Local monks were responsive to local people, not to the state whose center was far away from their communities. The monasteries were fully supported by local people, and it was the elders of the communities who, by consensus, bestowed honorific titles upon the monks and chose local abbots.

The Reverend Noah A. McDonald, an American Presbyterian who lived in Siam from 1860 to 1870, observed how traditional Buddhist education worked. "The temples or monasteries are the common schools of the country. Every priest can take to the temples with him as many pupils as he can teach, so that at almost every temple can be found a nice collection of boys, making a very respectable school. These boys besides being taught the rudiments of their own language, [the simple rules of arithmetic], and the tenets of the Buddhist religion, act also as servants to the teacher, propelling his boat when he goes out on the river, and doing other like menial tasks for him. They live on the surplus rice which is left, after the priests are satisfied." MacDonald noted, "It is consequently rare that a male can be found who cannot read or write his own language." The missionary also observed that the bond between teacher and pupils was very strong. "Every pupil is taught to hold his teacher in special reverence, which lasts through life."

McDonald continues, "There is scarcely any other field, in which modern missions have been established, where the introduction of the Gospel has met with so little opposition as in Siam proper, and especially during the late reign [of King Mongkut, 1851–68], and so far during the present [Rama V, 1868–1910]. It is equally just to say that there is scarcely any other field which has been so barren of results. Pure Buddhism appears to yield more slowly to the power of the Gospel than any other false system. Even Brahminism itself yields more rapidly. The Siamese have the utmost confidence in the strength of their own religion to withstand the power of the Gospel, and hence that stolid indifference which they manifest to the introduction of the Gospel amongst them."

Lunet de Lajonquière, a Frenchman who traveled in

Siam in 1904, wrote, "[The missionaries'] small clientele is made up almost exclusively of Chinese and of persons of mixed blood, without obviously taking into account those Europeans who for the most part belong to the reformed churches. Their efforts are mainly in the territories of the Upper Menam, where they have found very attentive listeners among the Karen and Kha." As Lunet de Lajonquière further observed, "The Protestant missionaries, the Presbyterians, Baptists, and so on, mostly American, appear to have made no more converts than the Catholics have in orthodox Buddhist circles [among the Dhammayut sect]."

In the nineteenth century it was the adherents of local Buddhism as taught by local Buddhist masters, many of whom appear in this book, that the Protestant and Catholic missionaries found difficult to convert. The strength of local Buddhism derived from the people's devotion to their teachers, their faith *(saddha)* in the Dhamma that they practiced, and their belief in nibbana as the ultimate goal of their religion. In his journal Bishop Pallegoix wrote that one of the obstacles in the way of gaining converts to Christianity was the fact that the education of youth took place in the monasteries. "The Buddhist sect imposes on all boys a strict obligation to pass a few years in the monasteries under the monks' leadership. The King's sons are not exempt from this." (Here, Pallegoix misunderstood the local custom. Bhikkhu ordination was, and still is, voluntary, not imposed.) The bishop continues, "It is easy to conceive that all these young people, when they have come back to the lay state, would be strongly attached to the superstitions they have drawn from the monasteries from a tender age." Western missionaries of the nineteenth century had difficulty understanding the Buddhist notion of *saksit* (sacred) power as it inhered in the landscape, in sacred objects, or in persons. They perceived local customs, religious practices, and the Buddhist masters who taught and practiced them as superstitious.

Carle Zimmerman, a sociologist from Harvard University, traveled all over Siam in 1930 and 1931 in order to conduct a survey of rural populations. After his investigations in the north, northeastern, southern, and central regions of Siam, Zimmerman reported, "The people of Siam also have a high spiritual or non-material standard of living. The exposing of children, the sale of children, the consecration of female children as temple prostitutes, child-marriage, crude and unhuman practices, all these and similar behaviors which might be considered as evidence of a low spiritual standard of living are not to be found among the Siamese." Like many European travelers of his time, Zimmerman found that before the economic development boom that began in the 1960s, villagers in rural Siam were generally not materialistic and rarely greedy. Zimmerman further observed that the "Siamese have a high development of art, sculpture, silver work, niello work, silk and cotton weaving, lacquer work and all of the other practices considered important to artistic life. Even in the most primitive communities, one can find a door-plate, a dish, a piece of weaving, a temple, a carved end-gate of a bullock cart which may be justly called a real work of art. Considering the general Oriental situation, the standard of living in this country is about as high as can be maintained at present."

Frank Exell, the schoolmaster turned banker, said in a memoir, "The one solid fact was that the Siamese had a well-established religion of the highest quality and their confidence in it was such that they had no objection to Christian or any other missionaries doing their best. Their firm belief was that the Christians were far more likely to end up as Buddhists and King Mongkut did not hesitate to say so." Exell had been a teacher in Bangkok for five years and a commercial bank manager in the north and the south for a total of nine years. He last saw Siam in 1936. In the memoir *Siamese Tapestry*, published in 1963, Exell bemoaned the fact that "Siam is no longer a country 'known to a few.' Its charm as a 'backwater' has long since gone. It is now a country of 'progress' whose voice is heard in international circles." By then state Buddhism had been dominant for six decades, and local abbots had been largely replaced by sangha officials. At the conclusion of another memoir, *In Siam Service*, published in 1967 when Thailand was ruled by a military government, Exell wrote, "One could only hope that leaders of true calibre would be found."

SOURCES

Sir John Bowring, *The Kingdom and People of Siam: With a Narrative of the Mission to That Country in 1855* (1857), vol. 1, pp. 119–120. Bishop Bigandet's observations appear on pp. 309–310 of Bowring's work. The same passage was cited by Lillian Curtis in *The Laos of North Siam* (1903), pp. 101–102. In *Amongst the Shans* (1885; 1970), pp. 233–234, Archibald Ross Colquhoun begins his citation of this same passage with the words "[Bishop Bigandet], famed for his learning and just appreciation of the people, fully testifies to the high position that women hold."

Shway Yoe (Sir James George Scott), *The Burman: His Life and Notions* (1927), p. 110.

John Crawfurd, *Journal of an Embassy from the Governor-General of India* (1967), p. 348; and *The Crawfurd Papers* (1915), p. 142.

H. Warrington Smyth, *Five Years in Siam, from 1891 to 1896* (1898), p. 281.

Ebbe Kornerup, *Friendly Siam: Thailand in the 1920s* (1999), p. 20.

Carl Bock, *Temples and Elephants* (1884; 1986), pp. 317–318.

Sir Ernest Satow, *A Diplomat in Siam* (1994), p. 85.

Daniel McGilvary, *A Half Century among the Siamese and the Lao: An Autobiography* (1912; 2001), pp. 144–145. Westerners and the Siamese elite generally referred to both the Tai Yuan and the Lao as "Lao."

Holt S. Hallett, *A Thousand Miles on an Elephant in the Shan States* (1890; 2000), p. 370.

William Clifton Dodd, *The Tai Race* (1996), pp. 306–307.

Archibald Ross Colquhoun, *Amongst the Shans* (1885; 1970), pp. 233, 292, 295.

Lillian Johnson Curtis, *The Laos of North Siam* (1903), pp. 100–119.

A. Cecil Carter. *The Kingdom of Siam* (1904), p. 45.

P. A. Thompson, *Lotus Land* (1906), p. 61.

Lucien M. Hanks, *Rice and Man* (1972), p. 81.

F. K. Exell, *In Siamese Service* [1922–36] (1967), pp. 188–189, 191; *Siamese Tapestry* (1963), pp. 32–33, 192; and *In Siamese Service*, p. 210.

Reverend N. A. McDonald, *A Missionary in Siam (1860–1870)* (1871; 1999), pp. 45, 95.

Lunet de Lajonquière, *Siam and the Siamese: Travels in Thailand and Burma in 1904* (1906; 2001), p. 47.

Jean-Baptiste Pallegoix, *Description of the Thai Kingdom or Siam* (1854; 2000), p. 416.

Carle C. Zimmerman, *Siam Rural Economic Survey 1930–31* (1999), pp. 227–228.

44

THE GREEN BUDDHA OF THE GROTTO

WESTERN EXPLORERS and thudong monks who traveled through the forests of Siam and Laos often saw Buddha images, large and small, in sacred caves. Between 1881 and 1893, when James McCarthy was conducting surveys for Siam's government that took him all over the north, he investigated many caves. When he was in Nan, a principality in northern Siam ringed by high mountains, McCarthy wrote, "We visited the cave opposite the mouth of the Nam U, the ascent to which was made easy by a flight of steps. It was not very large but contained from one to two hundred images, varying from 3 inches to as many feet. A beautiful little pagoda built within looked charming in the glorious sunlight." Local people generally believed that many of the Buddha images in the caves had been there since ancient times. Upon entering a cave or a wat they usually paid homage to the Buddha images there. Villagers did not keep Buddha images in their homes. In the days when village life was not yet ruled by money, it was unthinkable that anyone should wish to remove images from caves or monasteries.

Since becoming a thudong monk in the 1940s, Ajan Chuan (b. 1920) lived in a number of isolated caves in the forests of northeastern Siam. One of his favorites was Worship Cave on Ox Mountain. Ajan Chuan told his disciples that a very long time ago hunters and forest villagers came upon Worship Cave and found a number of Buddha images there, some of which were made of gold.

They were afraid to remove any Buddha statues, however, for fear that the spirits guarding the sacred caves would punish them. When they returned to their villages they told their relatives what they had seen. Since time immemorial the people's belief in guardian spirits has protected these images.

In 1964 Ajan Chuan and his fellow thudong monks returned to Worship Cave, intending to spend the next four rains retreats there. When the villagers came to offer food to the thudong monks, they said they were hoping to see the golden Buddhas. The monks helped the villagers search for the images, but to their dismay no gold Buddhas were to be found in the cave. The monks surmised that some people must have taken the Buddha images out and sold them for cash. Local people believed that the golden images were still in the cave but were being kept hidden by the spirits.

Unlike devout villagers, Westerners who came upon Buddha images in caves had no fear of guardian spirits. Those who wished to take a few images home with them did so without scruple. A Dutchman identified only by his last name, Klaasen, came to northern Siam during the first decade of the twentieth century when the mountains and jungles were still formidable places. Klaasen, who lived and worked in Siam for thirty-five years, was not an antique hunter and knew the law forbidding the removal of religious statuary, but when he saw a green jade Buddha image in a jungle cave somewhere beyond Chiang Mai, he could not resist the temptation to take it.

Many years later, in the 1950s, Klaasen met Ludwig Koch-Isenburg, a German zoologist, at a hotel in northern Thailand. The Dutchman proposed a trek to the cave. Klaasen, who knew his way around, persuaded a government official in Chiang Mai to give them permission to stay at a solitary forest rangers' station high up in the mountains. Koch-Isenburg, who wrote about their trek, described the scene. "And so we moved into a small stone building at an altitude of about sixty-five hundred feet. Solid walls of virgin forest stood practically within touching distance outside our windows. At sunrise thousands of birds filled the air with their songs, and the melodious 'hoo-hoo-hoo' of the white-hand gibbons rang out of the woods."

The two men set out early the next morning along a narrow jungle path that "grew wilder and more tangled. The majesty of this primary forest so overwhelmed us," the zoologist wrote, "that we had no desire to talk. Lianas thick as my arm hung from the trees. The aerial roots of banyan trees were strangling the trunks of other trees, and the pale Thai vanilla unfolded its alabaster blossoms in the eternal twilight. Everything was dripping with moisture, and we crept with infinite caution over the tree trunks that made rude bridges over the gorges cut by racing mountain streams. In the crowns of the trees above our heads innumerable voices screeched, but on the ground it was shady and still."

Klaasen was retracing his way back to the green Buddha cave that he had stumbled upon thirty years before. As they drew closer to the cave, Koch-Isenburg wrote, "Far away and rising from what seemed infinite depths, I could make out the rush of falling water. We left the path and headed in the direction of the sound. Before us, sheer precipices dropped off into frightful chasms. On Klaasen's suggestion I took off my shoes, so that my bare feet could grip the smooth stone. Clinging to the vines of climbing plants, we let ourselves down, crept around fallen rocks, slid down cracks worn by the water. The noise of the waterfall came closer and closer. Suddenly unfiltered sunlight streamed down upon us, illuminating a wild, magnificent scene. All around us plants and trees had shot up in inconceivable lushness. Swallow shrikes and barbets screamed shrilly; thrushes trilled; and with loud 'hoo-hoos' a troop of long-armed gibbons fled from our presence. The apes had come down to the water to drink. We had come," Koch-Isenburg continues, "to the bottom of a wide ravine whose floor was completely covered by a shallow, crystalline stream. Holding our shoes in our hands, we leaped from stone to stone in the bed of the river. To our right the cliff walls loomed up toward the blue sky; to our left stood an impenetrable wall of green foliage."

Koch-Isenburg was in for a surprise. "The ravine narrowed," he tells us, "and suddenly I cried out in amazement and stopped in my tracks. A gigantic recumbent Buddha had been carved out of the rock. One arm was outstretched along the body, the other was propping up the head; the eyes gazed, mysterious and unfathomable, into the timeless green and golden virgin jungle. The overhang of the cliff, like the dome of some tremendous cathedral, protected the work of art from dampness and decay. Only then did I realize that we had entered a mighty grotto in the rock. In front of the Buddha's face stood a vessel containing rods of incense, and I saw with some surprise that my Dutch friend was lighting them. With reverent expression he performed the prescribed censing ritual. I waited tactfully in the background until his private devotions were over and he had turned to me again."

Klaasen led Koch-Isenburg to a little niche in the rock at the feet of the Buddha. "Carefully he picked up a carving that stood there and handed it to me. I stared spellbound at the ancient image. Never, it seemed to me, had I seen finer, more artistic work." The small Buddha had been carved out of green jade, and the sight of it left the German zoologist spellbound. "The stone countenance in my hands seemed to be alive. The firmly closed mouth was smiling, but with a significant, understanding, and kindly smile such as I had never seen on a human face.

The eyes gazed inscrutably into another world. Whether it was due to the magic that emanated from this remote, paradisiacally beautiful place, or to this masterpiece of a vanished age, I do not know, but a tremendous feeling of happiness surged through me. I felt a deep sense of gratitude, though I could not have said for what." The Dutchman then told the German scientist that the statue had this effect "upon everyone who sees it." Klaasen next confessed that he had once been so "overwhelmed" by it that he "became a thief."

In the 1920s, Klaasen told his young friend, "there was not yet any path into the wilderness. I was tramping around this region, along with two natives. We had been gathering orchids, and the boys were carrying heavy packs. At the point where you and I left the path, I noticed large white-hand gibbons chasing one another in play under the trees. As soon as we appeared they vanished, but their exuberant cries suddenly began to sound from so far below us that I realized at once that we were close to a deep gorge into which the animals had dropped. I ordered my porters to wait and started in pursuit of the apes."

After coming upon the grotto, Klaasen discovered the green Buddha in the niche and "instantly felt its unfathomable spell," saying to Koch-Isenburg that for him "this statue breathed and lived. For centuries it had absorbed the roar of the water and drunk in the sublime repose of the forest. And all that seemed to pour over into me from its jade face. I must have lingered in that gorge for more than two hours, plotting how to make off with the green Buddha. The natives were waiting for me above; I could scarcely have concealed the statue from them, for I was wearing nothing but a pair of shorts and a khaki shirt."

Before daybreak the next morning Klaasen returned to the sanctuary. "I had to fight a terrible battle with myself," he told his companion, "before I reached out my hands and plucked the statue from the spot where it had probably stood for centuries. I was defiling a temple, offending the most sacred things of an alien religion. Certainly there must be a curse bound up with such blasphemy. And in fact, the very moment I put the sculpture into my pack, I thought I heard a burst of insane laughter. I shuddered to the marrow of my bones and threw scared looks up the wall of rock, where there were so many crevices and caves in which a spectator might lurk." Regaining his composure, Klaasen attributed the sound of laughter to a mockingbird.

Carrying his jade treasure, Klaasen returned to his headquarters six hundred miles south of Chiang Mai. Even after reasoning that he would soon be returning to Holland, where avenging spirits could not follow him, he found no peace. He bought "a small statuette of Buddha made of solid gold. Its money value," Klaasen said, "must be approximately the same as the value of the stolen jade Buddha. . . . We materialistic Westerns think we can balance everything by arithmetic and pay for anything on earth. I traveled back all that enormous distance and set the gold Buddha in the empty place on the altar. But this act of restitution did not buy me inner peace. Nevertheless, a few months later, I was ready to start for Holland, and by that time I had at least regained enough peace of mind so that I could sleep at night."

Klaasen succeeded in smuggling the statue out of the country, but "back in misty Holland, whenever I looked at my Buddha," he said, "I felt a stabbing pain in my chest. What an earthly paradise I had given up! I would sit lost in thought for hours, and all the magic beauty of that ravine in the jungle would pour through my heart."

After working out a new contract with his firm, Klaasen returned to Siam. As soon as he could get away from his job, he traveled back to the north. He had decided to return the green Buddha to its home. "By now it had become completely clear that I must return my stolen Buddha to the sanctuary if I were ever to be a free man again."

The closer he got to the cave temple the better the Dutchman began to feel. But when he entered the grotto, he said, he "sprang back in horror. Before the altar an ancient monk in yellow robe was kneeling. The pedestal of the jade Buddha, on which I had placed the golden image, was empty. The monk rose as if he had sensed my presence and came toward me. His eyes held a look of infinite kindness as he bowed his head and raised his clasped hands to his forehead in greeting. Like a sinner caught in the act, I stood before the man. The stolen Buddha burned like fire in my hands, and, acting under a mysterious compulsion, I held it out to him. A repressed smile played around his lips—or so it seemed to me—and quietly, as though it were the most natural thing in the world, he turned and replaced the statue on its pedestal." The monk said quietly, "I have waited for you, Brother."

Klaasen learned that the monk, a hermit, had watched the theft from his cave in the rocks above the grotto. He could have stopped Klaasen, "But true to the rules of his religion, with its respect for others," the Dutchman told the German, "he had let me commit the robbery. He could have called out to me, but had he done so the farang [Westerner] would have lost face, would have been shamed."

Taking a deep breath, Klaasen revealed to his German companion that he then became a Buddhist and for a long while "wore the yellow robe and trudged about the country with the begging bowl," returning to the gorge from time to time. "All our European haste and disquiet has fallen away from me. I have come to realize that quiet equanimity is the highest good that we can achieve in this life," the Dutchman concluded.

SOURCES

James McCarthy, *Surveying and Exploring in Siam* (1900), p. 83.

Ajan Chuan Kulachettho, *Prawat Phra Ajan Chuan Kulachettho* (1981), p. 82.

In his book *Khun Det* (1969), Sujit Wongthes used the vehicle of the short story to reveal that in 1960s Thai government officials hired people to dig beneath stupas in ancient cities to obtain artifacts for private collections or sale as antiques.

Ludwig Koch-Isenburg, *Through the Jungle Very Softly: A Quest for Wild Animals in the Far East* (1963), pp. 167–178.

GLOSSARY

The Buddhist terms translated below convey the meanings commonly accepted by ajans of local traditions. These may depart from standard definitions.

abhiñña: Supernormal or supramundane knowledge, possessed by a buddha, an arahant, or a bodhisat. The six *abhiñña* are psychic power, divine hearing, perceptions of the thoughts of other beings, recollection of previous births, divine eye, and knowledge concerning the eradication of one's own impurities and passions. The first five *abhiñña* are regarded as mundane; the sixth is considered supramundane.

ajan: Teacher; often romanized as ajarn or ajahn. (Pali: *acariya*)

arahant: One who has attained enlightenment and reached the highest stage of holiness, whose mind is totally free of greed, anger, and delusion.

ban: Village or community. For most of the nineteenth century a village was a community with a locally appointed chief. After the formation of the modern nation-state the village became the smallest administrative unit in Thailand. Several villages make up a commune or subdistrict *(tambon);* a number of *tambon* in turn make up a district *(amphoe);* a number of districts make up a province *(changwat);* a number of provinces make up a region. (Prior to 1938 a number of *muang* made up a *monthon.)*

bang: A village by the water (canal, stream, river, or sea).

bhavana: Mental development, meditation; to meditate.

bhikkhu: A Buddhist monk.

bhikkhuni: A fully ordained Buddhist nun.

bodhisat: Local term for one who strives, over many lives and through determined practice of the spiritual perfections (*parami or paramita*) to attain full awakening as a Buddha and thus benefit all beings. (Pali: *bodhisatta;* Sanskrit: *bodhisattva*)

Buddha: The Fully Awakened One; the Enlightened One.

Dhamma: The truth of the way things are; the teachings of the Buddha that reveal that truth. (Sanskrit: *Dharma*)

dhamma: Phenomenon; mental object; nature; all things, mental and physical, conditioned and unconditioned. Realities of nature. (Sanskrit: *dharma*)

doi: A word that means mountain in the northern region.

dukkha: Suffering, unsatisfactoriness of conditioned existence.

Jataka: Stories from the Buddha's previous lives.

jhana: A deep state of meditative concentration in which, at its deepest levels, one experiences no sensory awareness other than tranquility, purity, and mindfulness centered in the heart.

karma: The principle of cause and effect; volitional action by means of body, speech, or mind.

kasina: A class of meditation techniques in which the practitioner concentrates on a particular image, commits it to memory, and recalls the image as a way to achieve meditative absorption or full concentration.

khruba: A teacher who is a monk.

klot: A large, portable umbrella equipped with a mosquito net, used by thudong monks for shelter while meditating on trails or when camping overnight in wilderness areas.

kuti: The small, hut-like living quarters of a monk, made of wood or bamboo, and usually built on stilts, or a room assigned to a monk in a one-story building. The *kuti* of an abbot of a royal wat is larger and built of more durable materials.

Luang Pho: Affectionate term of respect for an old monk. Literally, "Revered Father."

Luang Pu: Revered Grandfather.

mae chi or *mae khao:* Female white-robed ascetics.

maha: Title given to monks, and sometimes novices, who have studied Pali and passed at least the third level of Pali examinations.

metta: Loving kindness; universal love.

muang: Kingdom or principality; in ancient chronicles, designates both a town located at the hub of a network of interrelated villages and all the towns and villages ruled by a single lord.

Nak-dhamma: Literally "Skilled in Buddhist teachings," a collection of formal Dhamma courses created by Prince Wachirayan (1860–1921), head of the Dhammayut order.

nibbana: The ultimate goal of Buddhist practice; liberation from all greed, hatred, and delusion. (Sanskrit: *nirvana*)

Pali: The ancient language in which the scriptures and related texts of Theravada Buddhist teachings were first written down. In Bangkok, Pali texts are written and printed in Bangkok Thai script; local Buddhist texts were written in Khmer or Yuan (Northern Thai) scripts.

pañña: Wisdom, understanding. (Sanskrit: *prajña*)

parami: The Ten Perfections; the ten stages of spiritual perfection on the path to Awakening. (Sanskrit: *paramita*)

pariyatti-dhamma: The study of Buddhist scriptures.

Patimokkha: Precepts observed by Theravada monks that consist of 227 disciplinary rules.

patipatti: Practice; not only the practice of formal meditation but also of *sila, samadhi,* and *pañña* (virtue, concentration, and wisdom).

phra: The honorific for monks; Buddha images, and relics.

rishi: Holy man, hermit.

saksit: The sacred; that which is beyond the five physical senses and is unexplainable by mere rationality. The power of saksit, according to local traditions, inheres in the landscape, in sacred objects, monks, and lay renunciants. The ultimate saksit is the attainment of nibbana.

sala: A multipurpose, open-sided, roofed structure mounted on posts used as rest house, preaching hall, and meeting place.

samadhi: The stable, clear, calm condition of the mind when it is completely centered, still, and focused on one point; a collective term representing a number of meditative states, of which *jhana* is one example.

samnak: Residence or school where a group of monks and novices or pupils study under a teacher.

samsara: The cycle of death and rebirth endured by those who have not attained *nibbana.*

sangha: The monastic community; in official usage, the institution of Buddhist monks.

sangharaja: Administrative head of the sangha.

sati: Mindfulness.

sila: Morality, moral discipline, virtuous conduct; the application of wisdom within a social group that brings peace because it does no harm.

somdet: Initial element in the titles of high-ranking monks in Bangkok's sangha hierarchy, roughly equivalent to a cardinal in the Roman Catholic hierarchy.

sutta: A discourse of the Buddha transmitted by his disciples. (Sanskrit: *sutra*)

Tai: Ethnolinguistic family of related peoples scattered from South China westward to Assam in India and southward to the Malay Peninsula. Within the borders of Thailand, Tai peoples include the Siamese, Yuan, Shan, Lua, and Lao.

thudong: Ascetic or austere practice. A thudong monk is one who keeps some of the thirteen ascetic practices over and above the general monastic code *(vinaya).* The word *thudong* in local terminology also means a pilgrimage made on foot by an ascetic monk. (Pali: *dhutanga*)

thung: A savannah-like area; a vast space covered with tall grasses.

Tipitaka: The three baskets of Buddhist scriptures consisting of the Vinaya (disciplinary rules for monks and nuns), the Sutta (discourses of the Buddha and leading disciples), and the Abhidhamma (psychological and philosophical analyses); called "baskets" after the containers which held the original manuscripts.

uposatha, ubosot, or *bot:* Ordination hall; building in a wat where important religious ceremonies and rituals are performed; Buddhist holy days based on the phases of the moon.

vinaya: The Buddhist monastic code of discipline.

wat: A place of residence for monastics; temple of worship; a community center for monastics and laypeople.

ILLUSTRATION CREDITS

Fig. 1   Map by David K. Wyatt.

Fig. 2   Map by David K. Wyatt.

Fig. 3   P. A. Thompson, *Lotus Land* (1906), facing p. 275.

Fig. 4   Thipakosa, *Prawat Somdet Phra Phutthachan (To)* (1971).

Fig. 5   Map by David K. Wyatt.

Fig. 6   John Crawfurd, *Journal of an Embassy to the Courts of Siam and Cochin China* (1828; 1967), p. 78.

Fig. 7   Crawfurd, *Journal of an Embassy.*

Fig. 8   Thompson, *Lotus Land*, facing p. 168.

Fig. 9   Thompson, *Lotus Land*, facing p. 122.

Fig. 10   Henri Mouhot, *Travels in Siam, Cambodia and Laos 1858–1860* (1864; 1989), p. 43.

Fig. 11   Wat Bophitphimuk.

Fig. 12   Map by David K. Wyatt.

Fig. 13   Thomas W. Knox, *Adventures of Two Youths in a Journey to Siam and Java* (1880), p. 124.

Fig. 14   Map by David K. Wyatt.

Fig. 15   Mouhot, *Travels in Siam*, p. 87.

Fig. 16a Thompson, *Lotus Land*, facing p. 180.

Fig. 16b Thompson, *Lotus Land*, facing p. 180.

Fig. 17a Thompson, *Lotus Land*, facing p. 72.

Fig. 17b Thompson, *Lotus Land*, facing p. 72.

Fig. 18   Knox, *Adventures of Two Youths*, p. 100.

Fig. 19   Thompson, *Lotus Land*, facing p. 60.

Fig. 20   Maxwell Sommerville, *Siam on the Meinam from the Gulf of Ayuthia* (1897), p. 202.

Fig. 21   Sommerville, *Siam on the Meinam*, p. 192.

Fig. 22   Knox, *Adventures of Two Youths*, p. 170.

Fig. 23   *Buddhology: Luang Pho Charan laoruang Luang Pho Doem.*

Fig. 24   Map by David K. Wyatt.

Fig. 25   Mouhot, *Travels in Siam*, facing p. 120.

Fig. 26   *Phra Maha Wira Thavaro, Prawat Luang Pho Pan, Wat Bang Nomkho.*

Fig. 27   Map by David K. Wyatt.

Fig. 28   Knox, *Adventures of Two Youths*, p. 335.

Fig. 29   Map by David K. Wyatt.

Fig. 30   Pallegoix, *Description of the Thai Kingdom or Siam* (1854; 2000), p. 164.

Fig. 31   Lucien Fournereau, *Bangkok in 1892* (1998), p. 110.

Fig. 32   Fournereau, *Bangkok in 1892*, p. 156.

Fig. 33   Sommerville, *Siam on the Meinam*, p. 137.

Fig. 34   Thompson, *Lotus Land*, facing p. 40.

Fig. 35   Knox, *Adventures of Two Youths*, p. 156.

Fig. 36   Map by David K. Wyatt.

Fig. 37   Map by David K. Wyatt.

Fig. 38   Holt S. Hallett, *A Thousand Miles on an Elephant in the Shan States* (1890), p. 349.

Fig. 39   Map by David K. Wyatt.

Fig. 40   Map by David K. Wyatt.

Fig. 41   Mural panel, Wat Suwannaram, Thonburi, photographed by Umaphon Soetphannuk.

Fig. 42   Phra Maha Pun Punyasiri, *Banthuk Somdet Pa* (1894).

Fig. 43   *Historical Illustrations: Wat Phra Chetuphon* (1982), p. 135.

Fig. 44   Map by David K. Wyatt.

Fig. 45   James McCarthy, *An Englishman's Siamese Journals 1890–1893* (1983), p. 57.

Fig. 46   Mouhot, *Travels in Siam*, facing p. 134.

REFERENCES

Alabaster, Henri. *The Wheel of the Law*. London: Trubner, 1871.

Anuson 80 pi Luang Pho Kasem Khemako (Commemoration of Venerable Father Kasem Khemako's 80th Birthday). Bangkok, 1991.

Apinan Poshyananda. *Modern Art in Thailand: Nineteenth and Twentieth Centuries*. New York: Oxford University Press, 1992.

Bacon, George. *Siam: The Land of the White Elephant*. New York: Charles Scribner's Sons, 1892.

Bassenne, Marthe. *In Laos and Siam*. Translated by Walter E. J. Tips. Bangkok: White Lotus, 1995 (French edition, 1912).

Batson, Benjamin A. *The End of the Absolute Monarchy in Siam*. Singapore: Oxford University Press, 1986.

Bock, Carl. *Temples and Elephants*. 1884. Reprint, Singapore: Oxford University Press, 1986.

Bowring, Sir John. *The Kingdom and People of Siam: With a Narrative of the Mission to That Country in 1855*. 2 vols. London: John W. Parker and Son, 1857.

Brereton, Bonnie Pacala. *Thai Tellings of Phra Malai : Texts and Rituals concerning a Popular Buddhist Saint*. Tempe: Arizona State University, 1995.

Bua Nanasampanno, Phra Maha. *Prawat Than Phra Ajan Man Bhuridatta Thera* (Biography of Phra Ajan Man Bhuridatta Thera). Bangkok, 1971.

———. *Patipatha phra thudong kammathan* (Wandering Meditation Monks' Conduct). Bangkok: Cremation Volume, Chu Sitachit, 1973.

———. *To the Last Breath: Dhamma Talks on Living and Dying*. Udonthani: Ban Tat Forest Monastery, 1992.

371

————.*Yotnam bon baibua* (Dewdrop on Lotus Leaf). Udonthani: Ban Tat Forest Monastery, 2000.

Buddhadasa Bhikkhu. *Lao wai mua wai sondhaya attachiwaprawat khong than Buddhadasa* (As Told in the Twilight Years: The Memoirs of Venerable Buddhadasa). Edited by Phra Pracha Pasannadhammo. Bangkok: Komon Kimthong Foundation, 1986.

————. *Heartwood of the Bodhi Tree.* Edited by Santikaro Bhikkhu. Translated from the Thai by Dhammavicayo. Boston: Wisdom Publications, 1994.

————. "Nibbana for Everyone." In *Keys to Natural Truth.* Bangkok: Mental Health Publishing, 1999.

Buddhaghosa. *The Path of Purification (Visuddhimagga).* Translated by Bhikkhu Nanamoli. Kandy: Buddhist Publication Society, 1979.

Butda Thavaro, Phra Ajan. *Luang Pu Lao Wai* (Stories Venerable Grandfather Butda Told Us). Bangkok, 1994.

Campbell, Reginald. *Teak-Wallah: The Adventure of a Young Englishman in Thailand in the 1920s.* 1935. Reprint, Singapore: Oxford University Press, 1986.

Carter, A. Cecil. *The Kingdom of Siam: 1904.* Bangkok: The Siam Society, 1988.

Chah, Phra Ajahn. *Food for the Heart: The Collected Teachings of Ajahn Chah.* Introduction by Amaro Bhikkhu. Boston: Wisdom Publications, 2002.

Chaiyawong, Khruba. *Phra Chaiyawongsanussati.* Lamphun: Wat Phra Buddhapada Huai Tom, 2000.

Chantichai Krasaesin. *Somdet Phra Phutthachan (To).* 2 vols. Bangkok: Khurusapha, 1964.

Chanya Suthiyano, Phra Maha, comp. *Chiwit lae ngan khong Than Paññananda* (The Life and Work of Venerable Paññananda). Nonthaburi, 1991.

Charan Thithadhammo, Phra Ajan. *Buddhology: Luang Pho Charan laoruang Luang Pho Doem* (Buddhist Technology: Venerable Father Charan's Recollections of Venerable Father Doem). Singburi: Wat Amphawan, 2001.

Chuan Kulachettho, Phra Ajan. *Prawat Phra Ajan Chuan Kulachettho* (Memoirs of Venerable Teacher Chuan

Kulachettho). Edited by Suriphan Maniwat. Bangkok: Cremation Volume, Phra Ajan Chuan, 1981.

Chuen Thaksinanukun. *Luang Pho Ngoen: Thephachao haeng Don Yai Hom.* Bangkok, 1962.

Cochrane, W. W. *The Shans.* Vol. 1. Rangoon, 1915.

Colquhoun, Archibald Ross. *Amongst the Shans.* 1885. Reprint, New York: Paragon Book Reprint, 1970.

Cone, Margaret, and Richard Gombrich. *Perfect Generosity of Prince Vessantara.* Oxford: Clarendon Press, 1977.

Crawfurd, John. *Journal of an Embassy from the Governor-General of India to the Courts of Siam and Cochin China.* 1828. Reprint, Kuala Lumpur: Oxford University Press, 1967.

Curtis, Lillian Johnson. *The Laos of North Siam.* Philadelphia: Westminster Press, 1903.

David-Neel, Alexandra. *Magic and Mystery in Tibet.* New York: Dover Publications, 1971.

De Lajonquière, Lunet. *Siam and the Siamese: Travels in Thailand and Burma in 1904.* Translated by J. H. Stape. Bangkok: White Lotus, 2001 (French edition, 1906).

Dhida Saraya. "The Development of the Northern Tai States from the Twelfth to the Fifteenth Centuries." Ph.D. diss., University of Sydney, 1982.

The Discourse on the All-Embracing Net of Views: the Brahmajala Sutta and Its Commentaries. Translated by Bhikkhu Bodhi. Kandy: Buddhist Publication Society, 1992.

Dodd, William Clifton. *The Tai Race: Elder Brother of the Chinese.* 1923. Reprint, Bangkok: White Lotus, 1996.

Early Missionaries in Bangkok: The Journals of Tomlin, Gutzlaff and Abeel 1828–1832. Edited by Anthony Farrington. Bangkok: White Lotus, 2001.

Exell, F. K. *Siamese Tapestry.* London: Robert Hale, 1963.

———. *In Siamese Service.* London: Cassell, 1967.

Finlayson, George. *The Mission to Siam and Hue, 1821–1822.* London: Oxford University Press, 1988.

Fournereau, Lucien. *Bangkok in 1892.* Translated by Walter E. J. Tips. Reprint, Bangkok: White Lotus Press, 1998 (French edition, 1894).

Grindrod, Katherine. *Diaries of Katherine Grindrod, Siam 1892.*

Vol. 1. Transcribed by R. S. Hill. Hong Kong: University of Hong Kong, 1982.

Gunaratana, Henepola. *The Path of Serenity and Insight: An Explanation of the Buddhist Jhanas.* Delhi: Motilal Banarsidass, 1985.

Hall, Harold Fielding. *The Soul of a People.* 1898. Reprint, Bangkok: White Orchid Press, 1995.

Hallett, Holt S. *A Thousand Miles on an Elephant in the Shan States.* London: William Blackwood and Sons, 1890.

Hanks, Lucien M. *Rice and Man.* Chicago: Aldine Publishing, 1972.

Historical Illustrations: Wat Phra Chetuphon. Bangkok: Wat Phra Chetuphon, 1982.

Horner, I. B. *Ten Jataka Stories.* London: Luzac, 1957.

Inter-Ethnic Relations in the Making of Mainland Southeast Asia and Southwestern China. Edited by Hayashi Yukio and Aroonrut Wichienkeeo. Chiang Rai: Center of Ethnic Studies, 2000.

Jory, Patrick. "Thai and Western Buddhist Scholarship in the Age of Colonialism: King Chulalongkorn Redefines the Jatakas." *Journal of Asian Studies* 61, no. 3 (August 2002): 891–918.

Jottrand, Émile, and Mrs Jottrand. *In Siam: The Diary of a Legal Adviser of King Chulalongkorn's Government.* Translated by Walter E. J. Tips. 1905. Reprint, Bangkok: White Lotus, 1996.

Kamala Tiyavanich. *Forest Recollections: Wandering Monks in Twentieth-Century Thailand.* Honolulu: University of Hawai'i Press; Chiang Mai: Silkworm Books, 1997.

Keyes, Charles F. "Millennialism, Theravada Buddhism, and Thai Society." *Journal of Asian Studies* 36, no. 2 (February 1977): 283–302.

Khaisaeng Kittiwacharachai, comp. *Butda Thavaro: Chiwit kanngan lae lakdhamma* (Butda Thavaro: His Life, Work and Dhamma's Teachings). Bangkok: Dhammasapha, 1994.

Khantipalo (Laurence Mills). *Calm and Insight: A Buddhist Manual for Meditators.* London: Curzon Press, 1987.

———. *Buddhism Explained.* Chiang Mai: Silkworm Books, 1999.

———. *Noble Friendship: Travels of a Buddhist Monk.* Birmingham, England: Windhorse Publications, 2002.

Knox, Thomas W. *Adventures of Two Youths in a Journey to Siam and Java.* New York: Harper & Brothers, 1880.

Koch-Isenburg, Ludwig. *Through the Jungle Very Softly: A Quest for Wild Animals in the Far East.* Translated by Richard and Clara Winston. New York: Viking Press, 1963 (German edition, *Im Reich des grunen Buddha*, 1959).

Kornerup, Ebbe. *Friendly Siam: Thailand in the 1920s.* Bangkok: White Lotus, 1999.

La Chanthophaso, Phra Ajan. *Kamson Luang Pu La* (The Teachings of Venerable Grandfather La). Edited by Withaya Chupan. Chiang Mai, 1989.

La Khempatato, Phra Ajan. *Chiwaprawat Luang Pu La Khempatato* (A Life Story of Venerable Grandfather La). Bangkok, 1989.

Le May, Reginald. *An Asian Arcady: The Land and Peoples of Northern Siam.* Cambridge: W. Heffer & Sons, 1926.

Luang Pho Phra Maha Surasak 72 pi (Commemoration of Venerable Father Maha Surasak 72nd Birthday). Washington, D.C.: Wat Thai, 1997.

McCarthy, James. *Surveying and Exploring in Siam.* London: William Clowes and Sons, 1900.

———. *An Englishman's Siamese Journals 1890–1893.* 1895. Reprint, Bangkok: Siam Media International Books, 1983.

McDonald, Rev. N. A. *A Missionary in Siam (1860–1870).* 1871. Reprint, Bangkok: White Lotus, 1999.

McGilvary, Daniel. *A Half Century among the Siamese and the Lao: An Autobiography.* 1912. Reprint, Bangkok: White Lotus, 2000.

Medicinal Plants of Thailand: Past and Present. Bangkok: National Identity Board, 1992.

Mongkhon Danthanin. *Pa chumchon Isan kap Ko Jo Ko* (Forest Communities in Isan and the KJK). Bangkok: Local Development Institute, 1991.

Mouhot, Henri. *Travels in the Central Parts of Indo-china (Siam, Cambodia and Laos) during the Years 1858, 1859, and 1860.* Vol. 1. London: John Murray, 1864.

———.*Travels in Siam, Cambodia and Laos 1858–1860.* 2 vols. Singapore: Oxford University Press, 1989.

Mulholland, Jean. "Thai Traditional Medicine: Ancient Thought and Practice in a Thai Context." *Journal of the Siam Society* 67, part 2 (July 1979): 80–115.

Murdoch, John B. "The 1901–1902 'Holy Men's' Rebellion." *Journal of the Siam Society* 62, part 1 (1974): 47–66.

Nak Khoso, Phra Ajan. *Kan Thudong Phua Nibbana* (Wandering to Attain Enlightenment). Bangkok: Cremation Volume, Mrs. Ariya Hiranyanon, 1979.

———. *Samanera Bunnak thieo kammathan* (Novice Bunnak Wandered to Meditate). Bangkok: Maha Chula Buddhist University, 1992.

Nanthapanyaphon, Phra. *Chiwaprawat Luang Pu Dun* (A Biography of Venerable Grandfather Dun). Surin, Thailand: Cremation Volume, Venerable Grandfather Dun, 1985.

Neale, Frederick Arthur. *Narrative of a Residence in Siam.* 1852. Reprint, Bangkok: White Lotus, 1996.

Norden, Hermann. *A Wanderer in Indochina: The Chronicle of a Journey through Annam, Tong-King, Laos, and Cambodia with Some Account of Their People.* London: H. F. & G. Witherby, 1931.

Nyanaponika Thera. *The Vision of Dhamma: Buddhist Writings of Nyanaponika Thera.* Edited by Bhikkhu Bodhi. York Beach, Maine: Samuel Weiser, 1986.

Nyanatiloka. *Buddhist Dictionary.* Kandy: Buddhist Publication Society, 1980.

P. Bunsanong. "Luang Pho Son" (Venerable Father Son). *Sun Phrakhruang* 3, no. 55 (March 1991): 34.

Paisal Visalo, Phra. "Buddhism for the Next Century: Toward Renewing a Moral Thai Society." http://www.bpf.org/ tsangha/phaisan.htm [August 2003].

———. *Buddhasasana thai nai anakhot: naeonom lae thangok chak wikrit* (The Future of Thai Buddhism: Crisis, Trends and Solutions). Bangkok: Sotsi-Saritwong Foundation, 2003.

Pallegoix, Jean-Baptiste. *Description of the Thai Kingdom or Siam: Thailand under King Mongkut.* Translated by Walter E. J. Tips. Bangkok: White Lotus, 2000 (French edition, 1854).

Paññananda Bhikkhu. *Chiwit khong khaphachao* (My Life). Bangkok: Wat Cholaprathan, 1983.

Pasanno Bhikkhu. "The Foundations of Virtue and Right View." *Forest Sangha Newsletter*, July 2002, 1–5.

Pasanno Bhikkhu and Amaro Bhikkhu. *Broad View, Boundless Heart.* Redwood Valley: Abhayagiri Buddhist Monastery, 2001.

Pattaratorn Chirapravati, M.L. *Votive Tablets in Thailand: Origin, Styles, and Uses.* Kuala Lumpur: Oxford University Press, 1997.

Phatsakhon Chuthaphutthi. *Phra Phuttharup lae singsaksit* (Buddha's Images and Sacred Power). Vol. 3. Bangkok, 1982.

Phra Khru Khosonsakhonkit (Thongsoem Sumedho). Bangkok, 2000.

Phra Khru Nonthasankhun (Somsak Nanthasaro). Thonburi: Cremation Volume, Venerable Teacher Somsak Nanthasaro, 1997.

Phut Thaniyo, Phra Ajan. *Thaniyata Therawathu.* Bangkok: Cremation Volume, Phra Ratsangworayan, 2000.

Piyanat Bunnag et al. *Wat Nai Krungthep 1782–1982* (Buddhist Monasteries in Bangkok, 1782–1982). Bangkok: Chulalongkorn University, 1982.

Ponroj Angsanakul. "Phap sathon sangkhom thai nai kitchakam faphanang" (Folklore Scenes in Thai Murals). In *Borankhadi.* Bangkok: Silapakon University, 1983.

Prasert Na Nagara. *Ngan charuk lae prawatsat* (Articles on Inscriptions and History). Nakhon Pathom: Kasetsat University, 1991.

Prawat Luang Pho Nong Inthasuwanno (A Life Story of Venerable Father Nong Inthasuwanno). Suphanburi: Wat Amphawan, n.d.

Prawat Somdet Phra Phutthachan (To Brahmarangsi). Bangkok: Lan Asoke Press, n.d.

Prawat wat changwat Samut Songkhram (A History of Monasteries in Samut Songkhram Province). Bangkok: Cremation Volume, Sangharaja Plot Kittisophano, 1962.

Prawat Wat Rajaburana (A History of Wat Rajaburana). Bangkok, 1995.

Prawat wat thua ratchanachak (A History of Monasteries in Thailand). Vol. 1. Bangkok: Religious Affairs Department, 1982.

Prayudh Prayutto, Phra Maha. *Dictionary of Buddhism.* Bangkok: Mahachula Buddhist University, 1985.

———— (Phra Dhammapitaka). *Luang Pho pua wat pua ban* (Venerable Father for the Wat, for the Village: Twentieth Anniversary of the Death of Phra Methidhammasan [1887–1979]). Bangkok, 1999.

Pun Punnasiri, Phra Maha. *Banthuk Somdet Pa* (Diaries of Cardinal Father). Bangkok: Cremation Volume, Sangharaja Pun Punnasiri, 1984.

Ratchakitchanubeksa (Royal Thai Government Gazette). Vols. 16–18. Bangkok, 1899–1901.

Sangiam Phumphawat. *Somdet phra sangharaja samai chakri wong* (Sangharajas of the Chakri Dynasty). Thonburi, 1964.

Sanitsuda Ekachai. *Seeds of Hope*. Bangkok: Thai Development Support Committee, 1994.

Santikaro Bhikkhu. "Buddhadasa Bhikkhu: Life and Society through the Natural Eyes of Voidness." In *Engaged Buddhism: Buddhist Liberation Movements in Asia*, edited by Christopher S. Queen and Sallie B. King. Albany: State University of New York Press, 1996.

Satow, Ernest. *A Diplomat in Siam*. Edited by Nigel Brailey. Stirlingshire, Scotland: Paul Strachan-Kiscadale, 1994.

Shway Yoe (Sir James George Scott). *The Burman: His Life and Notions*. London: Macmillan, 1927.

Siriwanwiwat (Wanna Wanno), Phra Khru. *Namta somphan* (An Abbot's Tears). Ratburi: Wat Lak Hok, 1987.

Smyth, H. Warrington. *Five Years in Siam, from 1891 to 1896*. New York: Charles Scribner's Sons, 1898.

Sombat Kongsoi. *Kao Phra Ajans* (Nine Venerable Teachers). Bangkok, n.d.

Sommai Premchit. *Mahawetsandon chadok botwikhro thang watthanatham lae sangkhom* (The Maha Vessantara Jataka: A Sociocultural Analysis). Chiang Mai: Toyota Foundation, 2001.

Sommerville, Maxwell. *Siam on the Meinam from the Gulf to Ayuthia*. London: Sampson Low, Marston, 1897.

Srisaka Vallibhotama. "Political and Cultural Continuities at Dvaravati Sites." In *Southeast Asia in the 9th to 14th Centuries*, edited by David G. Marr and Anthony C. Milner. Singapore: Institute of Southeast Asian Studies, 1986.

———. *Aeng arayatham Isan* (A Northeastern Site of Civilization). Bangkok: Mathichon, 1991.

———. *Phra khruang nai muang Siam* (Amulets in Siam). Bangkok: Matichon, 1994.

Sujit Wongthes. *Khun Det.* Bangkok, 1969.

———. "Pai Song Phinong" (A Trip to Song Phinong), *Sinlapa Watthanatham* (Art and Culture) 13, no. 10 (August 1992): 92–98.

Suphon Nachom. *Chiwaprawat lae patipatha Phra Ajan Fan Acharo* (Biography of Venerable Teacher Fan Acharo). Bangkok, 1977.

Suriphan Maniwat. *Thanasamo-nuson* (Remembering Thansamo). Bangkok: Cremation Volume, Venerable Grandfather Chop Thansamo, 1996.

Suriyavudh Suksavas, M.R. "A Dvaravati Votive Tablet Depicting the Palelaya Episode." *Muang Boran* 10, no. 3 (July–September, 1984): 76–82.

Swearer, Donald K. "Myth, Legend and History in the Northern Thai Chronicles." *Journal of the Siam Society* 62, part 1 (1974): 67–88.

Swearer, Donald K., and Sommai Premchit. *The Legend of Queen Cama: Bodhiramsi's Camadevivamsa, a Translation and Commentary.* Albany: State University of New York Press, 1998.

Tej Bunnag. *The Provincial Administration of Siam 1892–1915.* London: Oxford University Press, 1977.

———. *Kabot R.S. 121* (Rebellions of 1902). Bangkok: Thai Watthanaphanit, 1987.

Thiphakosa, Phraya. *Prawat Somdet Phra Phutthachan (To).* Bangkok: Cremation Volume, Phongnat Sawat-chuto, 1971.

———. *Prawat Somdet Phra Phutthachan (To).* Bangkok: Cremation Volume, Thawisak Wiradet, 1972.

Thiphawan Phiyakhun. "Tamnan Ban Tale Noi" (A History of Little Sea Village). In *Saranukrom Watthanatham Paktai* (Encyclopedia of Southern Thai Culture), vol. 3, p. 1288.

Thittila, Ashin. *Essential Themes of Buddhist Lectures.* Rangoon: Department of Religious Affairs, 1987.

Thompson, P. A. *Lotus Land: Being an Account of the Country and the People of Southern Siam.* Edinburgh: Riverside Press, 1906.

Thongsoem Sumedho, Phra Ajan. *Phra Khru Khosonsakhonkit.*

Samut Sakhon: Cremation Volume, Venerable Teacher Khosonsakhonkit, 2000.

Toem Wiphakphotchakit. *Prawatsat Isan* (A History of Isan). Bangkok: Thammasat University Press, 1999.

Uttama, Phra Ajan. *Luang Pho Uttama 84 pi* (Commemoration of Venerable Father Uttama's 84th Birthday). Compiled by Phensi Wacharothai. Bangkok, 1991.

Waen Suchinno, Phra Ajan. *Luang Pu Waen Suchinno (Venerable Grandfather Waen's Life Story).* Chiang Mai: Cremation Volume, Venerable Father Waen, 1985.

Wanna Wanno, Phra Palat. *Phra Khru Wichaisilakhun.* Ratburi: Wat Lak Hok, 1975.

Wat Intharawihan, Bang Khunphrom. Bangkok: Wat Intharawihan, 1994.

Wilson, Constance M. *Thailand: A Handbook of Historical Statistics.* Boston: G. K. Hall, 1983.

———. "The Holy Man in the History of Thailand and Laos." *Journal of Southeast Asian Studies* (September 1997): 345–364.

Wira Thavaro, Phra Maha. *Prawat Luang Pho Pan, Wat Bang Nomkho* (A Life Story of Venerable Father Pan, Monastery of Cow's Udder Village). Chonburi: Cremation Volume, Venerable Grandfather Nen, 1997.

Wirada Thongmitr. *Khrua Inkhong's Westernized School of Thai Painting.* Bangkok, 1979.

Wiriyang Sirintharo, Phra Ajan. "Prawat Phra Ajan Man." In *Prawat Phra Ajan Man chabap sombun* (A Life Story of Venerable Teacher Man). Bangkok: Cremation Volume, Grandmother Man Bunthrikun, 1978.

Wyatt, David K. *The Politics of Reform in Thailand: Education in the Reign of King Chulalongkorn.* New Haven: Yale University Press, 1969.

———. *Siam in Mind.* Chiang Mai: Silkworm, 2002.

———, trans. and ed., *The Nan Chronicle* Ithaca, N.Y.: Southeast Asia Program Publications, 1994.

Zimmerman, Carle C. *Siam Rural Economic Survey 1930–31.* Bangkok: White Lotus, 1999.

More Comments about *The Buddha in the Jungle*

"*The Buddha in the Jungle* is enchanting, charming — casting a spell on the reader and invoking visions of another world and another time. A lost world of simplicity and beauty in harmony with nature, where gentle and good people lived close to the earth, in close contact with animals and birds, traveling by rivers and canals and mountain paths, and celebrating the cycles of passing seasons. This book is Buddhist magic."

—Santidhammo Bhikkhu,
Atammayata Buddhist Monastery, Washington

"A heart-warming narrative of the wandering lifestyle of Theravada Buddhist monks in rural Thailand between roughly the mid-nineteenthth century and the mid-twentieth century. It is full of accounts of monks and their relationships to lay devotees in the villages, as well as snakes, wild elephants, tigers and ghosts. The book shows the central role of mindfulness and meditation in a non-violent way of life. The *Buddha in the Jungle* captures the most authentic expression of Thai Theravada Buddhism in which wisdom, inner repose and freedom of being takes central place for the monks."

—Christopher Titmuss, *Dharma Life*

"*The Buddha in the Jungle* consists of forty-four tales from pre-industrial Thailand. It is a real world of bugs and raptors and venomous creatures mixed with innocents, holy men, and pure magic. These are tales not unlike koans—to be savored, a few at a time. Not only do they tell us something about the abbots and lay-people and Buddhism, they give a comprehensive feel for what it was like to be in Siam in that innocent time. It *isn't Anna and the King of Siam*. It's forty-four times better."

—Wing Luke, *Ralph: The Review of Arts,
Literature, Philosophy and the Humanities.*

"*The Buddha in the Jungle* is an important and lovely book which . . . carries some important messages. More than any conventional work of history or anthropology, this book conveys a very tangible sense of what the landscape was like and how life was lived in old Siam."

—Chris Baker, *Bangkok Post.*